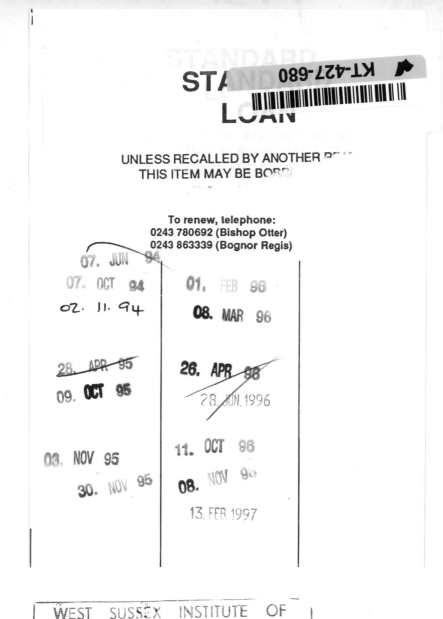

Starting English teaching

This book is aimed at teachers new to the teaching of English. Its main focus is the secondary classroom, but primary teachers too will find here much to interest them. Taking the National Curriculum in English as a starting point, but not necessarily the last word on the subject, Robert Jeffcoate looks at the theoretical issues involved in thinking about English. He argues that teachers must ultimately decide for themselves in defining goals and planning the curriculum. He shows the reader how to go about developing a repertoire of skills in the different curriculum areas: reading, writing, speaking and listening, literature, drama and knowledge about language, and in general classroom management. His suggestions are illustrated with detailed examples of classroom practice and with many quotations from pupils' own work.

Robert Jeffcoate taught English in secondary schools for 12 years and has also taught in primary schools and in higher education. He is the author of *Positive Image* and *Ethnic Minorities and Education*. He divides his time between teaching and writing.

Teaching Secondary English Series
General editor: Peter King

This series provides a focus for a variety of aims and teaching styles in contemporary English teaching. It is designed both for new teachers who want a simple guide to good practice, and for more experienced teachers who may want to revitalize their own teaching by considering alternative ideas and methods.

Also in this series

Encouraging Talk
Lewis Knowles

Encouraging Writing
Robert Protherough

Teaching the Basic Skills
Spelling, Punctuation and Grammar in Secondary English
Don Smedley

Marking and Assessment in English
Pauline Chater

Using Computers in English
A Practical Guide
Phil Moore

Teaching A Level English Literature
A student-centred Approach
John Brown and Terry Gifford

My Language, Our Language
Meeting Special Needs in English
Bernadette Walsh

Starting English teaching

Robert Jeffcoate

London and New York

First published in 1992
by Routledge
11 New Fetter Lane, London EC4P 4EE

Simultaneously published in the USA and Canada
by Routledge
a division of Routledge, Chapman and Hall Inc.
29 West 35th Street, New York, NY 10001

Typeset in 10/12pt Baskerville by
NWL Editorial Services, Langport, Somerset

Printed and bound in Great Britain by
Biddles Ltd, Guildford and King's Lynn

A catalogue reference for this title is available from the
British Library.

ISBN   0–415–05430–3
ISBN   0–415–05356–0 (pbk)

Library of Congress Cataloging in Publication Data
Jeffcoate Robert.
    Starting English teaching / Robert Jeffcoate.
        p.   cm. – (Teaching secondary English)
    Includes bibliographical references (p.   ) and index.
    ISBN   0–415–05430–3. ISBN   0–415–05356–0

    1. English language – Study and teaching (Secondary) –
Great Britain.   2. Language arts (Secondary) – Great
Britain.   I. Title.   II. Series.
LB1631.J37   1992   92–9353
428'.0071'214 – dc20   CIP

In memory of my mother, who introduced me to literature, and for my father, who made me think about how to write

Contents

General editor's preface

A student on her teaching practice in an 11–18 comprehensive school was heard to comment to a class teacher who was supporting her in school, 'My degree doesn't take me very far. What I want more than anything else is lots of practical advice about how to get my head round the National Curriculum, and how to think about what I've done'. When the teacher said he hoped she was in fact receiving such support from school staff she replied, 'Well, yes but really I need a sort of overview that I can carry around with me – something to fit your advice into my own thinking kit'. This book of Rob Jeffcoate's could well serve her as just that sort of overview.

Rob Jeffcoate is an English teacher with experience in primary, secondary and teacher training. He returned recently to teaching in secondary schools and this book not only distils his wide experiences of teaching but also records his sudden immersion in the brave new world of the National Curriculum. His fortuitous return to the world of the secondary English teacher at such a momentous era of change means that he can look at the new curriculum and its context with the eyes of an experienced insider and an onlooker at one and the same time. This gives him a perspective that is uniquely framed to be of help to someone struggling as a new teacher to come to terms with the National Curriculum.

It also means that he genuinely understands the position of the new teacher. In his first chapter he writes of his personal return to the classroom. His diary and commentary reveal thoughts and feelings which will instantly be recognised by a student at the beginning of her teaching practice. Chapter 2 locates the present curriculum through an account of the milestones in the development of English as a school subject. Together these two chapters provide a context which will be new to beginning teachers, but through which they may see how the latest changes affecting the English curriculum do not spring new born out of nowhere but come clothed in a history and step out of a perspective which when understood by the reader permits the development of a critical viewpoint.

The remaining chapters of the book are full of practical advice and classroom examples of the main activities within the English classroom. The framework within which this advice on the knowledge and pedagogical skills is set is, of course, the National Curriculum. Rob Jeffcoate's approach to this curriculum may serve to illustrate the value of his book. He assumes the beginner teacher needs to know the full practical implications of the curriculum for English, but he never forgets that the properly professional approach to its implementation is by way of critical reflection upon it. There are aspects of it which might be challenged and Rob Jeffcoate uses personal experience and an individually committed stance to explore these and criticise them. He does so not in the spirit of someone preaching a true way or a single answer to what should be taught, but because he believes that every new teacher must learn to analyse and reflect upon that with which she is involved. Living the unexamined curriculum, like living the unexamined life, is the way to ignorance and prejudice. He allows that not everyone will agree with his own analysis but presents his own arguments in the hope that this serves as a model for reflective teaching. If the beginner teacher is taught simply to accept the National Curriculum in all its present form she will become part of a deprofessionalised teaching force.

Rob Jeffcoate's view of the National Curriculum can itself be argued with – and I, for one, would take issue with him over, for example, his view of the place of media studies. But that is his very point. His book is written from a personal perspective in an attempt to encourage not only the development of a wide repertoire of pedagogical skills but also to help us be thinking teachers. The value of his book is that he speaks with a highly personal voice and his words 'reek of the real'. Any of us, whether new to the profession or whether experienced but in need of a rekindling of our critical fires, will benefit from this lively, combative and individual view of what it means to teach English now. This book is part of the Teaching Secondary English series published originally by Methuen and now by Routledge. The books in this series are intended to give practical guidance in the various areas of the English curriculum. Each area is treated in a separate volume in order to gain the necessary space in which to discuss it at some length. The aim of the series is twofold: to describe good practice by exploring the approaches and activities reflected in the daily work of an English teacher in the comprehensive school; and to give a practical lead to teachers who wish to try it out for themselves a wider repertoire of teaching skills and ways of organising syllabuses and lessons. Taken as a whole, the series does not press upon the reader a ready-made philosophy, but attempts to provide a map of the English teaching landscape in which the separate volumes highlight an individual feature of that terrain, representing its particular characteristics while reminding us of the continuity between these differing element in the overall topography.

It is at the level of the practical that any synthesis of the various approaches to English can be gained, and to accomplish this every teacher must be in possession of a rationale and an awareness of good methods wherever and however they have been achieved. By reading the books in this series it is to be hoped that teachers will be encouraged to try out for themselves ideas found effective by their colleagues, so gaining the confidence to make their own informed choice and planning in their own classrooms.

Peter King
March 1992

Preface

This book is intended, as the title suggests, for English teachers at the outset of their careers in secondary schools. To those of you who fall into this category it is directly addressed. At the same time I hope that others interested in English teaching, particularly primary school teachers, will find it of value: many of the examples of classroom practice and children's writing are taken from a Liverpool primary school in which I have worked on an intermittent voluntary basis since 1989. The book's origins can be traced to three short-term posts I held between 1987 and 1989 after a decade away from English teaching – two as an English teacher in comprehensive schools, the third as a university lecturer in education with responsibility for the English method work of undergraduate and postgraduate students. Collectively these experiences made me think again about the subject and the kind of support, including books, beginners are most likely to benefit from.

My return to English teaching forms the basis of Chapter 1 and establishes the personal nature of the book. Beginning like this has several advantages, to me at least. First of all, and most obviously, it enables me to introduce myself to you. Second, it provides a model – written reflection on practice – for you to consider emulating. This is widely regarded as a necessary ingredient in successful teaching and recommended by many initial training institutions. Third, it immediately sets before you a sample of classroom reality which I can draw on in subsequent chapters. Fourth, it establishes not only a personal approach to thinking about English teaching but also a historical one. Addressing the different issues in the subject from a historical perspective is the point of departure with which I feel most at ease.

The book's starting-point had in a sense, of course, to be the National Curriculum, or such of it as was visible at the time of writing, together with the Kingman and Cox reports, which created the basis of the statutory provisions in English. I have assumed a degree of familiarity with all three. Inevitably, by the time you read this, you will know a good deal more about the implementation of the National Curriculum, especially as regards the vexed issue of assessment, than I do as I write. Taking it as a starting-point, however, is not the same as accepting it without demur or regarding it as immutable. Critical dissent and practical considerations have already forced changes in the original design, and there will almost certainly be others before all the provisions are finally in place. This, it should be stressed, is unlikely to happen before the end of the century.

Critical dissent from the statutory provisions in English is one of the features of this book. Chapter 3 contains a general critique of them; Chapter 4 takes issue with the expectation that pupils can and should be taught to speak standard English; and I have deliberately omitted one topic the provisions include – media studies. Although I have, like other English teachers, made use of radio, television, audio and video cassettes, films, records and photographs to enrich classroom practice, I have never thought of them as part of the subject's content. Whether media studies deserve to be included anywhere in a crowded curriculum is also doubtful. The fact that some of the media – television, local radio, film, audio and video cassette – play a large part in many pupils' out-of-school life is certainly not in itself, as is sometimes implied, an argument for their occupying a similar position in the curriculum. Indeed, given that so much of their content is trivial and ephemeral, it is, if anything, an argument against.

The place of media studies is one of several controversial issues in English teaching. It is also one, I am well aware, in which my view is that of a small minority. I am equally aware that it is easy for someone comfortably removed from the classroom to exclude an element of the National Curriculum on conscientious grounds, when for a practising teacher to do so might result in dismissal or at least blighted career prospects. In planning the book I considered broaching matters of controversy in the manner of an Open University course unit – describing and analysing the range of opinion while playing down or even omitting mine. In the event, whilst retaining something of the OU approach, I found complete evenhandedness too much of a strain and opted instead to write a book founded on my own viewpoint. I sincerely hope this stimulates rather than inhibits you in developing yours.

One implicit premise of the National Curriculum I fully endorse is that you should think of yourself, in becoming an English teacher, as developing a repertoire of pedagogic skills to complement the repertoire of linguistic skills so often stated as the overall aim of the subject for pupils. From your degree course you will, no doubt, have received a grounding in English literature and been to some extent exposed to literary theory or cultural studies. You have probably already discovered that knowing about English literature for degree purposes is a very different matter from knowing how to teach it in school and puzzled over the possible relevance of the academic theory of the undergraduate seminar to the everyday life of a comprehensive school classroom. You may also have learned that literary knowledge has to be supported with linguistic knowledge, which you may or may not have acquired as part of your degree. You need to know at least some linguistics and certainly about its application to the teaching of language awareness, reading and writing, and English as a foreign language. With all these aspects of English teaching I have therefore attempted to give you some assistance, even if the modest length of the book has meant that it is less than I would have ideally liked.

From Chapter 2 onwards the book is organised around what I take to be the salient issues in English teaching, arranged in more or less logical order – moving from general and theoretical questions to more specific and practical ones. Obviously, as a reader, you have some freedom to make your own way through the book. If you are not interested in my personal history, you can start at Chapter 2; and, if you are not interested in the history of the subject, you can start at Chapter 3. Alternatively you may choose to focus on the issues which most concern you – language awareness or drama, for example. However, if you do, I should warn you that there is considerable cross-referencing between chapters.

I am indebted to more people for the ideas and practice contained in this book than I have space to mention, but I would like to acknowledge debts to: the English departments and my pupils at Moorclose High School, Middleton, Greater Manchester, and

Prescot School, Knowsley, Merseyside, in the spring terms of 1987 and 1989 respectively; my undergraduate and postgraduate students at the University of Keele during the academic year 1987–8; Susan Dransfield and her classes at St Sebastian's RC Primary School, Liverpool, between 1989 and 1991; Maureen Davies for talking to me about the teaching of reading; James Stredder for all I have learned from our four years' collaborative teaching of Shakespeare and for his comments on Chapter 8; Tony Fairman for stimulating discussions on language and education going back longer than I can remember and for his comments on Chapter 9; and Peter King, general editor of this series, for his overall observations and support.

Parts of the book have already appeared in *The Times Educational Supplement* and *Shakespeare and Schools*, albeit in different form. I have also taken the liberty of reproducing one piece of children's writing from my first book, *Positive Image*. The remainder was composed by my pupils at Prescot School or Susan Dransfield's at St Sebastian's. In the interests of readability I have kept in-text references to the bare minimum. Recommendations for further reading can be found at the end of each chapter and in the bibliography.

Finally, because there is no other obvious place for it, I would like to urge you here to join the National Association for the Teaching of English (NATE), if you have not already decided to do so. Although it can be faulted for the piety and defensiveness of some of its public pronouncements, and criticised for its role in the emergence of an occasionally doctrinaire orthodoxy on English teaching in recent years, NATE has managed to remain a broad church, and membership includes receipt of two excellent journals – *English in Education* and *The English Magazine* – besides a reduced rate for attending its invariably lively and sociable annual conferences.

R.J.

The author wishes to thank R.S. Thomas for permission to reproduce his poem 'January' on p. 158.

This morning the village school opened. I had twenty scholars. But three of the number can read: none write or cipher. Several knit, and a few sew a little. They speak with the broadest accent of the district. At present, they and I have a difficulty in understanding each other's language.

(Charlotte Brontë, *Jane Eyre*, 1847)

She would make everything personal and vivid, she would give herself, she would give, give, give all her great stores of wealth to her children, she would make them *so* happy, and they would prefer her to any teacher on the face of the earth.

(D.H. Lawrence, *The Rainbow*, 1915)

Chapter 1
English teaching revisited (1987–9)

At school . . . I enjoyed the inestimable advantage of a very sensible, though . . . very severe, master. . . . At the same time that we were studying the Greek tragic poets, he made us read Shakespeare and Milton as lessons: and they were the lessons too, which required most time and trouble to bring up, so as to escape his censure. . . . In our own English compositions . . . he showed no mercy to phrase, metaphor, or image, unsupported by a sound sense, or where the same sense might have been conveyed with equal force and dignity in plainer words. . . . He sent us to the university excellent Latin and Greek scholars, and tolerable Hebraists. Yet our classical knowledge was the least of the good gifts, which we derived from his zealous and conscientious tutorage.

(Coleridge, *Biographia Literaria*, 1817)

When will the bell ring, and end this weariness?
How long have they tugged the leash, and strained apart
My pack of unruly hounds: I cannot start
Them again on a quarry of knowledge they hate to hunt,
I can haul them and urge them no more.

(D.H. Lawrence 'The Last Lesson', *Love Poems*, 1913)

RETURN TO THE CLASSROOM (1): 1987

The school I returned to for the spring term of 1987, after an absence of nine years from the classroom, was a 14–18 high school serving a socially deprived area in an old Lancashire mill town, now subsumed within Greater Manchester. It was not the ideal school for someone no longer in the prime of youth and short on recent classroom experience. Built as a secondary modern in the mid-1950s, along severely functional lines, it suffered from most of the ills of urban working class comprehensives in the mid-1980s. Academic standards were poor (16+ results being the worst in the LEA), staff morale was low, discipline was shaky, and absenteeism and unpunctuality among pupils were chronic. The crumbling fabric of the buildings, whose appearance was not improved when person or persons unknown tried to set them on fire, and the depressing physical environment, added to the aura of gloom and despondency. Playground duty afforded an unprepossessing vista of litter, graffiti-daubed walls and smokers' huddles in the foreground, and decrepit mills and council estates in the background.

Yet the school's ethos was not wholly uncongenial, educationally or socially. Apart from the state of the buildings, there was no evidence of underfunding, if anything the reverse. Staffing was generous, resources seemed plentiful and the curriculum embraced everything one would expect, including the recent CPVE and TVEI initiatives. In addition, the staff were friendly and supportive, especially when, in the headteacher's words, I 'met a pupil coming down the street the wrong way'. The English department was outstanding in its commitment; and the pupils were, by and large, extremely affable, several of them producing excellent, and gratifying, work.

I was given the timetable of the head of department, who was on secondment, with one or two minor adjustments. This comprised: two lessons each with the Upper Sixth (for revising Milton's *Comus* and *Samson Agonistes*) and Lower Sixth (for teaching *Henry IV Part 1* and Brian Friel's *Translations*), and all the lessons of three fifth year classes (the top 16+ – forerunner of GCSE – set, the bottom non-examination set and a low ability CSE Literature set) and one fourth year class (the top set, who were in the first cohort to take GCSE). I decided to keep a weekly journal; the following excerpts chart my progress.

5 January
Well, I survived the first day and am feeling duly shattered, even though I only taught three lessons – *Henry IV* with the Lower Sixth, R.S. Thomas's 'January' to the fourth year and a discussion lesson with the top fifth in preparation for a discursive essay, which they are all short on in their files (AIDS,

inevitably, was the topic we ended up with). It was curious, starting all over again. I felt like a true novice, except with the fourth years, who are going to be a delight to teach. The fifths were boisterous, not unintelligent, but awkward, with minds of their own as to what should go on in a lesson, and not overkeen on work. The sixth were nice but stodgy. God, how schools get me down – the architecture, the social control aspect, the dinginess, the gloom, the pettiness.

6 January
Two days, and it feels like two years. I've met all my classes and they seem to be the usual mix of the conscientious, the idle and the badly behaved, but none is as bad as those I knew in Birmingham ten years ago. I was on playground duty at break and I had to stop a fight – two small 14 year olds thrashing away to no great effect. H. was with me. 'Are those two having a fight?' I asked her. 'No,' she said, 'only fooling around. . . . Well, er, maybe they are.' It was a result of one throwing coffee over the other. . . . The bottom sets are as sad and hopeless as they always have been everywhere, and I find it hard to get angry with them. The bottom fifths filled out a personal questionnaire for me. 'What is the happiest memory of your childhood?' was one of my questions. 'Losing my virginity,' wrote one boy. Much macho bravado but much anxiety underneath. To the question 'Are you frightened of anything?' the same boy replied, 'Yes, death.' It is amazing what affluence their talk reveals – computers and videos at home, holidays abroad, fashionable clothes. And this is a deprived area with a high rate of unemployment!

11 January
What of my first week? I survived it but the emphasis was very firmly on survival, and I've already got into my old Birmingham habit of counting the minutes to the end of the lesson, the lessons to the end of the day, the days to the end of the week, the weeks to the end of term – not that it's anywhere near the awfulness of Birmingham, though I did have to stop one boy assaulting another with a chair on Friday afternoon. The worst part of my week was the three lessons with the CSE Literature group. Most of them have no intention of doing any work and are quite happy chatting, scribbling on the desk and gazing out of the window.

17 January

One afternoon this week the Head closed the school early because of the snow, for the benefit, it transpired, of the staff living over the Pennines. Many pupils interpreted this as a hint to stay off for the rest of the week. Attendance isn't good at the best of times but then it is a 14–18 school and a significant minority have already had enough of classrooms by the time they arrive. It really is a glorified secondary modern school so far as intellectual and social range is concerned, and the general atmosphere is grim. 'No one's interested in education here,' said a Maths teacher to no one in particular, 'no one could give a toss.' He didn't say whether he was referring to the staff or the pupils or both. Either way, he wasn't being quite fair. Some staff care, and so do some pupils. I would certainly except the English department from his remark, though C. shocked me the other day when she said, 'English Literature is a dinosaur.' She and one or two of the others seem to think media studies more relevant.

I have also been shocked to discover that the course work system is being widely abused in this part of the world. It never was in Birmingham in the 1970s nor in the early days of CSE. The whole point of course work is that it is a fairer way of assessing what pupils have achieved. Now it seems to be almost as much the teacher's work as theirs, so strong is the pressure to be seen to have good results. No doubt in middle class areas parents are making their contributions too. This doesn't augur well for GCSE, which can be 100 per cent course work. Whatever the demerits of traditional exams, at least the examiner knows it's the pupil's own work, not a collaboration between pupil, teacher, parents and God knows who else.

I had a few modest successes this week after a bad start. An active approach to Lawrence's 'Snake', reassembling its cut-up parts plus a choral reading, went down well with the fourths, and one boy astonished everyone by picking up the reference to the albatross and retelling the whole story of 'The Ancient Mariner'. On the debit side, my supposedly good fifth year, most of whom need a collective boot up the rear, complained I was pushing them too hard. Is a week too short a time to do an essay in? I think not. One of the girls then referred disparagingly to 'all them snobby books', by which, it turned out, she meant the likes of Jane Austen and the Brontës. With my bottom fifths I'm concentrating on simple tasks and getting some success, but they don't half make me want to weep.

24 January
It was a bad week, on the whole, a few victories but mostly defeats. There was a traditional fifth year parents' evening on Monday – as useless as such occasions always were – five minutes each, nothing useful said and the parents you really want to see not there or too obviously weak to exert any influence over their offspring. In fact the fifth year top set, most of whose parents I saw, have emerged as a very unsatisfactory group to teach. Because they're all over the place with their course work, it's virtually impossible to teach them as a class and very hard to establish a working relationship with them. Several are so far behind, especially with their literature, that I've almost given up with them. A handful I'd gladly strangle; and I occasionally catch myself hoping they come a cropper. Only a minority will do well.

On Wednesday there was a crisis staff meeting over curriculum, staffing, discipline, truancy and all sorts of other things. It was heated and acrimonious, and I was astonished at how rude some staff were to one another and to the Head. A few are as badly behaved as some of the pupils. The other day one of them called a boy a 'fucking twat'. The school is in crisis – there's no doubt about that. Attainment, discipline and attendance all leave much to be desired. The trouble is that the staff as a whole don't pull together. Only a minority use the staff room as a social base, and there were faces at the crisis meeting I had never even seen before. Unionism is another problem. Its influence is very evident and it looks as though there are going to be days of action later in the term. 'Industrial' action is completely out of place in a state school.

My English colleagues, on the other hand, are always friendly, supportive and enthusiastic. We meet every Thursday to talk things over. I needed them this week for my worst moment so far. I had to have three obnoxious girls ejected from my CSE Literature set. Their behaviour was impossible – screaming, shouting and throwing things around. They've been in trouble all week and one was subsequently suspended. On the positive side things are going tolerably well with the bottom fifth year set, as long as only the regulars (i.e. half the number on the register), with whom I have established some kind of rapport, are present. On Friday I tried *Romeo and Juliet* on them, the story plus possible modern applications – Northern Ireland, black and white. It went really well. They showed interest in Shakespeare and one borrowed a copy of *Macbeth*. They also expressed interest in my African experience and wanted to know whether I'd had a black girlfriend and why I hadn't married her. I've finished *Lord of the Flies* with the top fourths. Most of them found it difficult, which gives some idea of the school's academic range. Now I must think of something imaginative to do with it.

1 February

Survival continues to be the theme at school. Only a couple of good lessons in the week – drama on *Lord of the Flies* with the fourths and *Macbeth* with the bottom fifths as a follow-up to last week's successful *Romeo and Juliet*. Other members of staff seem to think I've been quite adventurous, and I do believe I have. I wish I was better at discipline, though . . . I tried a discussion on unemployment with the bottom fifths. It didn't work at all. They didn't want to discuss it, just as they don't want to discuss nuclear war or anything else that's terrible and about which they can do nothing. The careers teacher told me that 75 per cent of the fifths go on to the YTS scheme and most of the others go to college or stay on for a sixth year. Only a tiny handful get actual jobs, and these are mostly of the 'lads of dads' variety.

8 February

Just when I thought things were getting better I had a 'do' with a pupil in the class I supervise for H. once a week. Colin his name is, and a more pathetic specimen it would be hard to imagine – ugly, ungainly and unwashed. He became extremely disruptive and I asked him to accompany me to 'referral'. He refused and ran out of school. It later turned out he'd been the victim of a poison pen letter from two boys mocking his smelliness. . . . The week ended in better style. H. said how pleased they were with the way I'd settled in. I returned the compliment by saying it was a pleasure to work in such an English department, which it is. I only wish I'd achieved more. I depressed C. by saying the school was a dump in my view and experience. She has very little to compare it with. At least in Birmingham there were the Asians to raise the academic tone and West Indians to inject some vitality.

15 February
Only a week till half-term and I'm in ecstasy at the prospect. Nothing fresh to report except that a boy in my class was suspended for throwing a metal rod at a teacher. This is the same teacher said to have called a pupil a 'fucking twat'; perhaps the boy was that pupil. . . . At last some of my classes are starting to produce good work, both on literature and in creative and discursive writing, and that's given me a real glow. . . . How I hate Mondays. I'm all right once I'm into the swing of the week.

28 March
Only two weeks left, slowly winding down. I'm throwing everything I can at the fourth year, D.H. Lawrence at the moment – one always tries to impose one's own enthusiasms. To my amazement most of the top fifth year have completed their course work in both language and literature. Next week we have to mark and moderate it all internally before the external moderators get their hands on it. What a business! One boy in the top set, a truly objectionable character, has been expelled after I caught him copying out someone else's work and submitting it as his own. 'Dickhead!' he snarled at me in the corridor after the Head had given him his marching orders. . . . I must say how I've enjoyed teaching Milton to the Upper Sixth, besides being appalled by their ignorance. When I started with them, they couldn't tell me what a metaphor was, nor a sonnet.

11 April
The last two weeks were typical end of term weeks. The dramatic highlight was that I got punched on the nose or on the glasses, to be exact, which cut into my nose on the impact of the blow. It was an accident, or at least the blow was not meant for me. Two of my bottom set fifth year boys were playing Cluedo in a small group in the post-course period. Suddenly a row erupted between them over an allegation of cheating. I was at the other end of the room playing Scrabble with another group. Before I could intercede the row had become a violent fight, with desks and chairs flying as in a Western saloon brawl. I dived in and grabbed one of the combatants and shouted to the biggest boy present to grab the other. As I pulled the first boy away, the right hook meant for

him hit me. The shock of that stopped the fight. The rest of the class rallied round and several members of staff appeared to haul the offenders off for chastisement. I felt a bit weak for a while, but more from the shock of being struck for the first time in my adult life than anything else, and I soon recovered. Subsequently the offenders, with both of whom I enjoyed a reasonably good relationship, had to write me letters of apology. These were semi-literate and rather pathetic in a way. One of them read:

Dear Mr Jeffcoate,
I would like to apologise about what happened with John and I and I am very sorry for what I done to your nose and I will never do what I done again I hope that you will accept my apollogey and I hope that John has apologised as well,
thankyou,
Dean

It was a bad week generally for discipline at school. A much worse incident concerned a young woman on the staff who had a notice stuck on her back in a fourth year science lesson saying, 'Follow me for a fuck.' The end of term itself was amicable enough. I think I genuinely did make a favourable impression on the staff. Despite having to commute eighty miles each day, I was never away and late only twice because of car problems. I prepared my lessons religiously, got fifth year course work finished, marked all assignments promptly and generally did all that could reasonably have been expected of me. Two classes gave me presents and 'Thank you' cards, and in the very last lesson of all I had a little tea party with my bottom fifth year set. At the end several of the boys shook my hand solemnly, including the boy who struck the blow. For me it was mainly a relief that it was all over and I was still alive. I was also proud of having done a good job and of having shown I could still stay the course in a rough urban secondary school. It made me think about education and about what a terrible failure the state system has proved for so many children after more than a hundred years. I shall write something about it, though I'm not quite sure what or who for.

What I eventually wrote was an article called 'Class of '87'. It concentrated on my experience with the bottom fifth year set in order to make the general point with which the last journal entry concludes. It was published in *The Times Educational Supplement* in the summer of the same year. Afterwards I rather regretted it, a feeling confirmed when a correspondent wrote to complain about its 'negative' and 'lugubrious' tone. For were not the fourth years, with whom I had achieved so much, equally a class of '87?

The untypicality of this particular experience, and indeed of much of my experience, skewed as it was towards underachieving, semi-anarchic city schools, was brought home to me the following academic year, when I was responsible for the teaching practice assessment of thirty-eight undergraduate and postgraduate students in almost the same number of comprehensive schools. The schools were in a mixture of urban and rural settings in the North Midlands, and only two of them significantly resembled the Greater Manchester school or reminded me of the schools I had taught at, and done research in, in a number of cities in the 1970s. The remainder exuded an encouraging aura of friendly, purposeful and orderly activity. I therefore decided that the next time I had the opportunity to write up a school experience I would try to rectify the balance and make the account as positive as the facts allowed.

RETURN TO THE CLASSROOM (2): 1989

My chance came in the spring term of 1989, when I was on supply at a comprehensive school in the Merseyside authority of Knowsley. Unfortunately, for my purposes, this school was much more akin to the Greater Manchester one than to those at which my students had been on practice. Although serving the more common age range of 11–16, and a former grammar school rather than a former secondary modern, its catchment area was very similar and it suffered from similar problems. Knowsley is one of the most severely disadvantaged LEAs in the country and regularly occupies the bottom of the league table for both 16+ and 18+ performance. Only 8.5 per cent of its school-leavers were awarded five or more GCSE grades A–C in 1990 as compared with 39.1 per cent in the London borough of Sutton and 19.4 per cent in neighbouring Liverpool. The school I taught at, however, is one of the authority's more successful ones. In 1988 approximately a quarter of its fifth year pupils gained an A–C grade in English (and a similar proportion in Maths – in each case, half the national success rate).

My timetable comprised: fourth and fifth year GCSE sets from the middle of the ability range, upper and lower band second year classes and a first year mixed ability group. This time I decided I would try to get closer to the reality of the experience by keeping a daily record of events and impressions. The following are excerpts.

6 January
It was a hell of a day, and I felt at the end as if I'd taught for a whole week. It started off badly with the lower band second year class, convincing me yet again of the wrongheadedness of all streaming systems, although the fact that I had not taught children of this age for ten years did not help. They reacted badly to my approach to drama teaching, admittedly developed for adults. To them drama simply meant group improvisation on a topic chosen by me. They refused to mix sexes, lacked discipline and several were genuinely disruptive. I then made a fatal error. Realising that the 'Fulvia is dead' dialogue from *Antony and Cleopatra* was too remote for most of them, I panicked and on the spur of the moment changed it to 'The headteacher is dead'. Some of the boys seized on this as an opportunity to ridicule their actual headteacher, improvising scenes in which he succumbed to AIDS or was caught in bed with the school secretary.

7 January
I did the solitary confinement role-play with the fifth years in the hope that it could lead into an assignment, and it seemed to go well. With the first years I continued with *King Lear*. We couldn't get into the drama room so we had to go into the hall. The Lear–Cordelia dialogue on 'nothing' was a great success, but thereafter I let the reins go too slack, and two girls had a fight in the corridor after the lesson. With the fourth years, in the afternoon, it was actually quite hard to know how to proceed with *Of Mice and Men*, since they are at different points in the story and some prefer to read on their own while others demand a class reading. They seemed keen, however, apart from a couple of semi-hysterical girls, but their folders are a shambles. Last lesson was the lower band second years again. I took three of the boys aside to reprimand them for the rude things they had written about the Head in their play scenes, but it did not seem to have any effect on the general standard of behaviour. This class is totally wild.

12 January
The first years watched what I thought was a rather pretentious production of an abstract fantasy by the Merseyside Youth Theatre. Afterwards they were very responsive when one of the actresses came to talk to them – to her, however, not to the play. They plied her with questions about her personal life and practical issues such as who had made the scenery. To my surprise I had a good drama session with the lower seconds, or the wild bunch, as I now call them, on Graham Greene's 'I Spy'. I've abandoned drama games with them; children like them don't need warming up. They also worked hard on their own fifty-word versions of the story. The upper seconds had already written stories continuing from where Greene leaves off, and I got them to mark one another's. This they did very responsibly. We finished the lesson with an interesting discussion of the issues raised by the story – gangs, smoking, stealing.

19 January
First two I had the wild bunch, and they were quite good for them. After some work on Greene's 'Case for the Defence', they set about their own murder stories. Two groups organised themselves exceptionally well – the third got nowhere. I was amazed; somehow I had touched the right button. Charlie, normally so badly behaved, organised his group particularly well, making many adult suggestions. They were really keen and needed no checking. The afternoon found them in more riotous mood when they tried to gatecrash my lesson with the upper seconds. This got them into trouble with the German teacher next door, who was supposed to be teaching them. At four o'clock the offenders came to apologise, laughing all over their faces. . . . The worst lesson today, however, was with the first year. They are a difficult class, essentially because so many of them are remedial and limited in what they can read and write. But I taught a bad lesson, knowing it was bad and unable to extricate myself. I wanted those who had been present last time to explain to those who hadn't, about a third of the class, how *King Lear* finished. They got confused, then I got confused; so I got irritable, and they got irritable.

26 January
Not only had the wild bunch rehearsed their plays in their own time, they actually brought in costumes and make-up. One play

was a variation on Hitchcock's *Psycho*, the other on Jack the Ripper. They were equally enthusiastic about writing out their scenes so I could pin them up on the board. One of the first years said to me he'd enjoyed *King Lear* but it had gone on too long. Drama with the upper seconds on the Victorian painting 'And when did you last see your father?' was the best yet. One boy said he was going to see *Richard III* with his parents at the weekend, which must make him pretty exceptional in this school.

27 January
To my astonishment most of the fourth years handed in their *Of Mice and Men* assignments on time. I feel relaxed with this class even though it does contain some awkward customers. In preparation for the next assignment I tried out some pair and group work on them. First, they had to complete a *curriculum vitae* for Steinbeck based on a six-page biography I had duplicated for them; then, using the same headings, they had to interview one another to see how much they could find out about their own lives. This should yield a number of possibilities for a biography/autobiography assignment. The whole class seemed to enjoy themselves for once.

30 January
The fourth years were not at their best today. Two of them, a boy and a girl, had a slanging match, during the course of which he called her a 'slut', disrupting the whole class. I sent them to the head of year. They came back saying they couldn't find him but promised there'd be no recurrence. I do hate all the abuse, aggression and squabbling that seems to go on between pupils these days. On the credit side, some members of the class had written promising assignments, so I read a couple of these out to try and calm things down. One boy in the fifth year has written a brilliant poem and incorporated it into his solitary confinement assignment. It resembles a ballad by Kipling, having an assured sense of rhythm. First year written work, on the other hand, is appalling almost without exception – in presentation, mechanics and content.

20 February
Several of the upper seconds had obviously worked really hard on their half-term assignments on Shakespeare. One produced

a full-scale typed-out project. The fourths have mostly finished their biography assignments, and now seem to be enjoying *A Taste of Honey*. It's ages since I've seen or read this play, and I must say it's worn better than most 1950s' 'kitchen sink' drama, though it creaks here and there. The fifth year, however, depress me; some give the impression they couldn't care less whether they finish their course work or not. 'It's not me doing this,' I snapped at one point, 'it's you.' They just shrugged their shoulders and looked glum. The first years, now understandably on class report, cheered me up. I read 'Spit Nolan' to them as an example of an autobiographical story, and then told them the story of how a friend and I had inadvertently saved the life of a man who'd taken a drug overdose. When it came to their turn, six volunteered to tell stories to the rest of the class. One boy proved a natural raconteur, enchanting his audience with a succession of increasingly horrifying tales which adroitly mixed fact and fantasy.

23 February
GCSE oral moderation in the afternoon – watching a video, marking the trial candidates, discussion with the moderator. It convinced me of both the undesirability and impossibility of oral assessment, since what you are in effect assessing is the candidate's personality. Interestingly neither accent nor dialect cropped up as an issue although several candidates had strong Yorkshire accents and regularly used non-standard forms. This is a welcome advance on the situation ten years ago. Two of my upper second years complained to me that no one had ever taught them how to punctuate, so in my absence at the moderation I set them an inverted commas exercise, using the Yobs cartoon from *Private Eye*, just to see how good or bad they were. Only a handful had significant problems. Those who finished had to carry on with their 'Fulvia is dead' scenes, many of which have turned out exceptionally well. It's funny to think what I have made of this simple suggestion, picked out of the Bullock report all those years ago. After school C. said how well I'd fitted in, using the very words H. used two years earlier. She also asked me if I would be interested in a permanent job in September, as K. is retiring. I said I was flattered, which I was, but it would kill me, which it would.

28 February
I asked the four fourth years who'd seen the dramatisation of *Of Mice and Men* at the Playhouse to give their comments to the rest of the class. Three had liked it, one hadn't. I then did tableaux with them to show how the relationships change in *A Taste of Honey*. Some of them found this a weird activity and said so, but they saw the point eventually, I think. To confirm whether they had, I asked them to see if they could represent the changes diagrammatically on paper. They worked well and produced some imaginative results. The lower seconds were keen to get on with writing up their play scenes, which pleased me, but Charlie remains a problem. R. suggested I have a word with F. about him. This I have done. Two of the first years appeared with letters of apology for yesterday's slanging match among the girls. K., head of first year, told me one boy had recited to her all the lines he had learned from *King Lear* with great pride.

2 March
I started *Macbeth* with the lower seconds. It was hard, however, to get them to concentrate on the story, and they weren't very good at learning their lines for the witches' scene either. But they were good, as you'd expect, at the murder, and worked hard at their spells afterwards. Working hard also seems to mean being noisy to them, unfortunately, even though Charlie had been taken out by F., a bit of an extreme move, I thought, but I'll have to go along with it. The first years were very rowdy too, mainly because of the disruption caused by the BCG tests, but they were attentive for the first part of 'The Ancient Mariner'. The upper seconds played the murder game in *Macbeth* superbly.

3 March
The first years were bad for the final part of 'The Ancient Mariner', restless and chatty, and I got very little done in drama because I insisted on complete silence before moving on to the next stage. 'This is a poo class,' said one of the keener boys, and I am afraid to say he's right. In the afternoon there was something of a calamity. I had a difficult third year class to supervise in CDT before rushing back to the other end of the school for the wild bunch. I found them being harangued by G. for knocking on the window to his room. After he'd gone, the

finger of suspicion pointed at John, a terribly mixed-up boy in local authority care with a tendency to run out of lessons. John claimed the main culprit was Tony, who promptly came up to hit him. I took Tony out for a talking to, which John interpreted as his cue to abscond. I tried to grab him and he started punching me wildly before running off. I reported the incident to F. who went in search of him. He was eventually found and persuaded to return and apologise. Then everything went quiet.

8 March
'You've certainly given them a classical education,' said C. to me today while admiring the work on Shakespeare, 'The Ancient Mariner' and the Greene stories now covering the walls of my room. She had summed up precisely what I had been trying to do all term, and I felt very chuffed. The upper seconds were superb in drama, miming the murder of Duncan as originally planned and as eventually executed. We also read the whole of the Porter's scene together, having borrowed copies from the fifth form, and I was pleasantly surprised at how well they read the text.

9 March
The lower seconds were even better than the uppers at the murder game in *Macbeth*, and then listened attentively to how the story developed. With the uppers I did a double drama session on the play in the hall. Particularly successful was my idea of applying the game of Grandmother's Footsteps to Lady Macbeth's sleepwalking. As I walked round the hall reciting the lines, the class had to follow me, repeating them phrase by phrase and freezing if I turned round. The first years carried on with illustrating their favourite verse from 'The Ancient Mariner' in order to make a frieze of the poem – very noisily, inevitably for them. One of the boys said to me, 'Sir, when are we going to do some proper English?' R.J.: 'What do you mean?' Boy: 'You know, exercises and stuff like that.'

10 March
Comic Relief Day. Several red noses and a general atmosphere of levity. The fourth years refused to work unless I forked out a fiver, which I duly did, somewhat to their surprise, although several of them then failed to keep their side of the bargain,

Jane and Rebecca being even more hysterical than usual. Now that *A Taste of Honey* is over, and most of the assignments are in, I've decided to round off the term with a selection of poems by Seamus Heaney, those which are clearly based on his childhood – 'Digging', 'Mid-term Break', 'Follower', 'Death of a Naturalist', 'Blackberry-Picking'. This may be a mistake, as their experience of poetry seems limited to children's verse and the likes of Roger McGough. However, I've explained to them that they have to do serious adult poetry for GCSE. The first years were impossible today. They're so bad at working together, and I was amazed yet again at the poverty of their vocabulary. We were doing 'Case for the Defence', and 'accused', 'victim', 'acquit' and 'prosecute' were among the words to bamboozle them. One girl has copied out the whole of 'The Ancient Mariner' in her best handwriting and done her own versions of the beautiful illustrations by Mervyn Peake. I was lost for appropriate words when she gave it all to me; it must have taken her ages.

14 March
I carried on with Heaney with the fourths but it was a real grind. He's simply too difficult for them. I gave each group a different poem to work on for presenting to the rest of the class. They struggled and floundered and most gave up. I can't see them doing a traditional assignment; probably the best idea would be a poem of their own on a childhood memory. Would this count as 'real engagement with texts', to use the GCSE jargon? The fifth year course work is all wound up, thank God, though I've still some oral assessment to do. The lower seconds have made a small wall display of their work on *Macbeth* – spells, posters, newspaper reports, a model of the Globe – nothing very substantial, but at least they've done something.

By the end of the term children's work adorned the walls of my room as well as the corridor outside. Below is a sample. All the pieces were written by first and second years, and most arose out of circumstances referred to in the excerpts above.

Alone
No one knows,
What it feels like,
To be all alone,
Except the man down our road.
He gets called names,
The children throw stones at him.
They don't know what it feels like to be
ALONE.

He has no wife,
She died.
He eats in the cafe
Because he can't cook,
He's too old.
People call him a tramp.
But he's not,
He's just
ALONE.

I feel sorry for him.
I wish I never grow old
And be
ALONE.

                    (Steven)

Haiku
I was born,
I grew up,
I died.
          (John)

Dark alleys,
The owl in the trees,
Scared.
                    (Ian)

Is there anyone
Stranded out there
In space?
                    (Kevin)

A tree in the dark,
Forming faces.
Lightning strikes.
               (Peter)

True Stories

I was going fishing for newts with my oldest brother and my auntie to a small pond. You have to cross a wide open field to get to the pond. The field is used by the children for playing football. It was on 3rd May 1986 when I was going for newts. As we were crossing this field a motorbike came from out of the nearby woods. I looked round. It was one of the Morgans who live on Hartfield Avenue. It was one of the oldest, Jason. I started to panic. I ran out of the way but straight into the path of the motorbike. It hit me. My leg was caught on the gear chain and it was dragging me round. He stopped. Before I knew it I was in the ambulance on my way to Whiston Hospital. When I reached the hospital the doctor put me to sleep so they could operate. They had to do micro surgery. I had 79 stitches in my leg, 26 in my head and my leg was fractured in two places. I was in so much pain. I was in hospital for six weeks. Jason Morgan came to see me. Then I went home. I had the bandage took off my leg and a plaster cast put on. My leg was in plaster for another 6 weeks. I took Morgan to court and the case is still going through.

(Colin)

My story is about a lad called Carl and he broke out of jail and he went to this house where a lady lived with her two kids. He went to her and she let him stay but she said to him he would have to stay in the loft. So he said, 'OK.' One day the police came and searched the house but not the loft so they went away to look for Carl and later on she said to Carl, 'Do not open the door to no one, help yourself to food and drink. I am going to my mother's for dinner and I will be back after.' So she went out and her mother said, 'You look strange today. What is the matter?' She said, 'Nothing is the matter.' She had dinner and then she went home. As she was coming in she opened the door and he had hung himself from the banister. She screamed and ran with the two kids all the way back to her mum's.

(Jenny)

My story is about a boy who was 22. He was on a robbed motorbike that was in good condition, and he left it outside a club. So two boys got on it and rode round everywhere. Also they went into a dual carriageway the other way round. And they crashed into the back of a bus, so the police said anyway, and one boy got killed. He broke his neck and died. His name was George Keenan and he was 22. A week later was his funeral and nearly everyone round his mother's went to it and they brought flowers and cards. Everyone of his friends went.

(Joanne)

Yesterday we wrote a story and I couldn't think of any story to do so I waited and I was thinking and I still couldn't think of anything. So I got a bit bored and after a bit the bell had gone so I am back today and I thought a bit and then asked our teacher and he told me to sit and think so I am here now writing a story about sitting and thinking.

(John)

King Lear
Dear Edmund,
I am writing to you for two things. One is to to tell you how much I love you and the other is to ask a favour. If you could think of a way to kill my husband, I would be very happy. I never really loved him. I loved you. If you can write back to me and give me your ideas, I would be very happy to help you,

Love,
Goneril (Maxine)

P.S. I love you X X X X X X X

Antony and Cleopatra

Antony:	Fulvia is dead!
Enobarbus:	Sir?
Antony:	Fulvia is dead!
Enobarbus:	Fulvia!
Antony:	Dead.
Enobarbus:	My Fulvia?
Antony:	I know it's hard but you must face it. She's dead. No one can change that. [*Enobarbus bursts out crying.*]
Antony:	Come on, a stiff drink is what you need. [*Antony hands him a whisky. Enobarbus drinks it*]
Antony:	Better?
Enobarbus:	Yes, thanks. [*Brief pause*]
Enobarbus:	She was so young.
Antony:	Yes, awful way to go, so much pain, awful . . .
Enobarbus:	How . . . how did she die?

Antony:	She slipped on a wet floor and knocked a knife off the table and landed on it, awful . . .
Enobarbus:	What was she doing in the kitchen anyway? She was supposed to be here with me. Her mother left her for me to look after. She trusted me. It was my fault, my fault! [*Enobarbus bursts out crying again.*]
Enobarbus:	Her poor mother. Does she know?
Antony:	No, we thought it would be best for you to tell her, if you're up to it.
Enobarbus:	Yes, you're right. I should, as it was my fault.

(Amanda; the first five lines,
of course, are by Shakespeare)

Macbeth
Two cats' eyes
Along with lashes,
Sprinkle on with plenty of ashes
A human's nose
Which first froze.
A frog's head
Stuffed with lead,
A dead man's finger
Which will linger, linger.
A rabbit's heart
With a bum to fart,
A cow's stomach,
Mixed in with a pig's tail,
Will never fail.
A woman's foot,
Dipped in soot,
A lizard's tongue
Which first was hung,
Four dogs' paws
Along with claws,
A jar of bats' wings
With a lot of bees' stings,
A baboon's teeth
Along with a wreath.

(Nikki and Lynsey)

BANQUO BLOODBATH: FLEANCE FLEES!
The famous thane Banquo was murdered today by two unknown assassins, whilst peacefully riding down a pleasant country lane with his son Fleance. The two attackers jumped out from behind a clump of trees and pounced on the two riders. After a fierce fight Fleance took flight and was forced to leave Banquo, whose body was later found face-down in a filthy ditch by the roadside. The exact time of the murder is unknown, as Fleance didn't have his watch on. However, we can exclusively reveal that we believe Macbeth to have hired the assassins. We received this information from a source who wishes to remain anonymous: 'I heard Macbeth tell the cut-throats, "Travel o'er to Banquo's favoured riding-place. Take thy blades and kill him and his son." We questioned Macbeth but he avoided answering by babbling something about a ghost appearing and disappearing and then fainting. One of the murder weapons was found near Banquo's body covered in Banquo's blood. Fleance himself is reported to have said, 'It was horrible! There was blood and steel everywhere. I had to leave my father and flee.' The assassins' names are not known but the authorities have issued photofit pictures of both men. These men are extremely dangerous and should not be approached.

(John and Scott)

I have included this sample of writing, not because any of it is outstanding for pupils of the authors' ages, but to give some idea of the range of achievement one can expect from a mixture of abilities in a teaching practice term. However, it does also represent a level of achievement in each individual case which the particular author could be proud of – in effect, an example of their best work. In the case of some of the authors – Jenny, for example, who was in a remedial withdrawal group for reading and writing – the weaknesses in their writing are somewhat masked by the fact that I have corrected spelling and punctuation to bring out the quality of the content. Jenny's uncorrected first sentence read: 'my story is I new a lab calleD carl and he brock out of Jail and he whent to this house were a laby lived will her two kiDs.'

A CLASSICAL EDUCATION

Although this second experience of returning to the classroom was, by and large, as depressing as the first, I remained determined to emphasise its positive features in writing it up. What I eventually wrote, with possible publication in mind, was a distillation of my journal entries, inspired by the head of department's remark, quoted in the entry for 8 March, 'You've certainly given them a classical education.' It provides a fuller statement of the ideological position hinted at in the journal entries.

> One of the most shameful moments in my teaching career occurred when I was head of English in a small Birmingham secondary school in the mid-1970s. The bane of my existence at that time was a fifth year CSE set whom I had also struggled with in the fourth year. As with many such classes, at the eye of the storm, as it were, was a small group of girls, mostly Asian, who beavered away industriously and seemingly oblivious of the mayhem surrounding them. One evening after school a member of this group, Shaheen, found me in the stock room. She stood for a moment surveying the piles of books, many of them relics of an earlier era when the school's intake had been bigger and more academically balanced, before her eyes settled on sets of half a dozen Shakespeare plays. 'Why don't we do Shakespeare, sir?' she asked.
>
> I no longer remember exactly what my reply was but it was to the effect that I could not begin to entertain such a possibility with a class as turbulent as hers. It was also the case that I had been seriously deflected from the main duty of the English teacher, the initiation of children into greater knowledge and appreciation of the English language and its literature, by the then fashionable preoccupation with issues of race, social class and gender which inevitably resulted in concentration on what was immediate and, more often than not, ephemeral and mediocre.
>
> Whatever my reply was, Shaheen did not look convinced by it. 'Well, can I read them?' she persisted, pointing to the sets of plays. The least I could do was give her a copy of each – *Macbeth*, *Julius Caesar*, *The Merchant of Venice*, *Romeo and Juliet*, *A Midsummer Night's Dream* and *Henry V*, if memory serves me right – to take away. A week or so later she reported that she had read and enjoyed them all. Her tone clearly implied that she

could see even less reason for her class not studying Shakespeare, having now read six of his plays, than she could before.

Memory of this episode has returned more than once to haunt and trouble me in the years that have elapsed since. It returned most recently, but to positive effect, last term when I was on supply in a Merseyside secondary school and searching for a rationale to give shape to my almost instinctive lesson planning. It came to me that what in a sense I was attempting to do was atone for, even exorcise, that memory by trying to recapture something of the pristine purity of my original dedication to the main duty of the English teacher twenty-five years ago.

The school in question was not so difficult as its Birmingham counterpart, though difficult enough. I had five classes – fifth and fourth year GCSE sets representing the middle of the ability range and, on the whole, well disposed towards work; upper and lower band second year classes; and a mixed ability first year. The upper band class were lively but a delight to teach, the other two more or less wild. They came into a lesson shouting, squabbling and jostling ('toy fighting', as they called it), and continued that way, except for brief intervals of peace, throughout its duration.

For these lower school classes I was free to teach what I wished and, disregarding the banding division on principle, devised the same curriculum for all three. I religiously eschewed anything smacking of my shameful Birmingham memory -- the wishy-washy arbitrariness of the thematic approach, the sentimental whimsy of children's literature (and the formulaic vulgarity of its offshoot, teenage fiction) and the insidious relativism of cultural and media studies. Instead I built firmly on the most reliable basis for curriculum planning ever put forward – Matthew Arnold's 'the best which has been thought and said in the world'. My core comprised *King Lear* and *Macbeth*, even though no set of the former was available, 'The Rime of the Ancient Mariner' and the short stories of Graham Greene. I filled in at the edges with other stories, poems and stimuli, and varied the programme slightly from one class to another, but essentially what all three classes experienced in English last term were these classics of adult literature.

A conservative aim and conservative choices of content, which is what many people would take mine to be, are by no means incompatible with a child-centred or active peda- gogy. Indeed, my choices were in part dictated by the extent to which they lent themselves to active methods and nurturing children's own creativity. In the case of Shakespeare, my first and second year classes worked on performing speeches, dialogues and individual scenes, learning some by heart (for example, the opening scene of *Macbeth* and the dialogue on 'nothing' between Lear and Cordelia); made up letters (from Cordelia in exile to Lear, from Regan and Goneril to Edmund); mimed (the murder of Duncan as originally planned and eventually executed); played drama games (Murder in the Dark for the killing of Duncan, Grandmother's Footsteps for Lady Macbeth's sleepwalking); and drew maps of Lear's Britain and Macbeth's Scotland. They also undertook more conventional tasks such as projects on Shakespeare's life and witchcraft and cloze tests to see how much they had understood or remembered.

'The Ancient Mariner' we read through, with me in the title role and good readers taking the parts of the narrator, the wedding guest and the other minor characters, before dramatising the opening encounter and the exciting bits of the mariner's narrative – the shooting of the albatross, the ship of death, the blessing of the water snakes, the sinking of the ship. Afterwards the children made a frieze of the story in small groups, illustrating one of its seven parts and finding a verse to go with their picture. The three Graham Greene stories – 'I Spy', 'Case for the Defence' and 'The Destructors' – I chose primarily because they are so dramatisable, and I used a mixture of tableaux, improvisation and role-play to bring them to life. They also provided openings for other material I was keen to experiment with – respectively, the well known Victorian painting in Liverpool's Walker Art Gallery 'And when did you last see your father?'; one of Liverpool's most famous legal cases, the Maybrick murder, which celebrates its centenary this year; and one of the very few decent plays specifically written for children, Rae Jenkins' *Julian*.

Having an ambitious plan of campaign does not, of course, necessarily issue in success. Some children found some of what they were asked to do difficult, confusing or dull. The map of Lear's Britain was left unfinished in one class, as was a model of the Globe Theatre in another. Scott complained that *Lear* had gone on too long, while Julie suddenly expostulated in the middle of Polanski's film of *Macbeth*, 'Sir, why isn't it in English we can understand?' and there was a general feeling, which I came to share, that the second half of 'The Ancient Mariner' was not nearly so good as the first half. For my own part I sometimes felt I was sinking beneath a tide of illiteracy, not to mention being driven to distraction by the sheer noise – in fact, not unlike Lear at the end of Act II in a speech we had worked on, 'You think I'll weep;/No I'll not weep:/I have full cause of weeping. . . . O Fool! I shall go mad.'

Yet, everything considered, the term was, I think, a success story. All three classes gave me the unmistakable impression that they appreciated having been admitted to cultural experiences, especially Shakespeare, often barred to them on the ground that they were too young, too dim or too badly behaved. At the end of term the first year, who had been on class report for most of it and were far and away the weakest and noisiest first year I have ever taught, presented me with a leaving card decorated with references to the work we had done and, in bold letters at the bottom, the question, 'Remember these?' (I sincerely hope they do.) By this time the walls of my room were filled with the children's writing and art. Surveying it, the head of English, who had supported me in my campaign throughout, commented, 'You've certainly given them a classical education.' It is the highest compliment I have ever been paid as a teacher, and I suddenly felt like the Ancient Mariner. The albatross of that shameful Birmingham memory had finally fallen from my neck.

FURTHER READING

Despite the obvious limitations to subjective and impressionistic accounts of classroom experience, they provide a necessary complement to theoretical discussion and more objective analysis. The one outstanding treatment of a young teacher's experience in our literature is to be found in D.H. Lawrence's *The Rainbow*, which you should certainly read if you have not already done so. Ursula Brangwen's experience (based on Lawrence's own and on that of the woman teachers he knew) was as an uncertificated teacher on £50 a year with responsibility for fifty-five Standard 5 elementary school children at the beginning of this century. Yet when I first read the novel fifty years after Lawrence completed it, as a young comprehensive school teacher on £50 a month with responsibility for five different classes of between thirty and thirty-eight pupils of varying abilities, I felt as though he was describing my experience. No fictional account of school life written since has achieved anything like the intensity of his vision; nor have any of the anthropological studies of classrooms which have proliferated in the last thirty years been able to match it for truthfulness.

Chapter 2

The subject of English

English is not a school 'subject' at all. It is a condition of school life.

(George Sampson, *English for the English*, 1921)

It is a characteristic of English that it does not hold together as a body of knowledge which can be identified, quantified, then transmitted.

(The Bullock Report, 1975)

English is all about your views and thoughts or a good story.

(Fourteen-year-old boy, quoted in
The Times Educational Supplement, 27 May 1988)

English is all just waffle, really. There is no grounding at all. . . . It is all blather.

(Imogen Stubbs, actress, commenting on having
gained a first-class degree in English
from Oxford University, interviewed 1991)

ENGLISH'S IDENTITY PROBLEM

'What *is* English?' With this emphatic question a postgraduate student of mine began an essay reflecting on his experience of the subject at school. That English has an identity problem (concerning what exactly it is), which sets it apart from the other academic subjects and causes anxiety and dissension among its teachers, has long been recognised. The first national report on English teaching, *The Teaching of English in England*, published in 1921 and usually referred to by the name of its chairman, the poet Sir Henry Newbolt, was particularly perceptive about the nature of the problem. Although it does not always press its analysis as far or as firmly as it might, it provides us with a useful starting point.

The report is best known for its remark, repeated by George Sampson, one of the members of its committee, in his own book *English for the English* published in the same year, that 'every teacher is a teacher of English because every teacher is a teacher in English'. The basic point is even older, dating back to the Board of Education's circular *The Teaching of English in Secondary Schools*, published in 1910. Since 1921 the first half of the remark – 'every teacher is a teacher of English' – has acquired the status of a truism, even though it does not necessarily follow from the simple fact of the second half – 'every teacher is a teacher in English' – and even though opinion has divided sharply over what the implications of accepting it are both for English teachers and for teachers of other subjects. The Newbolt report took the main implication to be that all teachers should be responsible for the quality of the English spoken and written in their lessons. While conceding that this interpretation posed something of a threat to the role of English teachers, the report could not quite bring itself to confront explicitly the simple question raised by its dictum: if every teacher is a teacher of English, why do we need English teachers?

The first facet of English's identity problem derives, then, from the fact that it is, in the words of the Cox report, 'both a subject and a medium of instruction for other subjects'. English teachers have to decide to what extent their responsiblities are subject-specific and to what extent they are cross-curricular, and, in the case of the latter, how they intermesh with the linguistic responsibilities of teachers of other subjects. The second facet of the problem was also clearly identified by George Sampson and the Newbolt committee. English is more than a school subject and more than a medium of instruction. It is, to quote Sampson, 'a condition of school life' and, in addition, for the great majority of children, to quote the report, a 'home' and 'life' subject. It is the language of their personal and social lives, both in school and without. English differs from other subjects because children know 'the beginnings' of it by the time they embark on statutory education and are receiving daily lessons in it quite 'independently of the school'.

The Newbolt committee was aware that this acknowledgement could be used to undermine its case for the centrality of English.

For, if it is true, as linguistics teaches, that children have mastered the rudiments of their mother tongue by the time they start school and receive daily lessons in it from other sources, what justification can there be for allocating it a central position in an overcrowded curriculum, given the demands of subjects which children do not know at all? This, in fact, is more or less what the representatives of a number of famous boys' grammar and public schools did say in their evidence to the committee. Provided a school had a good library, they argued, and gave children ample opportunity to use it and to express themselves through school magazines and drama and debating societies, there was no need for a subject on the timetable called English. Seventy years on you may well feel, as I do, some sympathy for their point of view. These schools drew their pupils, of course, in the main from educated homes in which standard English was as much the norm as it was at school. The Newbolt committee's principal concern was with children who attended elementary and secondary schools in the state sector and came from less favoured homes in which non-standard forms of the mother tongue often prevailed. The justification for giving these children lessons in English at school was, in the committee's opinion, that the daily lessons they received at home and elsewhere were at worst 'bad' and at best 'haphazard'.

The third and final facet of English's identity problem is that it does not appear to be about anything. The Newbolt report stresses several times that it is not a content subject, a point repeated fifty years later by the second national report on English teaching, *A Language For Life* (usually known, again after the name of its chairman, as the Bullock report), and quoted as an epigraph to this chapter: 'It is a characteristic of English that it does not hold together as a body of knowledge which can be identified, quantified, then transmitted.' The Newbolt committee's admission gave the representatives of the boys' grammar and public schools, in their evidence, a further reason for rejecting English's claim to a place in the curriculum. If it was not about anything, if it did not purport to transmit a body of knowledge, how could it be a subject at all? Once again you may well find it hard not to share a sneaking sympathy with what seems a reasonable enough point of view.

By that time, immediately after the First World War, English was already so entrenched in schools as to have acquired a content of a kind. George Sampson declared that it was about speaking and listening, reading and writing, study skills and literature. However, it was more often defined, theoretically and practically, in terms of the triad of composition, grammar and literature. This triad comprised a rather disparate amalgam of loosely linked activities and skills, some of which (those involved in composition) were already required by subjects like History and Geography, with an element of distinctiveness, and of objective knowledge, in English grammar and English literature. In something of an understatement the Newbolt report commented that English was not yet 'compactly enough built'. Developments since then, far from shoring up the edifice, have resulted in further disintegration and, some would say, total collapse into what Imogen Stubbs calls 'waffle' and 'blather'.

The first sign of disintegration was the separation of the triad at the beginning of the century into two subjects, English Language, covering composition and grammar (and other activities like precis and comprehension), and English Literature. The origins of the separation can be traced back to classical times. There had always been disagreement over whether the study of language should incorporate the study of literature and over the nature of the relationship between the two. What was new was the institution of a divorce between them in the school curriculum and examination system. When I was at secondary school in the 1950s I was not only entered for two separate subjects at GCE O Level but also, as often as not, taught by two separate teachers. Even as I write, for all the talk of the 'essential unity' of the subject in the last thirty years, the question of English literature's (or Literature's) relationship to English remains unresolved by those responsible for the National Curriculum and the GCSE examination.

The second important development has been the challenge mounted by the modern orthodoxy in English teaching to the idea of objective knowledge in general and English Literature (with a capital letter) and English grammar in particular. This has resulted in the disappearance from the English curriculum of such distinctive content as it did have. English Literature in the form I experienced it in the 1950s (that is to say, the canon from Chaucer to Lawrence) has been replaced by syllabuses which promiscuously mix *Macbeth* with *The Diary of Adrian Mole* and Australian television soap operas, while lessons on grammar have given way to courses in 'language awareness' which set relatively little store by children increasing their knowledge of linguistic terms and concepts.

There have been several attempts to shore up the edifice of English in the last thirty years through the imposition of organising principles derived from curriculum development – notably the topic or theme approach, which I shall be discussing in the next chapter. There have also been initiatives designed to overcome anxieties about content, and achieve a semblance of coherence, which have involved annexing other subjects' territory or new unclaimed territory. Many of the English course books for older pupils published in the 1960s and 1970s resembled social studies textbooks, while young forward-looking English teachers in those two decades were quick to move in on film and media studies as fruitful avenues to explore. In higher and further education this process has been taken one step further, largely under the influence of recent critical theory. There English has been subsumed under Communications or Cultural Studies or joined in alliance with them or Media Studies.

The diffusion of the subject has been defended by the orthodoxy on the ground that the true content of English is not literature (let alone Literature) or grammar or any of the other areas of knowledge the subject has concerned itself with over the century, but the child and his or her use of language. It is this child and language-centred view which underlies contemporary insistence on the 'essential unity' of English and pervades the statutory provisions of the National Curriculum.

English's problem of identity has not prevented its theorists and teachers from making bold claims – most of them unsubstantiated and unsubstantiatable – about its importance as a subject. George Sampson and the Newbolt report set the pattern for such claims – English 'includes and transcends all subjects' (Sampson); 'no form of knowledge can take precedence of a knowledge of English' (Newbolt) – and many have followed in their furrow. Evaluating those claims means coming to grips with the fierce ideological debate which has been such a feature of the subject's history and to which the identity problem has left it so susceptible. I have touched on the history already, or at least that since the First World War. We need now, I think, to examine it more closely. Space does not permit a full historical account, so I have opted for a version based on 'milestones' – key figures and texts – which, inevitably, has meant some oversimplification. If you are interested in a fuller account, you will find the most useful sources of it listed in the section on further reading at the end of the chapter.

MILESTONES IN ENGLISH TEACHING

Contrary to what has sometimes been maintained, English has a long history as a school subject. Ian Michael, who has examined that history in some detail through textbooks and teachers' descriptions of their practice, offers the following 'tentative outline' of the entry into the curriculum of the subject's 'principal components':

From early times	Reading, spelling and pronunciation; some oral expression; perhaps some drama, for which there is no textbook evidence
By 1525	Some written expression
By 1550	Snatches of literature
By 1586	Grammar
By 1650	More substantial literature; more sustained written expression
By 1720	Some explicit teaching of literature; linguistic exercises in, or derived from, grammar and rhetoric
By 1730	Elocution
By 1750	More substantial dramatic work
By 1770	More sustained teaching of literature; more attention to language and written expression
By 1820	History of the language
By 1850	History of literature

(Michael, 1987: 381)

English was first used as the name of a school subject in the late sixteenth century to cover the teaching of reading and spelling (then closely linked), grammar and rhetoric. By early in the nineteenth century the subject had spread generally to schools, and soon afterwards the first subject departments emerged and the first public examinations were introduced. Where it did not spread to, and met indeed, as we have seen, with considerable resistance, was the prestigious boys' grammar and public schools. To them it was the 'poor man's Latin' and properly confined to elementary schools, girls' schools and mechanics' institutes. The subject was further institutionalised in elementary schools after the 1870 Education Act and in secondary schools after the Education Act of 1902. Eventually the resistance of the prestigious boys' schools began to crumble too, and, by the time the Newbolt committee first met in 1919, English was set to replace Classics as the central civilising influence on the curriculum.

If one person could claim credit for the transformation in the status of English at the end of the nineteenth century and the beginning of the twentieth, it was the Victorian poet and critic, Matthew Arnold. For thirty-five years he was an HMI and mainly responsible for the inclusion of grammar, English Literature and learning poetry by heart in the curriculum of the first state elementary schools after 1870. More important, it was he who led the attack on the narrow instrumentalism of the Revised Code which held these schools in its thrall until 1897, and he who supplied English teachers with a philosophy which was to influence the Newbolt committee decisively and dominate the profession for the first half of this century. For Arnold the aim of the new state system was to overcome divisions of social class by providing all children with 'a general liberal culture' of 'the best which has been thought and said in the world'. The basis of such an education had to be the common heritage of the English language and its literature. Despite his efforts, however, it was what George Sampson called 'the dead hand' of the Revised Code which lay heaviest on many elementary and secondary school classrooms, even after its abandonment. The emphasis in English lessons in the early part of this century was decidedly utilitarian: the grammar grind, writing by numbers and literature as fact or moral homily.

Yet, at the same time, pioneers were beginning to show that two components of the triad, writing and literature, could be taught creatively and imaginatively. They drew inspiration principally from the German educationalist Friedrich Froebel and the American philosopher John Dewey. The alliance between the former's metaphor of the school as kindergarten, in which children are plants and teachers gardeners encouraging natural growth, and the latter's 'heuristic method', in which children learn through their own activities and discoveries, provided the foundation of what came to be known as the child-centred or progressivist philosophy of education. Intrinsic to this philosophy was a deep-seated belief in children's artistic creativity. The effect on English teaching was the encouragement of self-expression in oral and written work and the use of dramatic techniques such as mime and improvisation to enliven literature lessons.

The best known of the early pioneers was Caldwell Cook, who gave evidence to the Newbolt committee and taught at the Perse School in Cambridge. He followed Dewey in advocating active approaches to learning and stressed the value of imaginative writing for children's inner life. He was also the first to demonstrate how a theme, 'islands', could be used to stimulate a range of such work. To support his view that 'quite 70 per cent of our secondary schoolboys . . . can write creditable poetry and all you have to give them is permission', he published a series of anthologies of his pupils' writing between 1912 and 1917.

George Sampson and the Newbolt report

I have already indicated something of the historical significance of George Sampson's *English for the English* and the Newbolt report of 1921. Although the former was not the first individual book on English teaching in the modern sense (that honour seems to belong to J.W. Hales's *Suggestions on the Teaching of English*, published in 1869), nor the latter the first official pronouncement on the subject (having been preceded by the Board of Education's circular of 1910), they did together lay the basis for its theory and practice at least until the 1960s. The strength of Sampson's contribution derived from the fact that he was not, like most of the other committee members, a university academic or literary scholar, but an LCC district inspector who had taught for twelve years in the elementary schools ('the real public schools of England', as he rightly pointed out) of the capital's East End. This enabled him to temper the idealistic vision of a liberal and humane education, which he and the committee had taken from Matthew Arnold, with his knowledge of what was actually practicable in the classroom. His and their essential achievement was to identify and endorse the best of the practice of pioneers like Caldwell Cook and infuse it with the unifying philosophy of Arnold's vision.

It is remarkable how much of that philosophy and practice retains its pioneering flavour. Many ideas and suggestions which you might have imagined to have originated in the last ten years or so are to be found described and supported in the report's pages and Sampson's book. In addition to the general endorsement of a child-centred and active pedagogy ('The ideal teacher,' writes Sampson, 'is the one who does nothing while the class does everything'), the ideas and suggestions which strike me as surprisingly 'modern' are:

1 On reading and literature – the recognition of the importance of pupils forming the voluntary 'reading habit' (Newbolt); the relatively permissive interpretation of literature ('anything good to read extant in English' – Sampson; classics and modern authors 'rubbing shoulders' – Newbolt); and the support for experiential, as opposed to explicatory, methods of teaching and learning ('The reading of literature is a kind of creative reception' – Sampson; students as 'active participators', writing their own poems and making their own anthologies – Newbolt).
2 On writing – the encouragement given to children having a say in what they write, writing for 'a real purpose' (such as class magazines), commenting on one another's work (Newbolt) and teachers writing with them (Sampson).
3 On oral work – the argument for the importance of drama, discussions, debates, lectures, story-telling and teacher–pupil dialogue, both in themselves and as precursors to writing ('Oral work is . . . the foundation upon which proficiency in the writing of English must be based' – Newbolt).
4 On grammar – the rejection of set lessons in Latinate grammar (Sampson) in favour of some kind of 'pure' functional grammar related to children's speech (Newbolt).

The one respect in which Sampson and the Newbolt report are not in tune with the modern orthodoxy on English teaching is in the attitude they take to many children's natural speech and to the teaching of standard English. Both refer to the inarticulacy of elementary school children and to what the Newbolt report calls the 'evil habits of speech' acquired from the home and the street. For their language to be 'cleansed and purified', as Sampson puts it, speech training and elocution are required, as is systematic instruction in 'civilised' and 'educated' English. Neither Sampson nor the report has any doubt that the language of school should be standard English nor that all children should be taught both to write and to speak it. Their justification is that it is necessary for educational advancement beyond school and for wider communication now that English is an international language. There is the added implication that, if Arnold's dream of a common culture is to be realised, it has to be based on a 'common tongue', which can only be standard English. As no examples are given by either Sampson or the Newbolt report of the 'evil habits of speech' to which they refer, it is hard, seventy years on, to know quite what to make of that part of their position, especially in the case of the report, which takes a generous view of regional dialects and the need to maintain them.

In the 1920s and 1930s the battle lines were drawn up, which have not shifted much since, between those who followed Sampson and the Newbolt report in their advocacy of a child-centred philosophy and more active and creative methods, and those campaigning for teacher-directed and knowledge-based learning and a firm grounding in what are now known as the 'basic skills'. The debate was essentially a reformulation, admittedly with some very different emphases, of that between the liberal humanism of Arnold and the utilitarian instrumentalism of the Revised Code at the end of the nineteenth century. The overall child-centred philosophy was neatly summarised by the Hadow report on the primary school in 1931, when it argued that education was about 'activity and experience rather than knowledge to be acquired and facts to be stored'; while one of its adherents among English teachers, Greening Lambourn, writing in 1922, encapsulated the essential difference from the philosophy of its opponents as follows: 'Increasingly the modern teacher of English centres the child's attention on self-expression and leaves handwriting, grammar and spelling to improve incidentally or unconsciously.' Greatly reinforcing the rival view were the new public examinations, which remained substantially unchanged until the 1960s and stressed formal skills like essay and precis writing, clause analysis and the regurgitation of knowledge about literature.

Marjorie Hourd and the new Romanticism

After the Second World War the teaching of English was lifted by a second wave of writers and teachers promulgating child-centred and creative approaches. Prominent among them were a number of female educationalists – Marjorie Hourd, Dora Pym, Margaret Langdon, Sybil Marshall, Marie Peel – the titles of whose books – *The Education of the Poetic Spirit, Free Writing, Let the Children Write,*

An Experiment in Education, Seeing to the Heart – vividly convey the tenor of their beliefs. By general agreement the key text is Marjorie Hourd's *The Education of the Poetic Spirit*, published in 1949. The book is based on twelve years' experience in a socially mixed grammar school but also includes references to work with primary school children. Its attraction to me is that it is one of the first books on English teaching to recreate the authentic feel of classroom life. Consider, for example, the following snatch of dialogue between the author and two children during work on Arthurian legend:

Betty:　　　　Did Guinevere love Launcelot?

M.L.H.:　　　Yes.

Betty:　　　　But wasn't it wrong because Arthur was her husband?

M.L.H. (pause)*:*

Child:　　　　She loved Arthur as well, Betty, only she loved him differently.

(Hourd, 1949: 29)

Marjorie Hourd's historical significance is that she tried to undergird child-centred and creative approaches with a coherent body of theory. This she derived partly from the Romantic poets (Wordsworth on childhood, Keats and Coleridge on the imagination) and partly from psychology (including both the psychoanalysis of Freud and Jung and the developmental psychology of Susan Isaacs and Piaget). Her fundamental premises were that all children are creatively able (a 30 per cent advance on Caldwell Cook's view) and that the reading and making of literature served a therapeutic as well as an intellectual function. For her it was 'a means towards a fuller development of personality – a means . . . of growth'.

　　In terms of practice she made maximum use of drama (particularly, group improvisation and the writing and enactment of dialogue), on the assumption, already given currency by George Sampson and the Newbolt report, that children learn and benefit most when they are 'active participants' rather than 'passive recipients'. For material she relied almost exclusively on traditional and classical literature – ballads, myths and legends, miracle and mystery plays, Shakespeare, *Don Quixote*, *Pilgrim's Progress*, *The Iliad* – but as something to be experienced rather than taught. One class drew analogies between *Macbeth* and *Julius*

Caesar and Hitler and the recent war, while another envisaged a meeting between Don Quixote and Christian from *Pilgrim's Progress*. As regards children's writing, whilst acknowledging a debt to Caldwell Cook, she criticised the imitative element in his pupils' work and argued instead for 'free spontaneous expression', though aware that this was not to be confused with 'the completed artistic process'. When I started teaching in the early 1960s it was this 'free spontaneous expression' view of children's writing which predominated, so much so that the many anthologies of their poems published at that time consisted almost entirely of free verse. Since then the tide has turned in favour of the 'completed artistic process' view.

David Holbrook: forging a synthesis

David Holbrook was the George Sampson of the 1960s and easily the most important influence on my own early practice. The two books on English teaching which I remember reading with pleasure and excitement during my PGCE year were his *English for Maturity*, published in 1961, and Sampson's *English for the English*. Like Holbrook I had studied English at Cambridge and fallen under the influence of F.R. Leavis. When it came to teaching in a comprehensive school, I could see how Leavis's ideas on teaching literature might be applied in classes of older and abler pupils, but not how they might be applied in classes of younger and less able ones. Holbrook's achievement, inspired by his experience in secondary modern schools, was to build on what Sampson, Marjorie Hourd and others had already accomplished and, in effect, forge a synthesis between the literary moralism of Leavis and the creative approaches of the child-centred movement.

Holbrook shared with Marjorie Hourd an interest in psychology and a belief in the therapeutic value of appreciating and creating literature. With Sampson he shared an enthusiasm for Arnold's ideal of a liberal and humane culture. Two of the other major intellectual influences on him were also Victorian and in the liberal humanist tradition: J.S. Mill's *Autobiography* (in which Mill describes his discovery of 'the very culture of the feelings' while reading Wordsworth's poems), and Dickens's plea for the role of 'fancy' in education in the early chapters of *Hard Times*. The third, D.H. Lawrence, underlines Holbrook's more general debt to Leavis. His moralism – his fierce antagonism to materialism, the instrumentalist view of education and what he calls 'the new illiteracy' of the mass media – is essentially Leavisite, as are several of the educational aims stated in *English for Maturity* – exploring answers to the question 'How to live?', 'keeping the English word alive', and recreating 'a sound and active popular culture' comparable to that putatively destroyed by the industrial revolution.

Leavisite moralism is evident too in Holbrook's literary preferences for children. Yet it is in this aspect of English teaching that the impact of his secondary modern experience and the originality of his own contribution are also most apparent. Recognising that much of Leavis's 'great tradition', as well as academic literary appreciation, were beyond the capabilities of most secondary modern pupils, he recommended instead those classics which are accessible, traditional literature, such as folk songs and ballads, and a heuristic pedagogy in which children experience literature rather than discuss it. He followed the Newbolt report in regarding the Authorised Version of the Bible as fundamental to our culture, and therefore to English teaching, and added the Book of Common Prayer, famous hymns and the devotional poems of Donne, Herbert, Blake, Christina Rossetti and Hopkins.

From Arnold Holbrook borrowed the concept of literary 'touchstones' as aids in the choice of literature for children. The touchstone for fiction, he argued, should be *Huckleberry Finn*, and he berated those teachers whose choices fell so far below it for 'a kind of betrayal'. From Arnold he also inherited his commitment to poetry ('Teaching poetry is the centre of English') but his approach, emphasising the link with music and the experience of reading and listening to it, was peculiarly his own. This individuality is very apparent in his outstanding anthology *Iron, Honey, Gold*, which is full of variegated riches and served me well for many years. Prominent in it are ballads, folk songs and the poems of 'the simple poets, those who quietly ponder experience much as the immature spirit does' – Clare, Hardy, Edward Thomas, Frost, De La Mare. So far as 'making' literature is concerned, Holbrook's recommendations for practice are unmistakably those of the child-centred tradition – creative writing, oral work and drama.

John Dixon and the growth model

John Dixon's *Growth through English*, published in 1967, is an unlikely sort of book to have played a major part in the reconstitution of a subject, being but one delegate's response to an Anglo-American conference on English teaching held in the United States in the late summer of 1966. It was, of course, more than just that. It was also a response to a new mood in English teaching, on this side of the Atlantic at least, which had itself been partly inspired by the important developments in education then under way – comprehensivisation, experiments with mixed ability teaching and the introduction of the CSE examination. Although Leavisites like David Holbrook, Denys Thompson and Boris Ford also attended the conference, it was the representatives of the new mood – James Britton, Douglas Barnes and Harold Rosen – whose impact was to prove the more durable. Their power base was the London Institute of Education, then and still today the most influential centre for training English teachers in the country; and they were soon to capture another, the National Association for the Teaching of English (NATE), founded in 1963.

Growth through English did not mark a complete break with the past. The 'growth model' originated in Froebel's kindergarten metaphor, while Dixon's belief in the 'creative potentialities of *all* children', and his endorsement of drama, imaginative writing and personal responses to literature, located him firmly within the child-centred tradition. But it was a different version of the tradition from that of George Sampson, Marjorie Hourd and David Holbrook. Significantly omitted from it were the values of liberal humanism and any pretence to introduce children to 'the best which has been thought and said in the world'. Their place, at 'the vital core of English work', was given over to the child's experience and use of language – 'In English, pupils meet to share their encounters with life.' The aim of English, in the Dixon view, is to broaden the repertoire of experience and thereby of language use so that it in turn can better represent and order that experience. The effect is to make English synonymous with language development, which is precisely what it started to be called in many primary schools at around this time and has since become the basis of the modern 'unitary' approach to the subject.

From the late 1960s date two other facets of the modern orthodoxy endorsed in Dixon's book: scepticism about the possibility of objective knowledge and a relativistic view of literature. The former partly explains the reluctance to teach children about language ('it would be folly', wrote Dixon, 'for teachers of English to impose linguistic bodies of knowledge on pupils'); while the latter marks a very clean break with the past indeed. Literature since Dixon, to the horror of Leavisites, has been so broadly defined as to include not only literary material which could by no stretch of the imagination be classified as among 'the best which has been thought and said in the world' but also television, even bad television like Australian soap operas. The actual approach to literature, emphasising experience of the text rather than knowledge about it, is not new, having been advocated by the Newbolt report, but the importance attached to children's 'personal response' to it, and the way it relates to their own experience of life, certainly is. This new child-centred emphasis largely accounts for the movement away from classical and traditional literature to modern (supposedly more 'relevant') authors, children's literature and non-literary media which has been such a striking characteristic of English teaching in the last thirty years.

Striking too has been the transformation of the English classroom, and the view of teaching and learning this has entailed, for which Dixon can again claim some of the credit, or blame, depending on your point of view. It has become a workshop similar to an art or craft room, in which the teacher is an itinerant consultant and the often equally itinerant children engage in a variety of activities, predominantly those involving 'exploratory' talk and 'collaborative' group work. An American teacher of English commented sceptically, after visiting a number of such classrooms in 1969, 'time passed in the classroom is not easily distinguishable from time out of school'. This could certainly have been said about some of mine in the 1970s.

James Britton and the Bullock report

James Britton has probably been the most influential individual in English teaching in the past fifty years, although his influence on me personally has been slight, certainly when compared with that of George Sampson or David Holbrook. His importance was already evident at the time of the Anglo-American conference of 1966 and increased after the publication of *Language, the Learner and the School*, which he co-wrote with Douglas Barnes and Harold Rosen, in 1969 and of his own *Language and Learning* the following year. He played a major role in the Schools Council's work on English teaching in the 1960s and 1970s and was a member of the Bullock committee which sat between 1972 and 1974 and issued its report, *A Language for Life*, in 1975. However, it is not so much for pronouncements on English teaching that he or the report is best known as for pronouncements on language – specifically, for the concept of 'language across the curriculum' and the reassessment of the implications of the Newbolt report's dictum that 'every teacher is a teacher of English'.

Where Britton and the Bullock report differ sharply from Sampson and the Newbolt report is on the question of children's natural speech and its place in education. For them, far from needing to be 'cleansed' or 'purified' (as Sampson argued), children's talk is the means through which most learning takes place. This article of faith, which is what it is (rather than the matter of fact it sometimes masquerades as), led them to urge that all subjects, not just English, should increase the opportunities for 'tentative and inexplicit talk in small groups' and for what Britton called 'expressive' writing, by which he meant the kind of personal writing that is closest to speech. Complementing this attention to children's talk in the work of Britton and colleagues, and the second main strand in their contribution to 'language across the curriculum', was the emphasis they placed on the language of teachers and schools. This, they attempted to show, was more often than not an impediment to children making progress. If teachers wanted to engage children more actively and productively, they needed to shift the balance in the questions they asked from 'closed' to 'open' ones, as well as taking a critical look at the vocabulary and syntax of their subjects to see if they could not be made more accessible.

Behind the work of Britton and colleagues, and the deliberations of the Bullock committee, it is possible to identify the growing influence of modern scientific linguistics. This influence is apparent in the permissive view taken of children's natural speech, the reverent attitude to, and painstaking analysis of, raw data (in their case, tape transcripts of small-group discussions and dialogue between teachers and pupils), and in the relegation of literature to the status of one use of language among many. The Bullock report acknowledged the contribution made by Michael

Halliday's Linguistics and English Teaching project, which ran between 1964 and 1971 and produced the popular early reading materials *Breakthrough to Literacy* and the rather less popular *Language in Use* (Doughty *et al.*, 1971) (the only serious attempt in seventy years to meet the Newbolt report's call for a 'pure' functional grammar related to children's speech). From linguistics too – or applied linguistics, to be precise – comes the Bullock–Britton aim for English teaching – communicative competence, as first formulated by the American sociolinguist Dell Hymes in 1968.

The aim is no longer, as it was for the Newbolt report, George Sampson and generations of English teachers, to teach children to speak and write standard English, since that infringes both the child-centred principle of respect for children's natural speech and the linguistic principle according to which no one variety of a language is inherently superior or inferior to another. The aim instead is to start from children's natural speech and encourage them to build up a repertoire of use, so that in adult life they can match the social contexts they find themselves in with the appropriate language. The traditional and relatively simple, though by no means unproblematic, concept of 'correctness' has been replaced by the exceedingly fuzzy, and even more problematic, one of 'appropriateness'. Fuzziness has not prevented it, however, from taking its place in the modern orthodoxy on English teaching and thereby in the statutory provisions of the National Curriculum.

Communicative competence and the 'unitary' view of English as 'organic' language development have proved the lasting part of the Bullock report's legacy, rather than its 'language across the curriculum' recommendations, which generated much activity in schools but proved, in my experience anyway, unimplementable, simply because most teachers did not share the assumptions about language on which they were based and were not prepared to be 'put right' by English teachers who did.

Peter Abbs and English as art

Not everyone would include the work of Peter Abbs among milestones in English teaching. I do so essentially because he has solved English's identity problem, to my satisfaction if no one else's. In a number of books and articles over the last twenty years he has insisted that the subject of English should be classified in school as an arts subject analogous to music, dance, drama and art itself, and that it is therefore with these subjects that it should seek to make its political and pedagogic alliances rather than with the humanities or other languages. His justification is that English is 'centrally concerned' with 'creative mimesis' – the 'making and appreciation of literature' – not with language in a more general sense. The 'language across the curriculum' initiatives set up in the wake of the Bullock report inadvertently strengthened his case by enabling him to argue that, if language was every teacher's concern (in either the Bullock or the Newbolt interpretation), English teachers should concentrate on what was specific to them, literature. This solution was, I think, latent in Newbolt and in the liberal humanist tradition from Sampson to Holbrook; Abbs's achievement is to have made it explicit.

Abbs has much in common with Holbrook. He is unwaveringly hostile to contemporary consumerism and shares the same enthusiasm for forging a synthesis, though not so much between child-centredness and literary moralism as between children's creativity and the discipline of traditional cultural forms. For Abbs this means reviving the classical and Renaissance practice of writing according to established models, so that, for example, instead of producing exclusively free verse (as under one version of encouraging creativity), children are also expected to write ballads and sonnets. Abbs is generally unsympathetic to what he sees as the rival 'sociolinguistic' view of English (i.e. the 'language development' view of Britton and Bullock), because it leaves the subject ambiguously stranded between linguistics and social studies. However, he has not been wholly uninfluenced by the values of the 1970s, the decade in which sociolinguistics made its major impact on English teaching, particularly in respect of the emphasis he gives to those of 'community' and 'collaboration'. An arts subject, he maintains, requires collaborative performance or production within a community, while its classrooms should be 'busy' workshops in which teacher and learners are creative practitioners joined in 'collaborative methods of evaluation and production'.

Unfortunately for Abbs and those, like myself, who share his view of English as a 'literary expressive discipline', history has not gone according to plan. It is the rival 'sociolinguistic' view which has prevailed and now provides the basis of the National

Curriculum in English. In a way this should have been foreseeable. The 'literary expressive' view is simply not in accord with the perceptions of most pupils and parents or of society at large. Although there are certain aspects of the 'sociolinguistic' view which are not, either, notably its attitude to children's natural speech, its aim of communicative competence is widely subscribed to. The 'literary expressive' view, on the other hand, is not. 'Creative mimesis' in literature is in our society a fringe activity. To argue for an arts-based approach to English, as Abbs so eloquently does, is to argue for its marginalisation, to push it to the curriculum perimeter where arts subjects have long struggled to eke out an existence.

Kingman, Cox and the National Curriculum

I do not propose to summarise here the main recommendations of the Kingman and Cox reports or the statutory provisions of *English in the National Curriculum*, since I assume that you are more than familiar with them already. Instead I want to draw out what I take to be their historical significance. This does not lie in what any of them says about English teaching. None of the three publications can claim to be a major official statement in the mould of Newbolt and Bullock; all three are indeed conspicuously devoid of a coherent philosophy of English teaching. What is most striking about them is the signs of ideological tension they to varying degrees display between the tenets of the modern orthodoxy and the demands of conservative educationalists – in particular of the Conservative government directly responsible for their genesis. This tension was first evident in the furore created by the publication of the HMI document *English from 5 to 16* in 1984 (DES, 1984), which represented the first tentative step on the road to *English in the National Curriculum* (DES, 1990). The orthodoxy criticised the document both for presuming to spell out the objectives children should have achieved by certain ages and for including in them knowledge about language such as grammatical terms and concepts. A particular focus of its indignation was the expectation that at 16 pupils should be able to 'use the grammar and vocabulary of standard spoken English where necessary or appropriate'.

The publication of the Kingman report was awaited with considerable trepidation by the orthodoxy in 1988 because of the almost pointed exclusion of NATE and well known English teachers from its committee in favour of a rather idiosyncratic selection from the worlds of education, literature, linguistics and industry. In the event they breathed a collective sigh of relief. Although there were certainly statements in the report to take exception to, the general feeling was that it could have been much worse. Ideologically the report is an eclectic puzzle, which is perhaps unsurprising, given the composition of its committee. It freely mixes elements of the orthodoxy with old-fashioned liberal humanism (including an unacknowledged quotation from Arnold) and recondite linguistics. On language and teaching about language, its specific brief, the report reads like an uneasy amalgamation of Newbolt and Bullock. It follows both the earlier reports in rejecting a return to Latinate grammar and formal exercises but Newbolt, not Bullock, in insisting that it is 'as important to know about the structure of English as about the structure of the atom' and in stipulating that 'one of the school's duties is to enable children to acquire Standard English, which is their right', despite adopting, with Bullock, the orthodoxy's view that there is nothing intrinsically wrong with non-standard speech.

The Cox report of 1989 saw itself, accurately enough on the whole, as reflecting 'the growing consensus nationally about what constitutes good practice in the teaching of English'. The one respect in which it does not is, as with the Kingman report, its attitude to teaching standard English and about language. Despite, like Kingman, taking the conventional liberal view of dialect and non-standard forms, it still stipulates that by the age of 16 'all pupils should be in a position to choose to use standard English in speech where appropriate'. On teaching about language it is equally ambiguous. Decontextualised grammar exercises are rejected, but some kind of linguistically sound knowledge about language is required, though it stops short of specifying a list of terms and concepts to be taught.

The ideological tension evident in the two reports and the statutory provisions finally proved insupportable. In the summer of 1991 the Conservative government declined to publish the teacher-training materials developed by the Language in the National Curriculum (LINC) project, which had been set up in the wake of the Kingman report to equip teachers with the linguistic knowledge required to deliver the National Curriculum.

It had been clear from press reports for some time that this project had been hi-jacked by the orthodoxy, like the National Curriculum itself; so it came as no surprise (to me at any rate) when the government rejected its relativistic notions of language and literature and its preoccupation with issues such as linguistic diversity and language and power, and demanded instead a return to the formal teaching of grammar and of correctness in spelling, punctuation and syntax.

IDEOLOGIES IN ENGLISH TEACHING

It is impossible to review the history of English teaching without being conscious of ideological conflict. A number of the authors and books discussed so far have devoted some space to elucidating different views of the subject, although they have not usually taken advantage of the concept of ideology (here used in its everyday non-Marxist sense of a system of ideas). Some have distinguished three views, others two. The Newbolt report labelled its threesome: English for the purposes of ordinary communication, English as the scientific study of language and English in 'the highest sense' as 'the channel of formative culture for all English people'. The Bullock report translated the first and third into English as skills and English for growth and replaced the second with English for social change. The concept of English for growth came, of course, from John Dixon and ultimately, by way of Marjorie Hourd and others, from Froebel. Dixon also drew a tripartite division in views of the subject and identified a skills model in opposition to his preferred growth model. The other view he called 'cultural heritage', presumably to distinguish his version of growth from that of Holbrook, Marjorie Hourd and the Newbolt report.

When I first turned my attention to the topic of ideologies in English teaching in 1973, in a higher degree essay, it seemed to me too that there were three such ideologies. These I labelled creative Romanticism (corresponding to the growth model), literary moralism (corresponding to the Leavisite version of the cultural heritage view) and linguistic pragmatism (a combination of the skills model and applied linguistics). Two years later, in her book *The Preachers of Culture*, Margaret Mathieson made a similar division into Romantic progressivism, literary anti-industrialism and the new left, which Peter Abbs subsequently relabelled the progressive movement, the Cambridge school and the sociolinguists. Two of these ideologies – my creative Romanticism and literary moralism – are quite clearly expressions of the general educational ideologies of child-centred progressivism and knowledge-centred humanism. The characterisation and placing of the third are more problematic. In my analysis of linguistic pragmatism I was right, I think, to identify the language-based view of English teaching as a defining characteristic and the functional linguistics of Michael Halliday and *Language in Use* (Doughty *et al.*, 1971) as a major influence. What I did not then perceive, but Margaret Mathieson did, was the equal importance to it of the work of James Britton and colleagues. She was right to detect a distinct left-wing flavour as well – in the rejection of 'high' culture, in the concern for the underachievement of working class children and children from certain ethnic minorities, and in the aim of 'liberating' or 'empowering' children so evident in the work of socialist English teachers in the 1970s.

She was also right in detecting considerable ideological 'convergence', both between creative Romanticism and literary moralism among English teachers belonging to the broad liberal humanist tradition of the Newbolt report, Marjorie Hourd and David Holbrook, and between creative Romanticism and sociolinguistics among socialist English teachers. Some commentators, like Peter Abbs, have therefore preferred to represent the ideological contest as a straight two-cornered fight between a literature-based view, for which his label 'literary expressivism' might be suitable, and a language-based view, which Margaret Mathieson refers to as 'Romantic radicalism' but might be better characterised, by analogy, as 'linguistic expressivism' in order to emphasise that it covers a broad sweep of ideological territory from Bullock and Britton to overt socialism.

The Cox report, on the other hand, is more expansive, identifying no fewer than five views of English teaching. To English as growth, cultural heritage and skills (which it calls 'adult needs'), it adds a cross-curricular view and a cultural analysis view. This fivefold classification is, on the whole, neither very helpful nor very illuminating. It is certainly inferior to Margaret Mathieson's, not only because it says so little about any of the views it identifies but also because it fails to note either the 'convergence' between 'personal growth' and 'cultural heritage' or the 'divergence' between literature-based and language-based versions of 'personal growth'. The 'cross-curricular' is not a distinctive view of English teaching, in my opinion, being but one manifestation of the sociolinguistic ideology. The same might be said of 'cultural analysis', because of its roots in linguistics and Marxism, although such impact as it has made on schools has been since the categorisations of Mathieson and Abbs were published.

Cultural analysis is a product of what is usually known as critical or literary theory. If you have done a degree in English in the last ten years or so, you will probably have been exposed to a hefty dose of it and naturally wondered how it connects, or ought to connect, with English teaching at school. This is a contentious issue. My own view, as a liberal humanist, is that its influence has happily been negligible. Its more blatant weaknesses – obscurantist jargon, vapid theorising and arrogant elitism – render it highly unsuitable for application to everyday English teaching in primary and secondary schools. Even on its own theoretical high ground it is weak, riddled with unfalsifiable assertion and elementary philosophical errors like pragmatic self-refutation ('an occupational hazard' of post-Saussurean literary theorists according to one critic, Raymond Tallis), and seriously hampered by its dependence on Marxism.

Its defenders have claimed that its influence lies behind a number of recent developments in English teaching – the demise of Literature (with a capital letter), the rise of media studies, the promotion of writing as 'multi-layered process' and the deployment of more active approaches to texts. There is some truth in this claim, although it is essentially *post hoc* rationalisation, since all four developments antedated the importation of critical theory from the continent of Europe in the 1970s. Indeed, by one of the curious ironies of history, media studies, now dominated by neo-Marxist analysis and prose, actually originated in a classic expression of literary moralism, *Culture and Environment* by F.R. Leavis and Denys Thompson, published in 1933.

Cox's fifth view of English teaching, 'adult needs', is synonymous with the skills model identified by John Dixon and others. It is utilitarian instrumentalism in its pure form and not so much an ideology among English teachers, though it is not unknown in their ranks, as an ideology among teachers of other subjects, pupils, parents, politicians and the public at large. When the first year boy at the Knowsley secondary school, quoted in an extract from my journal in the previous chapter, translated his notion of 'proper English' into 'exercises and stuff like that', he was in his own way expressing this instrumentalist view. In my experience it is the dominant ideology among parents and those pupils old enough to have one, though they may well also concede that there is a place for 'cultural heritage', Shakespeare for instance, in secondary school and 'personal growth' in primary.

I hope this chapter has left you feeling clearer, rather than more confused, about different views of English and English teaching and hence better placed to start formulating your own. You may well feel, of course, that you are not ready to identify yourself ideologically or that your position is inconstant or that the map I have provided is inadequate. The Cox report adds some important qualifications to its own classification when it comments that it is not the only one possible, that the different views are not necessarily mutually exclusive or even that sharply distinguishable and that their appropriateness may depend on the age group taught. It also refrains from arbitrating between them and adopts a broadly eclectic approach, thereby allowing individual teachers some room (though far from complete freedom) for ideological manoeuvre. Deep down it seems to me to follow the modern orthodoxy in being based on the principal premises of the sociolinguistic ideology. Yet at the same time it manages to accommodate something of both liberal humanism and creative Romanticism as well as the instrumentalism of most parents and pupils. In this it is fairly representative. Very few teachers are likely to be pure adherents of one ideology or another in either theory or practice. Most find themselves straddling the three main ideologies and occupying a consensual middle position in the triangle of tension between them.

My own ideological position is, I trust, by now reasonably clear. It certainly ought to be from my essay 'A classical education' reproduced in the previous chapter. I started out in the tradition of Sampson and Holbrook as a liberal humanist who owed something to creative Romanticism (literary moralism with older and abler classes, child-centred creativity with younger and less able ones), whilst also acknowledging my duties to parents and pupils in respect of teaching utilitarian skills. In the 1970s I wobbled erratically in the direction of the sociolinguistic ideology but in the 1980s returned to the liberal humanist fold as a follower of Peter Abbs' 'literary expressiveness', without renouncing all I had acquired from sociolinguistics.

FURTHER READING

I hope you agree with me that a historical perspective is illuminating. It can have the effect of making one feel 'there is no new thing under the sun'. But each generation of teachers does seem to need to rediscover the wheel; and knowing the history can also provide the comfort of belonging to a tradition in which others have shared the same joys and tribulations. If you want to investigate the history of English teaching further, two invaluable books are *The Teaching of English from the Sixteenth Century to 1870* by Ian Michael and *The Teaching of English in Schools 1900–1970* by David Shayer. The early history of the subject is also covered to some extent in the Newbolt report and more recent history by David Allen in *English Teaching since 1965: How much Growth?* The best book on ideologies in English teaching is *The Preachers of Culture* by Margaret Mathieson. There are interesting discussions too in Allen's book, by Peter Abbs in *English within the Arts,* a group of PGCE students in issue 22 of *The English Magazine* (Daly *et al.,* 1989) and Chris Davies in the November 1989 issue of the *British Journal of Educational Studies.* On the possible relevance of critical theory to schools and English teaching, Rex Gibson's book *Critical Theory and Education* is enviably lucid and even-handed. You might also like to read *Literary Theory and English Teaching* by Peter Griffiths, although its effect on me was simply to confirm the view stated in this chapter. Indeed, at one point it actually summarises that view rather neatly: 'much literary theory . . . teeters along a thin borderline between stating the obvious and marshalling a complex of terms and concepts that seem to have little to do with human experience'. Otherwise all the books and authors here designated as 'milestones' in English teaching are worth reading.

Chapter 3

Developing an English curriculum

> Teaching is really a three-sided relationship; for the teacher has to select his material with an equal regard for its integrity and the nature of the child's interest.
>
> (Marjorie Hourd, *The Education of the Poetic Spirit*, 1949)

> At that time they had been immediately recognizable as Miss Brodie's pupils, being vastly informed on a lot of topics irrelevant to the authorized curriculum . . . and useless to the school as a school.
>
> (Muriel Spark, *The Prime of Miss Jean Brodie*, 1961)

> It seems an elementary mistake to demand a list of skills, proficiencies and knowledge as the basis of an English curriculum.
>
> (John Dixon, *Growth through English*, 1967)

CURRICULUM PLANNING IN ENGLISH: THE SEARCH FOR COHERENCE

Curriculum planning is especially difficult in English because of the identity problem analysed in the previous chapter. The subject's lack of inherent structure and agreed content, the paucity of obvious starting points and boundaries, the amorphousness and disparateness of its elements, the possibility that it might not be a subject at all (in the sense that Chemistry or History is) – all these have combined to make life very awkward indeed for those starting out and for the many in secondary schools required to teach English without being qualified to do so (one third of all English teachers, according to the commonest estimate). In my experience, it is curriculum planning which most taxes probationers and students on teaching practice, not the more publicised problem of maintaining discipline.

Everyone is agreed, whatever their ideological affiliation, that the subject of English must appear to make sense, even if in reality it does not. Over the past hundred years there have been a number of attempts to impose some semblance of coherence. The oldest solution recognised that the subject comprises disparate elements and allocated each one its own slot in the weekly timetable – Monday: creative writing; Tuesday: drama; Wednesday: comprehension, etc. This was the approach which held sway when I was at school and when I started teaching. It was never in practice as rigid as it may appear on paper because of the widely acknowledged need for flexibility, allowing activities which were going well to spill over from their prescribed slots into subsequent ones. Coherence under this 'separate elements' approach was achieved, in theory at least, by matching activities and reading material to the perceived stages of children's linguistic, intellectual and emotional development. A plethora of comprehension-based course books (e.g. *The Art of English 1–5*) and books on specific elements (e.g. *Understanding and Enjoyment 1–3*) were available to reinforce this largely bogus sense of progression.

The 'separate elements' approach has been out of favour now for thirty years without disappearing entirely because of the practical constraints of room timetabling for drama and library lessons. In an otherwise fluid week of three or four lessons of an hour or more, these still tend to be unmovable fixtures. The general principle of 'separate elements', however, is simply not in accord with the modern orthodoxy's insistence on the unity of English, and it has been replaced over the last quarter of a century by literature-based approaches, thematic and topic approaches and approaches amalgamating the two. The most coherent versions of these have divided the school year into discrete units or modules (say, six half-terms) focusing on particular aspects of literature (for example, myths and legends or a Shakespeare play), particular themes (for example, childhood or Caldwell Cook's islands) or units combining literary and thematic material (e.g. war poetry or romantic novels).

Although many schools have elected to combine literary and thematic approaches, there has been some tension between those teachers for whom the literary experience is paramount and the theme no more than a convenient link and those for whom the theme as salient human experience is paramount and the literary material subordinate to it. Either, for instance, one teaches *Lord of the Flies*, as I taught it in the Greater Manchester school (see Chapter 7), because it is an important novel which happens, in addition, to invite comparison with other novels with island settings. Or one teaches it as one of a number of possible imaginative responses to an important human experience (not necessarily islands in the case of *Lord of the Flies* – it could be childhood, gangs or good and evil), which is the way by and large I taught it in the 1970s.

Literary-thematic approaches have, at their best, undoubtedly given English more of a rationale and a shape than it had under the 'separate elements' approach. Adopting them has made teachers think hard about aims, content and method, and considerably encouraged departmental planning and co-operation. It has also signalled the end of the long reign of the comprehension-based course book, which was such a prop to me in my early years and which I, and many others, tended to follow slavishly and use indiscriminately. Nowadays, if used at all, it is likely to be selectively for particular passages or activities; or it may have been abandoned altogether in favour of a thematic anthology such as the pioneering *Reflections* published in 1963 or Penguin's very popular English Project of twenty years ago. Some English departments, perhaps the most forward-looking, have effectively written their own course books – identifying and mapping out units, selecting and collecting literary and other relevant material – which, whilst giving a new member of staff the comfort of a firm framework to start off in, still welcome fresh ideas and encourage individual initiative.

This is a big advance on the situation when I started out. I was introduced to the stock cupboard, directed to the course books and literature appropriate for my classes and left to fend for myself. This kind of *laissez-faire* regime can still be found, if my experience of supervising student teaching practice is anything to go by, but it is unlikely to survive the implementation of the National Curriculum. Nor is another kind of *laissez-faire*, popular in some circles in the 1970s, whereby children decide when to read, write and talk and what to read, write and talk about. The threat today is likely to be from the other end of the spectrum – over-prescription inhibiting fresh ideas and discouraging individual initiative. I have had students on teaching practice who were allowed a minimal area of discretion in their curriculum planning. The English syllabus prescribed, term by term, which themes and topics were to be done, which class novels were to be read, even a route through the bank of supporting materials which went as far as listing the homework assignments to be set.

Where literary-thematic approaches have conspicuously failed is, as with the 'separate elements' approach before them, in imposing on the English curriculum a convincing sense of progression. This is partly, in their case, because the choice of topics and themes often appears completely arbitrary, bearing no relation at all to what is understood of the structure of human knowledge. Children may not be unduly bothered by this weakness, having been inured to it in primary schools, where topics and themes have long been used, with varying degrees of success, to correlate subjects other than English and Maths. But teachers ought to be; and it is one reason why I at any rate now incline towards a literary rather than a thematic or topic basis of curriculum planning. Literary choices can, of course, seem arbitrary too, but I think I can make a better case for devoting the first few weeks with a new class of 11 year olds to *A Midsummer Night's Dream* than I can for a popular topic such as 'Myself'. Whereas the former is undoubtedly part of English and of 'the best which has been thought and said in the world', goes down well with 11 year olds and can be used to stimulate a range of exciting activities, the latter seems both too narrow and too amorphous, is only ambiguously related to English and may well already have been done, often more than once, in primary school.

When it comes to trying to establish continuity throughout the school, however, (from 11, say, to 16), literary approaches have been no more successful than thematic approaches. Both have followed the 'separate elements' approach in basing their claims to continuity on stages in children's natural development, and they seem to me equally contrived and spurious. Thematic approaches conventionally move from child-centred (e.g. Myself, Childhood) and imaginative topics (e.g. Adventure, Journeys) with younger pupils to more factual and socially aware topics (e.g. Crime and Punishment, Minorities) with older ones. Although there is some sense in this, to the extent that younger pupils find marshalling evidence and organising arguments more difficult, it does not in itself seem sufficient justification for such a prescriptive principle. Eleven year olds can enjoy and extract benefit from a topic on Crime and Punishment, as can 15 year olds in the case of Childhood. Similarly, with literature, although one can understand why it has been accepted practice to choose *A Midsummer Night's Dream* as the first Shakespeare children experience (the nature of the subject matter, the relative accessibility of the text) and leave the likes of *Hamlet* to the sixth form, there does not seem any compelling argument against doing *A Midsummer Night's Dream* with the sixth form or *Hamlet* with 11 year olds (in Chapter 8 you will find a description of the teaching of *Hamlet* to 7–10 year olds).

English in the National Curriculum (DES, 1990) does not pronounce on the competing claims of these different approaches, nor does the non-statutory guidance so far published, although both certainly attach importance to the principle of continuity. The assumption is clearly that it is for an English department or individual teachers to decide which is the most appropriate. In the present climate of corporate planning it is more likely to be a departmental than an individual decision. But, if you do find yourself in the position of having to decide – on teaching practice, for example – the important thing is to choose an approach which, whatever its weaknesses, makes some kind of sense to you, gives some kind of shape to your lessons over a term or a year and can be explained and partially justified to your pupils.

In making your choice you will need to bear in mind another principle which has been made much of in recent years and figures prominently in National Curriculum documents – the principle of balance. In English there are two respects in which the principle might need to be applied. First of all there is Marjorie Hourd's concept of teaching as a three-sided relationship. In deciding what to teach, and how to teach it, you need to strike a balance between your own interests, the children's interests and what she calls the 'integrity' of the material or what, in my case, would be the demands of 'the best which has been thought and said in the world'. Today, of course, the balance would have to be struck within the constraints of the National Curriculum.

The second application of the principle, endorsed in the National Curriculum, emphasises the importance of balance between the modes of language – speaking and listening, reading and writing – now the three profile components of the statutory provisions in English. The argument here is that, although certain lessons such as drama or library may be heavily tilted towards one, over a week, term or year the distribution of time between the three should be more or less equal, and that the ideal lesson both devotes some time to all three and tries to ensure easy passage, and integration, between them. A common extension of the principle, for example in GCSE, also requires that there should be balance within the modes of language – between informal/process and formal/product activities in oral work, across the main genres of poetry, drama, fiction and non-fictional prose in reading and between transactional, expressive and poetic writing.

Emphasis on what the Cox report calls the 'interrelatedness' of the modes of language is fundamental to the modern orthodoxy's notion of the 'essential unity' of English and to the National Curriculum, notwithstanding the latter's division of language development into three profile components. The Newbolt report laid the basis of the orthodox view in 1921 and it was well summarised by the Bullock report in 1975: 'We believe that language competence grows incrementally, through an interaction of writing, talk, reading and experience, the body of resulting work forming an organic whole.' A student of mine in 1987–8 inadvertently provided a good example of what this might mean in practice whilst reflecting on her experience of English teaching at school:

> Our teacher asked us to consider the nuclear weapons argument . . . the first lesson was spent reading and exchanging articles on all viewpoints on the nuclear arms race. The following week we held a debate on the issue, chaired by the teacher, and the written work set for this topic was to write a letter to a newspaper stating our views on nuclear weapons and our reasons for them. Our teacher sent some of these to the local newspaper, which printed them. I think everybody in the class felt involved with and benefited from this method of teaching.
>
> (Laurel)

You will find further examples of interrelatedness in practice described in this book: the *Hamlet* topic in Chapter 8, the work on Graham Greene's 'I Spy' in Chapter 7 and the language awareness unit in Chapter 9. However, I should warn you against trying to impose it on doctrinal grounds when the pedagogic justification is weak. Too often in schools nowadays, or so it seems to me, reading and writing, both of which require the isolation of pupils and an atmosphere of silent concentration, are disrupted by talk; I always remember the boy who said to me plaintively, on being issued with the term's class novel, 'Sir, can we just read this without having to discuss it?'

ENGLISH IN THE NATIONAL CURRICULUM: A CRITIQUE

Like most people I know, I am in favour of a National Curriculum in principle but not of the one now in force, which I find incoherent, overcrowded, too prescriptive and excessively preoccupied with objectives and testing. I am particularly opposed to a National Curriculum which is effectively controlled by the government of the day. Oddly for one owing so much to the tenets of Victorian liberalism, the Conservative government responsible for the 1988 Education Reform Act seems to have paid no heed to the warning given in that philosophy's classic text, John Stuart Mill's *On Liberty*, published in 1859. Whilst supporting the idea of statutory education for all, and of making 'a certain minimum of general knowledge virtually compulsory', Mill was adamant that this knowledge should be confined to facts, 'positive science' and 'instrumental' uses like foreign languages. He was equally adamant that it should not be governed by the state:

> That the whole or any large part of the education of the people should be in State hands, I go as far as anyone in deprecating. All that has been said of the importance of individuality of character, and diversity in opinion and modes of conduct, involves, as of the same unspeakable importance, diversity of education. A general State education is a mere contrivance for moulding people to be exactly like one another ... in proportion as it is efficient or successful, it establishes a despotism over the mind, leading by natural tendency to one over the body.
>
> (Mill, 1985 edition: 176–7)

Whatever general reservations you or I may have, however, we have also to accept that the National Curriculum is now a fact of school life. Its attainment targets, statements of attainment and programmes of study have statutory force as 'the starting point for all planning'. You are required by law to teach specified 'knowledge, skills and understanding' and specified 'matters . . . and processes'. This puts you in a very different position from me when I started out. I was free to teach as I wished, except with examination classes, of course. No one told me what to do or tried to stop what I was doing; and the only objections I can recall were from pupils claiming such-and-such activity or book was 'boring', a mother who found *Room at the Top* too 'sexy' for her daughter, an *imam* who took offence at what a pupil had told him of my sixth form General Studies course in comparative religion and Welsh colleagues in 1966 who accused me of insensitivity in asking children to write poems on the Aberfan disaster.

Yet the statutory provisions remain, at the time of writing, very much paper prescriptions, except in infant schools – confined within ring-binders and still to be enacted in the classroom. So far as English teaching in secondary schools is concerned, the final shape of Key Stage 4 is far from clear, as are the likely solutions to the major problems of the place of literature and teaching about language. As I emphasised in the preface, there is nothing final or immutable about the statutory provisions, which is why I have included a critique of *English in the National Curriculum* here.

Much of what is amiss with *English in the National Curriculum* has nothing to do with the statutory provisions for English as such but is the result of adopting an almost wholly inappropriate model for curriculum development – that of American rational curriculum planning. This, of course, affects all National Curriculum subjects. Responsibility rests, therefore, with the Task Group on Attainment and Testing (TGAT) and the Conservative government which introduced the Education Reform Act of 1988, although the Cox committee and the English section of the National Curriculum Council (NCC) must certainly accept some blame for applying the model so inelegantly and unimaginatively. The nature and provenance of the model do not seem to have been widely recognised, because of the TGAT's curious decision to replace its relatively familiar terms – aims, objectives, content, learning experiences – with newfangled ones – attainment targets, statements of attainment and programmes of study.

Rational curriculum planning, or the objectives model of curriculum development (as it is sometimes also known), emerged in the United States in the middle of this century as part of a campaign by educational psychologists and administrators, interested principally in assessment and evaluation, to knock some sense into teachers and some shape into the curriculum. According to rational curriculum planning the purpose of school is to change pupils' behaviour; society wants them to be different in certain identifiable respects when they leave school from the way they were when they began. This premise provides both a starting-point and a rationale for planning a curriculum. First of all teachers identify the overall aims embodying their educational philosophy, such as turning out good citizens, skilled workers and cultured thinkers. From these they derive more specific objectives which state what, in the words of the National Curriculum, 'pupils should know, understand and be able to do' at a given age or stage. Then they choose the learning experiences which they believe are most likely to lead to the achievement of these objectives; and finally, at a given age or the end of a stage, they assess their pupils to see whether the objectives have been achieved or not. For assessment to be feasible, of course, the objectives must be, in the nomenclature of rational curriculum planning, 'operational', that is to say, so precisely and unambiguously phrased as to leave no one in any doubt what they mean or refer to. Once the process is complete, teachers should be in a position to evaluate the success or otherwise of the curriculum and make any changes to the objectives or learning experiences which the pupils' performance in the assessment seems to suggest are required.

Rational curriculum planning undoubtedly does have a certain rationality about it, but it also has serious weaknesses, as a number of American and British critics have pointed out. The most obvious ones are practical. If objectives really are 'operational' there will be far too many of them to teach or assess. If they are not, they are likely to seem vague and banale. Both these weaknesses are clearly evident in the National Curriculum. Primary school teachers have complained that they cannot possibly assess all children on all attainment targets in all subjects and that some targets are so vaguely expressed that they could never be sure whether a child had met them or not. Moreover, rational curriculum planning ignores the fact that teachers simply do not plan by objectives. They plan by deciding what to teach and how to teach it – that is to say, by content and method. In addition, the richness and complexity of what they experience every day tell them that a more flexible and tentative model than that of pre-specified objectives is required which makes full allowance for individual creativity, hit and miss and unforeseen happy outcomes. On these practical counts rational curriculum planning is decidedly irrational.

A further major objection is that the objectives model is not applicable across the whole curriculum. Although some subjects (and certain aspects of others) – notably Maths, Science and Technology, which depend on a step-by-step acquisition of concepts and skills – can be made to fit the model, all certainly cannot. It is particularly unsuitable to the arts and humanities, where teachers and pupils are so often dealing in elusive qualities like imagination, creativity and sensitivity. What can be pre-specified in these subjects is likely to be limited to the activities teachers and pupils are to engage in. The outcomes will be various and essentially unpredictable. Certain objectives can, of course, be pre-specified in English, but these are invariably low-level and self-evident (for example, in the statutory provisions, 'spell correctly ... simple monosyllabic words ... which observe common patterns', AT 4, 2b; 'write fluently and legibly', AT 4/5, 6c). But what for many, including me, is the heart of the subject, its very *raison d'être* – the making and reading of literature – is simply not translatable into formulations of this kind. The uneven applicability of the model goes some way to explaining why in the National Curriculum there are seventeen attainment targets in Science, fourteen in Maths, five (and only three main ones) in English and three in Art.

There are also several philosophical objections to the objectives model which make it particularly inappropriate for a subject like English. The first concerns the place of content. In the model, curriculum content is reduced to an instrumental role as the means whereby objectives are achieved. In English, however (or, perhaps I should say, in my view of English), content is more important than this. It represents inherently worthwhile knowledge and experience. To borrow a famous example from Lawrence Stenhouse (the best of the model's British critics), the reason for choosing to do *Hamlet* with a class is that it is *Hamlet*, part of the cultural heritage, not that it may help pupils achieve certain pre-specified objectives for their age or stage. The second objection is that the model is a product of the ideologies of behaviourism and instrumentalism. How its society-centred, skills-focused and assessment-dominated view of education can be made to harmonise with the liberal humanist and child-centred ideologies which prevail among English teachers is far from clear. The final philosophical objection is that rational curriculum planning appears to make education synonymous with instruction and to some extent also raises the spectre of indoctrination.

When imposed from the centre, as in the case of the National Curriculum, the objectives model is also essentially anti-teacher – 'a stick with which to beat teachers', Lawrence Stenhouse once called it. Their expertise is devalued and any objectives they may have (to say nothing of the objectives of parents and pupils) are disregarded. Its imposition may sound the death knell of original and idiosyncratic teachers – of the Miss Brodies of the teaching profession, and it is well to remember that the subjects her pupils knew about which were not part of the authorised curriculum included Mussolini, the painters of the Italian Renaissance, skin care, menarche, Einstein, astrology and the love lives of Charlotte Brontë and herself.

These practical and ideological weaknesses suggest that John Dixon was right when he argued twenty-five years ago that it was 'an elementary mistake to demand a list of skills, proficiencies and knowledge as the basis of an English curriculum', and one can only wonder how the TGAT and the government came to make such a mistake and how the Cox committee and the English section of the NCC came to go along with it. I cannot believe they were unaware of it. Any English teacher reading the Cox report or *English in the National Curriculum* is bound to be struck by the conflict within them between the behaviourist ideology and prose of rational curriculum planning and the child-centred socio-linguistic and liberal humanist ideologies which prevail among English teachers. This conflict is one reason why both are so difficult to read and so greatly inferior, as educational testaments, to the Newbolt and Bullock reports.

If we now examine the statutory provisions for English in more detail, we find that some of the weaknesses in the attainment targets, statements of attainment and programmes of study are a direct consequence of adopting the objectives model, others are due to the particular version of it favoured by the TGAT and the government, while yet others appear to be the responsibility of the Cox committee, the NCC and whoever else had a hand in framing them. The most obvious weakness in the statements of attainment is that, like so many lists of objectives, they are both too many and too vague. This year I have been working off and on with a mixed ability top junior class of twenty-seven children in a Liverpool primary school, to whom, if my calculations are correct, nearly half the statements of attainment in English (over seventy at least) would be applicable, were Key Stage 2 statutorily in force. It would have helped if they had been clearly and unambiguously expressed, so that teachers were left in no doubt as to what was intended. Rarely is this the case, however. Vagueness and vacuity abound, as do those besetting sins of lists of obectives, unexplained evaluative adverbs – 'expressively', 'effectively', 'constructively', 'cogently' and, above all, 'appropriately' – which the appended non-statutory examples do little or nothing to elucidate. The teachers at the Liverpool primary school where I work say that *English in the National Curriculum* is the worst of all the subject documents for the meaninglessness of its verbiage – 'just waffle . . . all blather'.

Other weaknesses in the statements of attainment arise out of the government's decision to divide them into ten levels. The figure ten must have magical properties in official eyes; to lesser mortals it looks like a completely arbitrary figure. Certainly the Cox committee seem to have experienced considerable difficulty fitting their conclusions into such a straitjacket. The reason they give for this is that language development is not 'linear' but 'recursive'. I am not sure I understand what they mean by this or whether we know enough about language to make such emphatic pronouncements. It sounds to me suspiciously like an excuse for not having made a better fist of mapping the linguistic development which undoubtedly does take place as the child without serious problems in this area gets older. Most of the distinctions between levels that are made fall into a category that might be summarised as 'the same only more so'. For instance, AT2 3d, 'beginning to use inference, deduction . . .', becomes at 4c 'developing their abilities to use inference, deduction . . .'; AT1 7c, 'take an active part in group discussions, contributing constructively to the development of the argument', becomes at 8c 'take an active part in group discussions, contributing constructively to the sustained development of the argument'; and AT3 6a, 'write in a variety of forms . . .', becomes at 7a 'write in a wider variety of forms . . .'. Sometimes it is hard to see any 'operational' difference at all between the verbal distinctions made (for instance, between 'listen attentively, and respond, to stories and poems', AT1 1b, and 'listen attentively to stories and poems, and talk about them', 2c); and sometimes the committee seem to have simply given up, repeating at a higher level word for word what has already been stipulated for a lower one.

Finally, there are the weaknesses resulting from the objectives model's problem with knowledge and cultural experience. The Cox committee actually exacerbated this by prefacing all statements of attainment with the rubric 'pupils should be able to'. So, even though they are supposed to include 'knowledge, skills and understanding', the committee, in effect, converted them all to skills. The inevitable consequence is some very odd and unconvincing formulations for literary experience and linguistic knowledge. For example, strand (a) at levels 8, 9 and 10 in AT2 reads, 'read a range of fiction, poetry, literary non-fiction and drama, including pre–20th century literature'. Prefaced by 'pupils should be able to', this statement of attainment reads ambiguously. Does it refer primarily to the linguistic ability of pupils or to the opportunities made available to them by their teachers? If it refers to the former, one really has to ask what being 'able to read' Shakespeare and Dickens, two authors mentioned in the programmes of study, actually means. If the latter, the statements cease to be objectives in the technical sense, and one also has to ask why these opportunities are limited to higher levels of attainment. Most junior school children are incapable of reading *Hamlet* and *Great Expectations* in the full sense of the word 'read', but they can still experience and enjoy their stories. Similarly, in the case of knowledge about language (clumsily and arbitrarily divided up by the Cox committee between the three attainment targets), what common sense would suggest was best stated as curriculum content is awkwardly rephrased as skills objectives. For example, knowledge of the grammatical differences between spoken standard and non-standard English is prefaced in the Cox report by the feeble 'pupils should be able to talk about', which is replaced in the statutory provisions by the almost equally unconvincing 'pupils should be able to show in discussion an awareness of'.

This brings us on to the programmes of study. According to the pure version of rational curriculum planning, the relationship of learning experiences to objectives is one of means to ends. This seems to be the thinking behind the National Curriculum too.

The programmes of study are intended to 'support' the attainment targets, to indicate 'the essential ground to be covered to enable pupils to meet the attainment targets'. However, in *English in the National Curriculum* it is hard to discern anything remotely resembling this intended relationship or indeed any consistent relationship at all – except for repetition, since much of what appears under programmes of study is simply a rehash of what has already appeared under statements of attainment. Only the rubrics have been changed, 'pupils should be able to' becoming 'pupils should have opportunities to' or 'pupils should be taught that'. As with the original rubric, this results in some very peculiar and inelegant formulations: 'pupils should have opportunities to be helped to recognise that/to be enabled to use . . .'. Occasionally the formulation is actually nonsense. It is hard to credit that something like 'pupils should have opportunities to . . . have continuing opportunities to write in aesthetic and imaginative ways' is a statutory provision which has undergone the scrutiny of many eyes and brains. Just once or twice the changed rubric, and other verbal alterations, almost completely transform the tone of the provision. For example, AT1 7d, 'pupils should be able to show in discussion an awareness of the appropriate use of spoken language, according to purpose, topic and audience', has a very different flavour from 'pupils should be taught that Standard English is generally required in public or formal settings', which is one of the elaborations of AT 1 level 7 in the programmes of study.

The main weakness of the programmes of study is their flimsiness. They give only the barest outline of the 'ground to be covered' – Key Stage 2 in Reading (four years of school) merits only one page, Key Stages 3 and 4 (five years of school) only three – and offer minimal guidance on method when even an experienced teacher would welcome it. An experienced teacher needs no encouragement to use role-play or group discussion (two of the methods implicitly endorsed), but would very much like to know precisely how, for example, pupils are to be given 'increasing opportunities to develop proficiency in spoken Standard English' whilst at the same time being 'encouraged to respect their own language(s) or dialect(s) and those of others'. Without clear guidance on how they are to be 'operationalised', such injunctions are destined to remain mere attitudinising.

Despite this weakness, most of the teachers I know are starting their National Curriculum planning from the programmes of study, not from the statements of attainment. The reason for this, however, has nothing to do with any intrinsic merit in the former (though it may have something to do with weaknesses in the latter). It is simply that teachers plan by content, rather than by objectives and, on the whole, by year group. Although the statutory provisions do indicate something of the anticipated relationship between levels of attainment and age, the statements of attainment are geared primarily to the assessment of individuals not to the teaching of year groups. The programmes of study, on the other hand, are divided into Key Stages corresponding to existing divisions within and between schools and, even though the Key Stages are not subdivided into years (but again into levels), and only in writing is 3 distinguished from 4, they do offer teachers the security of a relatively familiar framework for their planning.

It might have been expected that the problem of flimsiness in the programmes of study would be addressed in the non-statutory guidance emanating from the NCC. The preliminary guidance for Key Stages 1–4, published in 1990, does not, however, augur well. It includes two interesting examples of curriculum planning in English (on folk-tales and story-telling) and some interesting discussion of specific aspects of the subject. But, on the whole, it simply repeats what is already in the statutory provisions and adds to the growing pile of platitudinous guff teachers have to wade through. For non-statutory guidance it is also remarkably prescriptive. The modest modals 'could' and 'might' are heavily outweighed by formulations such as 'teachers will need to', 'children must learn to', 'teachers should be sensitive towards', 'teaching and writing about literature necessarily requires'. Sometimes it is downright doctrinaire and provides further evidence that the National Curriculum in English has been hijacked by the dominant ideology of 'new left' sociolinguists – for example: 'Children should think of the first draft as an initial attempt'; 'The "essay" is too abstract a form to be appropriate for most pupils at this stage' (KS 3); 'historical and biographical details are relevant if they help to make sense of the text but should not be an end in themselves'; 'good drama is about discovering what is unknown rather than re-enacting what is already decided'.

The most striking defect (to me) in the statutory requirements for English, and in the supporting non-statutory guidance so far published, cannot be blamed on rational curriculum planning or the TGAT model of curriculum development. It is the complete failure even to attempt a solution to the subject's identity problem. At no point are we told where English begins and ends, which requirements apply to English as a subject and which to English as the medium of instruction or how the responsibilities of English teachers in regard to language development differ from and relate to the responsibilities of the rest of the staff. The implication seems to be that this difficult task falls within the obligations of schools (the 1990 non-statutory guidance actually says as much), even though the post-Bullock experience in the late 1970s unequivocally showed that devising and implementing a language across the curriculum policy is quite simply beyond the capacity of most staffs, certainly in secondary schools. At the very least it might reasonably have been expected that a document entitled *English in the National Curriculum* would try to outline, for Key Stages 3 and 4, a syllabus for an English department, as opposed to a general language development programme for the school as a whole. No such attempt is made. The three main attainment targets, albeit unexceptionable in themselves (like most general aims), are not goals for the subject of English but goals for language development across the curriculum, whereas the statements of attainment, presumably derived from them, are a mixture of the two.

What are the implications of this critique for curriculum planning? We are told that the statutory provisions 'will be the starting point for all planning'. Obviously, being statutory, they cannot be ignored, but it is very doubtful, at least in English, whether the statements of attainment and programmes of study can really fulfil that function, partly because of the inapplicability of the rational curriculum planning model, partly because of the failure to attempt a solution to the identity problem and partly because of the many weaknesses in their formulation. These short-comings rapidly become apparent once one sets about the teacher's principal task under the National Curriculum (excluding assessment, of course) – devising schemes of work and lesson plans.

SCHEMES OF WORK AND LESSON PLANS

By now you will almost certainly be in the middle of planning schemes of work – individually, as a department and as a school –

to meet the requirements of the National Curriculum. You may also have participated in local authority initiatives. What I want to do in this concluding section is raise some of the issues at stake by presenting examples of my own. First of all, however, we need to be clear what we are talking about. The non-statutory guidance of 1990 defines a scheme of work as a description of 'the work planned for pupils in a class or a group over a specified period'. This definition would, I think, be generally accepted. The same cannot be said for the document's idea of what a scheme of work should contain. In my view, for example, it should be limited to 'elements unique to English'. To ask that it should also include 'where English work supports and is integrated with other subjects', some of which would be better placed in a school policy statement on language across the curriculum, is expecting too much, at least of secondary school teachers of English. The same applies to others of the eight characteristics of a scheme of work listed in the guidance document, such as detailing provision for individual children or methods of monitoring progress. I would be satisfied if it simply met the first criterion and detailed 'the content and sequence of lessons'.

In 1990, before the start of the autumn term, the teacher of the top junior class at the Liverpool primary school referred to earlier asked me what I thought a scheme of work for the year ought to include to satisfy the statutory provisions in English. I did not know the class at the time but I knew their predecessors and the school well. So I sat down with the statutory provisions and worked one out. The first thing I did was to reduce the provisions – statements of attainment for levels 4 and 5, programmes of study for Key Stage 2 – to a single page of A4, as follows:

Summary of statutory provisions in English for year 6

1 *Oral work:*   Group discussion; drama (improvisation, role-play, learning lines); story-telling; presentation/performance (e.g. reading aloud, giving a talk, reciting a poem).

2 *Reading:*   Range of reading (e.g. folk tales from different cultures, adult as well as children's poetry); independent reading (reading log); response to literature (personal preferences, making own anthology, discussion of formal characteristics, e.g. plot); comprehension (distinguishing fact

from opinion, implicit from explicit meaning);
information/study skills (use of library).

3 *Writing:* Range of writing (chronological and non-
chronological, for different purposes and
audiences); handwriting (fluent joined-up);
spelling (prefixes, suffixes, inflectional endings);
punctuation of sentences and speech; use of
paragraphs, headings and subheadings; development of vocabulary (use of thesaurus); increased
use of more complex sentences (subordination)
and standard English; drafting, revising, proof-
reading.

4 *Language:* Differences between standard English and local
dialect; differences between social and occupational
groups; differences between reading and writing;
history of writing; fun with words (puns,
nonsense, deliberate misspellings).

A distillation of this kind reveals the size of the gap between the
statutory provisions and what one might actually teach. It includes
very few pointers for schemes of work or lessons, even though I
tried to increase the possibilities by separating out knowledge
about language, which I believe, in opposition to the modern
orthodoxy, needs to be taught explicitly. The provisions are best
thought of, therefore, not as a starting point for deciding what to
teach or how, but as a checklist to bear in mind while devising and
revising schemes of work to ensure that all the activities and
opportunities stipulated have been catered for.

When I set about devising the scheme of work itself, its content
came not from the statutory provisions but from me – from my
knowledge, experience (particularly of the class's predecessors)
and preferences. As it stands, it does not incorporate all the
distillation, though it would only require vigilance on the teacher's
part to make certain that nothing was omitted. It is intended to
occupy the half-morning daily slot allocated to English by many
primary schools and allows for the possibility that the teacher
might well want to reserve one or two sessions for individual silent
reading and work on the well established language development
scheme Ginn 360. I divided it into eight units – three each for the
longer autumn and summer terms, two for the spring – and
arranged them in a sequence which appealed to me but was also

flexible. Omitted from the scheme, because I felt they fell outside my competence, were any possible links with other subjects, although there are some fairly obvious ones with history, geography, science and technology. Given the crowded nature of the National Curriculum, any primary school teacher would be looking for opportunities to economise on time and space in this way:

Scheme of work in English for top juniors (year 6) in academic year 1990–1

1 *Charles Dickens*	Life and times; simplified versions of *Oliver Twist, Great Expectations, David Copperfield* (comparison with television and film versions and with original novels); dramatisation (improvised and scripted) of episodes from novels and life; reading aloud.
2 *Language awareness (a)*	Names; idiolect; girls' talk and boys' talk; variation according to age and generation; differences between spoken and written language (narration); standard English and local dialect.
3 *Poetry topic on animals*	Read and discuss a range of animal poems; children make and illustrate own anthologies; learning by heart and reading aloud; introduction to formal properties of verse (rhythm and rhyme); children write own animal poems.
4 *Group news-paper*	Analysis of newspapers (contents, layout, style); visit to local paper; each group creates an issue of its own paper, making use of software available.
5 *Story-telling*	Folk tales, myths and legends from a variety of cultures; children make up their own; telling stories to younger children; writing them for another audience (e.g. pensioners or pen friends).
6 *Language awareness(b)*	Different ways of communicating; writing systems and alphabets; other languages; history of English; spoken and written language (discussion); linguistic variation according to context (role-play); breaking the rules (misspellings, nonsense); introduction to grammar (parts of speech).
7 *Shakespeare*	Life and times; *The Tempest*, using active

	approaches (see Chapter 8).
8 *Theme on islands*	Reading fictional and non-fictional accounts (*Treasure Island, A Pattern of Islands*, etc.); drama, discussion and imaginative writing.

This scheme does, I hope you agree, have a satisfying balance and well-roundedness to it, even if it is essentially an expression of my own predilections and prejudices and limited by the arbitrariness which characterises all curriculum planning in English. Although it would, I think, go down well with a top junior class, it would be equally suitable for just about any secondary school class as well. In the event the class teacher did take up several of the suggestions. The class completed the Dickens unit (limited to *Great Expectations*, however) and the Shakespeare unit (based on *Macbeth*, not *The Tempest*), and undertook some work on animal poems and story-telling. That she did not take up more is a reflection of the pressure junior school teachers are under to cover the full range of National Curriculum subjects rather than of any reservations she may have had about the value of the other units.

During my time at the Greater Manchester and Knowsley schools, described in Chapter 1, I was responsible for devising schemes of work for a term. Only in the case of the bottom fifth year set at the former did this task defeat me. Because of the irregularity of their attendance I had to settle for a series of unconnected lessons – fifty-two, as it turned out, a tall order even for a knowledgeable teacher, and a very frustrating experience. The schemes I devised for the other classes antedated the National Curriculum, but you may still be interested in what I came up with. Here, first of all, is my scheme for the upper band second year class (now year 8) in the Knowsley school, as it was eventually taught rather than as originally planned, though the difference between the two was not great. The term was a short one and, allowing for staff development days, contained only eight full weeks. The class had two double lessons of approximately one hour and a quarter per week (including a single timetabled for drama) plus a single library lesson, which I sometimes left free for individual reading and sometimes incorporated into the scheme:

Scheme of work for upper band second year class (year 8), spring term 1989

Week 1	R.S. Thomas's poem 'January' (see Chapter 7 for details of content and method and examples of

	children's work).
Week 2	Graham Greene's story 'I Spy' (again see Chapter 7 for details).
Week 3	Victorian painting 'And when did you last see your father?' (note link with 'I Spy'); Graham Greene's story 'Case for the Defence' (linked to the painting through the idea of interrogation in court) – discussion, drama, writing of play scenes.
Week 4	Rae Jenkins's play *Julian* (continuing the idea of interrogation and introducing the topic of gangs); Graham Greene's story 'The Destructors' – discussion, drama, play scenes and stories.
Half-term assignment	Find out about the life of Shakespeare.
Weeks 5 and 6: Macbeth	Shakespeare's life, times and theatre; witchcraft; experiencing the play through active approaches (mime, movement, games, learning by heart – see Chapter 8); Polanski's film.
Week 7	A Victorian murder in Liverpool (the Maybrick case of 1889) – reading, discussion, drama, writing of various kinds.
Week 8	Poetry – Ted Hughes, 'The Thought-Fox', 'The Stag'; children find an animal poem they like, illustrate it, learn it by heart and perform it.

I have already explained the thinking behind my choice of content for this class in Chapter 1. It is, of course, a perfect example of a literature-based approach to planning, with somewhat of a bias towards drama. Interestingly, the links between the different elements (errant father, interrogation, gangs, etc.) for the most part occurred to me as I was going along rather than being pre-planned. Also literature-based is my second example of a scheme from the same school, this time for the fourth year GCSE class (now year 10) representing the middle of the ability range. In their case I had to bear in mind the constraints of the syllabus and ensure there was balance across and within the modes of language. They had three double lessons for English per week, including a slot for the library but not for drama:

Scheme of work for fourth year GCSE class (year 10), spring term 1989

| *Week 1* | Finish *Of Mice and Men* through class and individual reading; group discussion of ending |

	(assessed); choral reading of Lennie–George dialogue (assessed); set written assignment 1 (see Chapter 8).
Week 2	Work on assignment; class discussion on accent and dialect, starting from dialogue between Lennie and George (non-assessed); group translation and discussion of Robert Burns's 'To a Mouse' – why did Steinbeck take his title from it? (assessed).
Week 3	Completion of assignment 1; finding out about Steinbeck's life, interviewing friend to find out about his or hers; assignment 2 set – autobiography, biography of a friend or of Steinbeck.
Week 4	Return and discussion of assignment 1; work on assignment 2; assignment 3 set – examination conditions comprehension on newspaper article 'The enigma of Mrs Maybrick' (questions devised by me).
Week 5	Completion of assignment 2; discussion of differences between attitudes to sex and marriage in the 1950s and today (interview parents and grandparents, non-assessed); start class reading of *A Taste of Honey*.
Week 6	Return of assignment 2; finish *A Taste of Honey*; watch TV version on video; group performance of a section of dialogue (assessed).
Week 7	Tableaux of developing relationships in *A Taste of Honey*; pictorial representation of these (non-assessed); assignment 4 set – letter to Shelagh Delaney, episode rewritten as for a novel or added scene in which Geof or Jimmy returns.
Week 8	Completion of assignment 4; questionnaire on reading as preparation for wider reading assignment; the childhood poems of Seamus Heaney – 'Digging', 'Blackberry-Picking', 'Follower', 'Mid-Term Break', etc.

As you can see, the class covered a lot of ground, all pupils completing four written assignments (although the wider reading assignment and Seamus Heaney's poems were left rather in the air at the end of term). You will find further examples of schemes of work for particular units and modules described or referred to elsewhere in the book (for example, on R.S. Thomas's 'January' in Chapter 7 and on *Hamlet* in Chapter 8). One you might like to look at now is the language awareness module outlined in Chapter 9, as it was devised with the provisions of the National Curriculum in mind and provided the basis of units (2) and (6) in the Year 6 scheme of work on pp. 70–1.

Finally, in this section, I want to give you an example of the smallest unit in curriculum planning, a lesson plan. In my experience institutions of initial training often demand highly elaborate lesson plans from students – detailing aims and objectives, timing, materials to be used, almost a blow-by-blow account of what is to happen and why, followed by an evaluation of how things went. This is both excessive and unrealistic, bearing in mind the daily demands on the life of the ordinary classroom teacher. Written self-evaluation is a good idea (hence my keeping a journal); otherwise all that is really necessary for day-to-day teaching is a summary of what you and the pupils are to do. When I was supervising teaching practice I told students to forget about aims and objectives and the rest of the prescribed paraphernalia, unless they actually found abiding by the departmental formula useful, of course. What I wanted to see in their files was a brief statement of intended content – a kind of *aide mémoire* for themselves – plus an evaluation of the lesson afterwards. Here is an *aide mémoire* of my own, my notes for a drama lesson with the second year class on the one-act play *Julian*. We had already read it in class except for the ending:

Plan for a drama lesson with an upper band second year class (year 8)

1	*Mime*	Holding the torch in the dark, handing it on, dropping it; holding and handing on the tortoise; closing and opening the church door; throwing stones at the windows.
2	*Defining the acting space*	Establish the interior of the church in groups – where the door, nave, altar, stained glass windows all are.
3	*Dialogue*	In pairs work on dialogue between Finch and Julian – choose a manageable bit, practise different ways of saying it, learn it by heart, find suitable actions and movement for it.
4	*Improvisation*	Memorise the sequence of events so far in groups

	and try acting it out.
5 *Ending*	In groups work out what you think would be a good ending for the play; if time, read the actual ending.

I realise I have said nothing about one of the most important elements in curriculum planning, assessment, and very little about another closely related to it, evaluation. In the case of the former I do have something to say in the next two chapters. Otherwise it is really a question of waiting to see what form the national scheme of assessment in English at 7, 11, 14 and 16 eventually takes. Official noises from the Cox committee, the government and the Schools Examination and Assessment Council (SEAC) have been at pains to dispel many teachers' fears that the National Curriculum is going to be dominated by assessment to the detriment of teaching and learning. The assessment, we are told, will be 'the servant not the master' of the curriculum, an integral part of daily classroom activities, and take account of the subjective perceptions of teachers, parents and the pupils themselves. However, first reactions from primary schools to the first assessment materials have been almost wholly hostile – on the grounds of their disrupting teaching, upsetting children, revealing nothing, wasting time.

As for evaluation, the proposal for a national scheme of teacher appraisal appears to be in a state of suspended animation. There is nothing, however, stopping you implementing your own. The value of self-evaluation has already been commented on. This can be strengthened by asking pupils – at half-term, say – for their opinions on how you are doing and by asking colleagues to observe and comment on your lessons. When I suggested to my students in 1987–8 that they do the former on teaching practice, some of the staff at the schools they were attached to reacted with horror. Those students who took up the suggestion found the results of the exercise extremely illuminating.

FURTHER READING

Most writing about the curriculum is unnecessarily abstruse and jargon-ridden, and therefore best avoided. The two writers on the subject I would recommend, however, are Lawrence Stenhouse – *An Introduction to Curriculum Research and Development* – and

Douglas Barnes – *From Communication to Curriculum* and *Practical Curriculum Study*. Two interesting attempts to impose some kind of coherence on English teaching, prior to the advent of the National Curriculum, are to be found in Peter Doughty *et al.*, *Language in Use*, published in 1971, and David Jackson's *Continuity in Secondary English*, published in 1982. The former tries to provide a coherent but flexible English programme based on linguistics, while the latter aims to marry literary and language development approaches to pupils' maturation. If you are looking for ideas and suggestions on topics and themes, *Teaching English* by Tricia Evans and *Teaching English across the Ability Range*, edited by Richard Mills, are both very useful.

Chapter 4

Speaking and listening

Holofernes: *Via*, goodman Dull! Thou hast spoken no word all this while.
Dull: Nor understood none neither, sir.
(Shakespeare, *Love's Labours Lost*, c. 1593–4)

Beatrice: I wonder that you will still be talking, Signior Benedick. Nobody marks you.
(Shakespeare, *Much Ado About Nothing*, c.1598–9)

Mrs Durbeyfield habitually spoke the dialect; her daughter, who had passed the Sixth Standard in the National School under a London-trained mistress, spoke two languages: the dialect at home, more or less; ordinary English abroad and to persons of quality.
(Thomas Hardy, *Tess of the Durbervilles*, 1891)

ORAL WORK IN THE ENGLISH CURRICULUM

Oral activities in English are customarily divided into two groups, one labelled formal or product, the other labelled informal or process. If we look at the National Curriculum and GCSE, we can reduce product activities to the following: telling stories; making an audio tape (e.g. of a radio programme); delivering a report (e.g. on a book which has been read); dramatic performance, recitation and reading aloud; giving a talk or speech (e.g. on a hobby or controversial issue); and formal debates and discussions. Process activities can be reduced to: dialogue between teacher and pupils; dialogue between pupil and pupil; small-group discussion (e.g. of a poem read or a problem set); and improvised drama (including simulation and role-play). The distinction between process and product is not absolute (story-telling, discussion and drama can all be both, for example) but it is a useful one for teaching purposes, certainly far more so than the categorisation of oral activities in terms of communicative function favoured by some – narrating, describing, hypothesising, etc.

Historically schools have always acknowledged the importance of oral work, while defining education essentially in terms of reading and writing. The activities included in the curriculum, however, have, until recently, tended to come from the product category, precisely because of their closer relationship to reading and writing. Dramatic performance, for example, has been accepted as educationally worthwhile as long as there have been schools, and so have related activities such as making speeches, recitation and reading aloud. In the eighteenth century, as part of the standardisation of English, elocution (comprising pronunciation, articulation and the management of voice and gesture) was added to the curriculum. It was advocated by George Sampson and the Newbolt report in 1921 and still has its supporters today, despite being out of favour with the modern orthodoxy for its implicit denigration of children's natural speech. The final element in the product list, the formal debate, entered the curriculum in the nineteenth century, presumably as a response to the extension of the franchise.

As for the process activities, the art of conversation has always been regarded as a desirable social skill (though not necessarily one schools need concern themselves with), and teaching through dialogue is at least as old as Socrates. That talk between pupils, as well as between teacher and pupil, might be of educational value was recognised as early as the eighteenth century. It was certainly among the activities approved by the novelist and teacher Maria Edgeworth for the teaching of literature at the beginning of the nineteenth.

The basis of the oral curriculum in English was, then, firmly laid by the time of the Newbolt report. Drama; discussions and debates; story-telling; recitation and reading aloud; talks; and dialogue between teacher and learner – all these are explicitly recommended or implicitly recognised as educationally valuable in its pages. What has happened since is that elocution has been dropped and small-group discussion has been added – two changes which it would not be too much of a distortion to perceive as a single significant substitution of process for product. I have already commented, in Chapter 2, on the historical importance of the introduction of exploratory talk and collaborative group work into English teaching in the 1960s, as a result of the initiatives of James Britton and his colleagues. 'We started in May 1965,' wrote Harold Rosen at the end of that decade, 'and we started . . . with talk.'

I have also already registered my scepticism about the bold claim made for this innovation (that small-group discussion helps pupils make connections between school knowledge and their own, thereby facilitating learning and enabling them to forge new meanings) despite, or maybe because of, having made considerable use of such methods myself in the last twenty years. The representatives of the modern orthodoxy, including the Cox committee and everyone else who had a hand in the statutory provisions, appear to have no such doubts. Indeed, they actually seem to value process activities over traditional product ones, because, whereas the latter normally involve few performers and many listeners, these implicitly acknowledge that, in the words of the Cox report, 'listening and speaking are primarily reciprocal and integrated'. Not only is this a very narrow interpretation of 'reciprocal and integrated', it is also yet another example of the doctrinal assertion to which the modern orthodoxy is so prone. That reciprocation and integration, in this narrow sense, are a good thing is assumed rather than argued.

You are no doubt already engaged in sorting out your own position on the relative importance of process and product activities, and on the case for 'balance' between them. Mine is that I accept the case for balance whilst privately believing that product activities are of greater value, just as I accept the case for balance between the modes of language whilst privately taking the traditional view that it is primarily through reading and writing that knowledge is acquired and the mind developed. In the next two sections I want to look more closely at two activities, story-telling and discussion, which can be both process and product, are related to reading and writing and, though time-honoured, have attracted much recent attention. Of the other activities, drama, easily the most important form of oral work, has a chapter, Chapter 8, to itself, which also contains ideas you may find useful for recitation and reading aloud, whilst the giving of prepared talks and speeches, once set up, normally runs itself. All I would say, in connection with the latter, is that you should do everything within your power to get children to perform to the whole class (otherwise much of the benefit, in terms of developing the confidence to speak in public, is lost).

STORY-TELLING

One of the consequences of recent critical interest in narrative (that 'primary act of mind' in Barbara Hardy's famous phrase of 1968), or narratology as it is sometimes called, has been a renewed focus in educational circles on the telling of stories to and by children. This 'primary act' can take a variety of forms. Stories can be told by you, your pupils or by an outsider (a professional story-teller, perhaps); they can be live or pre-recorded on audio or video tape; they can be told to the whole class or to a friend or a small group; they can be uninterrupted or interactive (allowing for questions and forecasts); they can be true or made up; they can be retellings of traditional folk tales, myths and legends or of more modern fiction; and they can be told extempore or planned and polished like a written story. In the journal extracts in Chapter 1 two examples of story-telling are mentioned. In the first I described my surprise and pleasure at how well my versions of the stories of several Shakespearean plays went down with the bottom fifth year set at the Greater Manchester school. It is the second, 'story time' with the first and second years (now years 7 and 8) at the Knowsley school, that I want to concentrate on here.

My approach was simply to tell them that we were going to spend several lessons exchanging stories – true stories – of things which had happened to us, and that I was going to begin. My story, carefully rehearsed, was as follows, in its later written-down form:

> Some years ago I was walking on the Oxfordshire downs with a friend. It was a bitterly cold December day and almost the shortest of the year. Dusk was falling and it was obvious that the temperature that night would drop well below freezing. We were on a path in scrubland and returning to our car, which was parked in a minor road about 200 yards away. For some reason I happened suddenly to look to my left and saw in the gathering darkness the body of a man lying partly concealed under a bush. He was lying on his back and breathing loudly

through his nose, making a noise resembling a snore. At first I thought he was drunk but, when I stooped to smell his breath, I detected no alcohol. I shook him and shouted in his ear – without success. He seemed to be fast asleep. We clearly could not leave him where he was. He wore no overcoat, hat or gloves and would certainly not survive a night of below-zero temperatures. We then remembered that there had been a solitary house on the road near our car and went to raise the alarm. Its occupants were Polish immigrants who, by chance, had their daughter, a nurse, staying with them for the weekend. While they rang the emergency services, she returned with us to the man. Because it was now pitch dark, it took us a little while to find him. She turned him on his side to ease his breathing and covered him with a blanket she had brought from the house. The police and ambulance soon arrived. One of the police officers went through the man's clothes and removed a chemist's phial and a letter, which he read. From his reaction it was plain that the man had taken an overdose. The ambulance took him to hospital in Oxford, the nurse returned to her parents and my friend and I drove home. Next day my friend rang the hospital for news and was told that the man was comfortable and his wife was with him. Slowly it dawned on us that we had saved the life of a man who had wanted to die.

Although this story invites audience response (Who was the man? Why had he tried to commit suicide? Should he have been allowed to do so?), I told it uninterrupted in complete silence and did not ask for comments or questions at the end. I wanted it to serve as a stimulus and was interested to see how many pupils in the two classes, both of which were lively and talkative, would be prepared to come out to the front and tell a true story of their own extempore – something they did informally to their friends every day. In the second year class no one volunteered, and it took further stories from me to warm them up to the point where they were at least prepared to jot the outline of an anecdote down on paper. In the first year class, however, six children volunteered. Here are three of their stories, as later transcribed by me, with repetitions and expletives like 'um' omitted and speech punctuation added:

Right on Friday night at about quarter to five there was this boy called Ian ['Lee', correction from class] Lee I mean and he got murdered in Alamein Road right opposite me nan's house and he come in from a party and he jibbed the taxi and ran through the opening and the taxi followed him round and beat him up or this is what the CID think and he was lying on the floor and then the next day at half past five me nan looked out the window and saw a body there and thought he was drunk so she come out and told me auntie and then someone found him and looked at him and ran and then at about six o'clock the police come and marked it all off with orange banners and drew round the body and they put all little arrows down and put a Wendy house over him [laughter from class] and his head was all slit and there was a five-inch gap and he lived in our road and the police are still looking into it.

(Stacey)

It's a funny story this right there was this man and you know the Emperor Hirohito in Japan's died well this man in England he's a bit mad and he said he could make a psychic link to him through his mind and he said he'd already done it before he'd already been making psychic links to the Emperor Hirohito in his grave he's saying that he could talk to him and it was in all the newspapers and all this saying that he could do a psychic link to him at 2 o'clock he was going to do the link and he was talking to him and he was saying that he was sorry for all the bad things he'd done in his life and the man in England he had to tell all the people who Hirohito had hurt in the war camps that he was sorry and that he was dead now so he can't do much about it and he was having all these psychic links all the time and at the end they found the feller who had hanged himself just like Emperor Hirohito used to do to the people.

(Kevin)

The other night we were playing true dare right and we dared Melanie there was me Stacey Melanie and Paula come later and Alison and we dared Melanie to knock on this feller's door and I knew that he was dead creepy and Melanie didn't and she was going to say 'Is Mr Wilson there?' and run away and she knocked and went 'Is er er er aaaah' and screamed and legged it up the path and the feller went 'Ha ha ha ha ha' and started laughing and Melanie screamed the whole road down and ran and then Paula knocked and Paula didn't even know that he was horrible like that and she knocked and went 'Oh my God' and legged it up the path and the feller was going 'I'm telling your mother on you' and Paula just like was screaming and everything because he was dead ugly and he had black teeth and everything.

(Maureen)

In subsequent sessions other children came forward to tell true stories – things which had happened to them or which they had read or heard about – and one of the above narrators, Kevin, proved to have a seemingly inexhaustible store of factual and fictional anecdotes to draw on, which he related with considerable panache and some genuine feeling for the story-teller's art. For other members of the class, however, a public performance was asking too much, and they retired to the privacy of the stock room to tell the tape recorder their tales. A few claimed they had none to tell, although, when it came to writing the stories down (a perfect instance of natural 'interrelatedness' if ever there was one), only John persisted with this claim. What he and three of the others eventually wrote can be found under 'True stories' in Chapter 1. It would be reasonable to deduce from this small experiment that story-telling needs to be more carefully set up, if the shy are to be protected and the diffident encouraged. Posssibly a different kind of stimulus from the one I provided is required too; its dramatic content may have intimidated as many as it inspired, fuelling the feeling that they did not have a story worth telling.

I had the opportunity to try out another approach in 1990 as part of a language awareness module with a mixed ability class of top juniors at the Liverpool primary school (the 'predecessors' of the present top juniors referred to in the previous chapter) which is fully described in Chapter 9. The relevant week's focus was on the difference between talking and writing, and the idea for how to introduce it came from an article the class teacher had read in *Junior Education*. We told the children they were going to have to do four things: take it in turns in a friendship group to tell the story of something which had happened to them into a tape recorder; write the story down (first of all in rough, then, after discussion with me or the teacher, 'in best'); go back to their taped stories and transcribe them; and, finally, compare the written and transcribed versions and note down the main differences for class discussion. To start them off I played the recording of Stacey's story above.

The results were interesting but, if you are thinking of replicating the idea, you should be warned that the logistics proved tricky. This was a large class of thirty-five children, and the first phase of the exercise required seven tape recorders and seven power points. The teacher and I were in constant demand – for checking work, explaining again what was to be done next and fiddling with non-functioning tape recorders. By the end of the week, however, all the children had told a story on tape and the great majority had also completed the other phases. Many had provided illustrations for classroom display as well. Below is a sample of the stories, with the transcribed version preceding the final written version. You will notice that the children have interpreted 'transcribe', the meaning of which had been discussed with them beforehand, in slightly different ways:

> The boys were on the way to a footy match and four girls were in the minibus with them. We were on Sheil Road an um there was a taxi aswell it went in front of Sir. He went and banged into the back of the taxi. No one was really hurt and Mr H got the blame.

> One afternoon about 3.45 the boys and four girls were in the mini bus, on Beech Street and Mr H was driving the mini bus. The lights were on green and Mr H drove on. The taxi went right in front of the mini bus and there was a big BANG! David banged his head on the window, Scott jammed his legs in the chair but no one really was hurt. Mr H got the blame.
>
> (Natasha)

> One day I was going down to Michaels to ask him if he had any felts (an um) I got the felts an I was running up the street an these men had been working next door to us an they left all the rubbish every were so I so I fell over all the rubbish an me mum took the men to court an I got an an de got an one of the men would'ent pay an now he's payed an I got a lot of money.

> One afternoon about 1.30 I went down to my friend to borrow some pencils. When I was on my way up the street some workmen had left all their rubbish and I never saw the hanger on the floor. As I was running I fell over and hurt my arm. The next day I had to go to hospital. But when I fell over my mum took the workers to court but for my court case to come though it took 4 years. One of the workmen would not pay but now he has payed.
>
> (Dawn)

A went to me brother's flats and wen me and Katie were comming up the lift an we erd funny noises. We stayed for a lile bit then we went. An we were suppoest to go down but we went up. I remmembed that this lift does not go to de ground. I ran out and Katie folloed me. I tuck a step an Katie thought I was gona get back in so she ran in. I went to get back in but the door shut. Em she was, I could hear here skreming for me on the way down. She sent a man up to get me. I got in the lift and I went right up to the twenty forth floor. Soon I got down an me and Katie started laughing.

Once when I went to my brother's flats it was frightening. Because when me and Katie were comming up the lift we could hear strange noises. We stayed for a little bit then we went. On our way home we went up, in the lift insted of down. We went to the twelfth floor. I ran out because I rememberd that this lift does not go to the ground. So I ran out and Katie followed me. I took a step and Katie thought I was going to run into the lift. So she ran in. I went to run back in but the doors shut. Katie started scriming for me. She sent a man up to get me. Soon I got down and me an Katie started laughing.

(Catherine)

Me names Mathew it was a Thursday night it was raining 'ard an I was crossing by the lollopop man when an um when the lolopop man had his stick out a car came round the corner an did'nt see the stick an knocked me down (AARRHHHH) After shop people had phoned for an ambulance it came about half an hour later. the ambulance took me to hospatial an I waited about an hour for surgery an I had an I only had to have one stitch then I went home.

It was a Thursday night and it was rainning heavily and I was crossing by the lollipop man when a car came round the corner. The driver did not see the lollipop and she knocked me down. The people from the pizza shop phoned for an ambulance, it came about half an hour. The ambulance took me to hospatial an I waited half an hour to see a doctor then I got a stitch on my leg then I went home.

(Mathew)

One night we were going to cubs in my friends mums car the next minite we took a short-cut through an entree and we drove right into a 4ft puddle of water we looked out of the window then we had to get out into the water with rats, cold-water and bin bags then we had to dry all are feet. Then we still had to go to cubs.

One night we were on the way to cubs and it was raining cat and dogs and my friends mum was taking us up in her car. We were going to take a short-cut through a side-road. We drove right through at full speed then we stopped and we looked out of the window and found that we were in a 3ft pool of water. The car would not start so we opened the door and had to swim to the shallow end. There were rats, binbags and glass floating in the water. When we got out we dried our feet. The car was towed out we got in the car and still went to cubs.

(Vincent)

When it came to the fourth phase, commenting on the differences between the spoken and the written story in preparation for a class discussion, most children simply listed the differences irrespective of significance. Only Joanne showed any real awareness that some might be due to the mode of language being used. Here are her transcript, her final written version and her comments:

When I was on holiday me an me mum an me dad an Vicky and Joseph went the shops and I got lost I was looking everywhere for them but I couldn't find them and a man started following me so (um) I was running to the caravan and my mum and dad was there and the man was outside an me dad come out and told him to go away. So he just started shouting so me dad just went in [laugh] and locked the door (good by) [laugh].

When I was on holiday me, my mum, Vicky, Joseph and my dad went to the shops but I got lost. I was looking everywhere for them but I couldn't find them. A man started following me so I started running. I went into the caravan and my mum and dad were there and the man was waiting outside the caravan. So my dad went outside and told him to go away. The man started shouting. So my dad went in and locked the door and we never saw him again.

The first difference is on the transcript I keep saying 'an' but I don't say it on the proper writing. Another difference is I left the and out in the writing but I put it in on the transcript. On the transcript I said 'um'. I wrote I was running to the caravan on the transcript. I said my mum and dad were there but I didn't put it on the transcript and I put 'me dad' instead of my dad. and I laughed and said good by on the transcript.

It is possible that the greater productivity of the primary school class was in part due to the use of friendship groups, and of a more developed structure than obtained in the case of the secondary classes, but there were too many other factors in play to be emphatic about this. The class's close relationship with their teacher, whom they had known for several years, had a lot to do with it, I think, as did the fact that there were two of us in the classroom most of the time, chivvying and helping. However the use of group work does conveniently take us into the next section.

DISCUSSION

Discussion can cover a range of oral activities. In English it can refer, for example, to: comparing personal experiences, deciding on a course of action, working out the meaning of something read, revising something written, evaluating the merits of a performance, anticipating what might happen next and arguing a case. Argument is often thought of as the most typical, even the most important, discussion activity, and it has been suggested, by the likes of Jerome Bruner and Andrew Wilkinson, that it too is a 'primary act of mind' whose 'grammar' children learn early on. The point has also been well made that argument and narration are frequently interwoven by both children and adults. This book is an example. My general purpose has been to raise issues with you, and sometimes to develop a thesis. The easiest way of doing so, more often than not, has been through the narratives of the history of the subject and of my own experiences.

I want to devote this section to the most important kind of discussion that can take place in English lessons – the discussion of literature. My intention is to help you assess the claims made for three of the forms it can take – full-class, small-group led by teacher and small-group with itinerant teacher intermittently present – and decide whether any is likely to prove a rewarding method for you to employ. My example comes from 1989. The pupils involved were a small overspill class of 7–10 year olds in the Liverpool primary school and the subject was an episode in *Hamlet*. The children had experienced the story, principally through drama, up to the death of Polonius (for a full description of the work see Chapter 8), at which point the teacher divided them into groups reflecting the class's mixed age composition and gave each group a postcard reproduction of Millais's painting of Ophelia in the brook. The children's task was to decide what had happened to her. The following extract comes from the middle of group B's discussion. Its members were Martin (third year junior, now year 5), Lucia and Matthew G. (second year, now year 4) and Jenny (first year, now year 3). The class teacher (S.D.) was present at the beginning of the extract, but it is not clear from the tape how long she stayed, although she must have left before I arrived. We had adopted the role of peripatetic consultants customary among teachers when a class is engaged in this way.

S.D.:	What's it all about?
Jenny:	It's all about her, miss, lying in the water. Killed herself, in the woods, miss, going through the stream.
Lucia:	Miss, I think she wants to try and kill herself.
Jenny:	Miss, because she couldn't marry Hamlet and . . .
Martin:	It's just like she jumped in the water.
Jenny and Lucia:	And her father's dead and so she's lying down in the stream and she wants to get killed.
Martin:	It's just like she jumped in the water and she's flowing down the stream.
Jenny and Lucia:	I know, she looked at her father dead and she thinks there's nothing to do 'cause I can't marry Hamlet and there's nothing to do so she's killed herself 'cause she likes him very much so she's killed herself so she can end her life by committing suicide.
Matthew:	I thought she was in a tree.
Jenny:	And that's a ghost going through the water.
Matthew:	I know but I thought she was in a tree because she's lying down in the water.
Jenny:	And she's holding the flowers from where she's picked them.

R.J.:	What have you decided over here?
Lucia:	Sir, she's committed suicide lying in the stream because she can't marry Hamlet, sir, and her father's dead.
R.J.:	You're agreed about that, are you?
All:	Yes.
R.J.:	OK, why has she got flowers?
Lucia:	Sir, because she's going to kill herself and no one will know where she is and she wanted to go to heaven so she's put flowers on her [laughter].
R.J.:	Because she wants to go to heaven, that's why she's got the flowers – I see. She seems to be floating there.
Matthew:	And she can come down from heaven to visit.
R.J.:	Do you think she's alive there or dead?
All:	Dead, sir.
Lucia:	No, alive, sir, 'cause her eyes are open.
Matthew:	Well, she could still be dead with her eyes open.
Lucia:	Sir, she's probably showed somebody flowers and then killed herself and taken them into the water so that they'll know that she's dead.
Jenny:	And she's fallen in the water and she's floating on top of it.
Martin:	You'd think she jumped in the water.
R.J.:	You think she might jump in?
Lucia:	The only reason she's gone in there is because she's got no one to marry, nothing to do.

The teacher and I judged this a successful discussion. It was lively and engaged (with Jenny and Lucia often, as twice in the extract, speaking as an ensemble to such a degree that it was impossible to decipher who said what) and solved the problem set, to the children's satisfaction and to ours. My own intervention at the end was less successful, partly because I had not been present from the outset and was asking them to go over issues (Alive or dead? Suicide, accident or murder? Why flowers?) they had already resolved.

Once we were satisfied that all groups had reached some kind of conclusion, we followed the conventional formula of calling them together for a plenary session in which group representatives reported on their deliberations. This revealed that, although all agreed that Ophelia was dead, far from everyone shared group B's view on the manner of, or reason for, her death. The effect of this dissension was to take the class, as it were, back to the beginning again, so that all versions of what had happened could be thoroughly explored. A fascinating debate emerged, as rich in childish absurdity and irrelevance as in genuine insight, whose ebullient cut and thrust our single portable tape recorder managed partially to capture. The extract comes from the end, after rival views to group B's – notably the claim that Claudius had murdered Ophelia because he had discovered she had learned from Hamlet the truth about his father's death – had been, more or less, scotched; and when the class's attention had come to rest on the exact circumstances of her death, with minimal prompting from me. The extract begins with Paul and then Philip restating group B's original view, now the general opinion:

Paul:	I think she was sad about the way Polonius said she couldn't see Hamlet because he was too good and she went down to the river and drowned herself, she was so sad.
Philip:	Or it could be because she's got no life left because her dad's dead, she didn't have a mum and her father said that she couldn't marry Hamlet, she couldn't see Hamlet. So she's got no life left so she killed herself.
R.J.:	Yes, Lucia?
Lucia:	Sir, I think, you know when you told us that whose grave are they going to dig, sir, well I think she's been told that the gravediggers are digging her grave and she doesn't want to get killed so she kills herself. And when the gravediggers try to look for her, they find her in the sea, because then she's done nothing wrong when she comes to heaven.
Matthew G.:	It's suicide, that, Lucia, you know. It's suicide . . .
Laura:	She might have fell in accidentally and smashed her head on the stones.
R.J.:	Knocked herself out. Yes?
Philip:	Sir, she could have been looking at those flowers there, the white flowers, and someone pushed her in.

R.J.:	Yes? One at a time.
Paul:	I think she was climbing up a tree and she was trying to reach for the flowers in a tree and she made herself dizzy and she can't stand heights and she fell in the river . . .
Ross:	Sir, I think she was going to pick some flowers for her dad's grave and she tripped and fell in the water and drowned.
R.J.:	Any more suggestions?
Philip:	Sir, it looks like she was walking across the tree, sir, to try and stroke the robin. She was walking across the tree to try and get a good look at the robin and the robin flew at her and she went like that – 'Oh'.
R.J.:	The robin, did you say? Is there a robin in the picture?
Pupils:	Sir, yes, there is.
R.J.:	You're very observant. I hadn't seen the robin. Yes, Lucia?
Lucia:	Sir, she tried to grab some flowers to put on her father's grave. Then she fell in.
R.J.:	And didn't try and save herself or she couldn't swim?
Lucia:	Sir, she couldn't swim.
[confusion, several pupils talking at once]	
Patricia:	They never used to learn to swim in those days. She fell down.
R.J.:	Yes, Natasha?
Natasha:	If she fell in the water, she'd have cuts on her.
R.J.:	If she fell in the water, would she have cuts on her?
Natasha:	Like, off the trees or something. She'd have scratches or something.
Patricia:	If she fell backwards, she wouldn't . . .
R.J.:	Lucia, yes?
Lucia:	Sir, I think she tried to climb the tree to get this robin because she'd never seen a robin before. She tried to grab it and as she got it she fell and the robin flew away.
R.J.:	OK.
Matthew G.:	Lucia, the robin's still in the picture.

R.J.:	Right now. Yes, David?
David:	She might have been walking and looking at the robin. She stood on the bank and accidentally fell into the water.
R.J.:	Right. Yes, Philip?
Philip:	Sir, it looks like she might have been trying to climb up the tree to get the flowers at the top and the tree started to move, sir, and she went like that, sir, and she just went flying off into the river, sir.
R.J.:	OK. Well, we've had a lot of suggestions there. Just put your hands down.
Lucia:	Sir, I think she was climbing the tree and she was holding on to one of the branches and she fell back and the flowers've fallen on top of her.
Patricia:	But, sir, it wasn't ladylike to do those things then.
R.J.:	OK, well just listen now. Put your hands down. Listen, because this is what happened.

To explain what in fact happened, I told them about Ophelia's madness, the only aspect of the truth they had failed to anticipate, and then simply read them Gertrude's speech 'There is a willow grows aslant the brook' to confirm how right they had been. Collectively divining the truth was not the only respect in which the plenary session could be judged a success. The teacher and I were also struck by its fertility – the way the class bounced ideas (from the sensible to the preposterous) off one another, taking risks where adults probably would not, and by the extent of individual children's participation. Although dominated, like many full-class discussions, by a minority, and especially by the irrepressible Lucia who gave every sign of having fallen in love with the play, no less than thirteen out of a class of twenty-one made at least one recorded contribution.

After the *Hamlet* project had been completed, I interviewed the class in threes as an evaluation exercise. I undertook work of this kind in the 1970s while involved in educational research and found the results extremely revealing as regards children's perceptions of the curriculum, and so too, usually, did the class teachers concerned. This proved to be the case with the *Hamlet* interviews as well. The best of them took on a life of their own and became an opportunity as much for the children to continue exploring and consolidating their knowledge of the play, in the manner of the discussion of Ophelia's fate, as for me to try and assess how successful the class teacher and I had been. Here is an extract from the liveliest, that between Philip (third year junior), Lucia and Matthew G. (second year) and myself. You may find it helpful at this stage to read the full account of the project in Chapter 8 first.

Philip: I loved that part where we were playing with the swords.

Matthew: Me and Matthew C. couldn't stop fighting fast.

Lucia: I liked the part where you started them off.

Philip: I couldn't stop fighting because I just loved fighting, so it was just like that for ages and ages and ages, fighting with Andrew. It was dead funny.

Lucia: At the end it was very sad.

Matthew: I liked the part where I killed Claudius and I fell down and I stopped Horatio because I didn't want him killed and then I just liked that bit.

Philip: When we were fighting Andrew was going, 'Let me kill you, let me kill you, let me kill you,' just like that, wham, wham, wham.

Lucia: I liked the part where we were acting should we go to heaven or hell, all the questions.

Matthew: I wanted Claudius to go to hell.

Philip: Yeah, that was good. We never finished that.

Lucia: I know.

Matthew: I wanted Claudius to go to hell.

R.J.:   Did you. Why?

Lucia: Why?

Matthew: Yeah, because he done something wrong which he shouldn't have done.

Lucia: What did he do wrong? Oh yeah, he poisoned someone, was it?

Matthew: He poisoned Gertrude, he killed Hamlet junior's father.

Lucia: He poisoned Hamlet. Yeah, I think he should've gone to hell.

R.J.:   Well, it was accidental, the poisoning of Gertrude. He didn't mean that to happen, did

	he?
Philip:	But he meant to kill Hamlet junior.
Lucia:	How did he do it, though? What do you mean, "He didn't mean it"?
R.J.:	She drank the cup with the poison in it. She drank it without realising there was poison in it.
Lucia:	But why did Claudius put poison down his ear?
R.J.:	To get Hamlet to drink it. He wanted Hamlet to drink it but Hamlet wouldn't.
Lucia:	But why did he put the poison down his ear?
R.J.:	That was his father, Hamlet's father, he killed that way.
Lucia:	Why?
R.J. and Philip:	Because he wanted to be king.
Lucia:	Oh yeah, that's right. So he killed him to be king. You [i.e. Philip] wanted to be king.
R.J.:	He wanted to marry Gertrude as well. [Lucia laughs]
Philip:	No, I didn't want to marry her [i.e. Lucia].

Whether these examples of whole-class and small-group discussion could be cited to substantiate the orthodoxy's claim that 'exploratory talk' helps pupils set their own knowledge and experience against those of the text and thereby enables them to create new connections and meanings I leave you to decide. For my own part, I find it almost impossible to say what happened between the children and the play, except that, whatever it was, they enjoyed themselves. Undoubtedly much of *Hamlet* lay outside their knowledge of life and I never heard any of them make an explicit connection between it and what they already knew. Yet there was something about its story and its tangle of emotional and familial relationships which spoke to them powerfully and directly.

In formulating a policy on discussion, you are going to have to make three key decisions: how much discussion work to have, what balance to strike between small-group and full-class discussion and what part to play yourself. If you feel in need of advice, mine is that you should use discussion, and especially small-group discussion, sparingly, that is to say, when you believe it is pedagogically desirable and has a reasonable chance of success – and only after you have established a working relationship with a class. In the case of small-group discussion, I would recommend that you: start with pair work; ensure that groups really are small (never more than five), close together round a single table and as far away from other groups as possible; give them clear tasks (plus roles, if you think it necessary) and timetables; never hesitate to break up friendship groups whose productivity is poor; and, whenever possible, follow the classic formula of bringing groups together in the final phase of a lesson for a report back and full-class discussion.

The most obvious role for you to play, while group work is in progress, is that of itinerant consultant, learning when to intervene and when just to listen. In a concluding plenary, or any kind of full-class discussion, your obvious role is to chair it, although in classes you feel confident with I would urge you to experiment with pupils taking turns in this role, allowing you to adopt a back seat for observation. In case you think this is asking too much, I should add that in the spring term of 1991 I sat in on a student's discussion lesson with a fourth year class (year 10) who not only chaired their own plenaries but successfully operated in preliminary groups of eight – in defiance of my advice above.

For pupils to be able to chair their own discussions, you will first need to establish a model of chairmanship. On what this should be English teachers are divided. Personally I have long favoured the 'procedural neutrality' model associated with the work of the Schools Council Humanities Curriculum Project which Lawrence Stenhouse directed between 1967 and 1972. The aim of this model is to encourage pupils to submit to 'the discipline of the evidence' and thereby develop views on a rational basis. The role of the chairman, whether teacher or pupil, is to try and ensure that discussion is as thoughtful, fair and orderly as possible – by, for example, adroit questioning, restraining the voluble, protecting the shy and dealing firmly with all instances of rudeness. Specifically excluded from the role is the intrusion of the chairman's own opinions, unless the class actually ask to hear them. This may be asking a lot of teachers in respect of issues on which they are knowledgeable and about which they feel strongly, but the purpose of class discussion is to help pupils formulate views, not to provide opinionated teachers with a platform for propagating theirs.

Another important element in the work of the Humanities Curriculum Project was the use of tape-recording for purposes of assessment and evaluation, as exemplified by the *Hamlet* extracts above. Stenhouse believed strongly that classroom research should be done by teachers, not by outsiders. To this end the teachers involved in the project were encouraged to tape-record their lessons. This was also, of course, an important element in the work of James Britton and his colleagues at roughly the same time, although their focus of interest was different. Tape-recordings of pupils' discussions can be genuinely illuminating on what they can achieve on their own, as can those in which you figure, whether as participant in a group or as chairman of a full-class debate, on how you can facilitate rather than impede learning through your questions and contributions.

THE QUESTION OF SPOKEN STANDARD ENGLISH

The one respect in which the statutory provisions for speaking and listening are at odds with the modern orthodoxy on English teaching is over whether children should be taught to speak standard English. The orthodox view is that, although schools should certainly seek to broaden their pupils' repertoire in speaking and listening (making them 'polyglots' in their mother tongue, in David Crystal's phrase), it is for pupils to decide whether certain features of their natural speech, conventionally labelled 'non-standard', are inappropriate in certain circumstances and should be discarded. The statutory provisions, whilst broadly in line with the non-prescriptive gospel of contemporary linguistics, appear to imply a rather different view: 'From level 7, pupils should be using Standard English, wherever appropriate, to meet the statements of attainment'; in Key Stages 2–4 pupils 'should have increasing opportunities to develop proficiency in spoken Standard English, in appropriate contexts'; in Key Stages 3 and 4, for level 6, pupils 'should be guided towards the use of spoken Standard English in public or formal situations'.

For once I find myself taking the orthodox view. The most obvious defect of the view inherent in the statutory provisions is its impracticability. The evidence of over a hundred years of state education, for most of which a similar programme of intent has held firm, suggests that the great majority of children who do not speak standard English as 'a native dialect' (as the statutory provisions put it) have no wish to. Neither the provisions themselves nor the non-statutory guidance so far published give any indication how pupils are to be 'guided towards the use of spoken Standard English in public or formal settings' in defiance of their own wishes. One of the reasons the LINC project foundered in 1991, to judge by press reports, was that it appeared to dissociate itself from such an unimplementable project.

Any teacher knows that, outside the rarified atmospheres of independent and selective schools, with their restricted social class bases, pupils simply cannot be taught to speak standard English unless they have very strong personal motivation (e.g. an ambition to be a television newscaster) for wanting to change the way they talk. Later on in life, as we all know, some may start to do so, as a result of going away to college perhaps or for their own social or professional reasons. This, of course, is their prerogative, but it is remarkable how few people actually do, given the supposed social and professional advantages. The widely accepted estimate is that only a quarter of the population can be classified as speakers of standard English. I have even known teachers who regularly used non-standard forms ('done' for 'did', 'seen' for 'saw') in their ordinary staff room conversation.

Nor is impracticability the only problem with the statutory position. There is also the problem of definition. The assumption behind the statutory provisions, and the pronouncements of those taking up similar positions, appears to be that 'Standard English' exists in a simple identifiable form akin to that of the *Oxford English Dictionary*. Nothing could be further from the truth. Ron Carter, national co-ordinator of the LINC project, has called it 'a chimera, a phantom', and it is not surprising that so many would-be definitions end up in circularity. 'The dialect of educated people throughout the British Isles' is one I came across recently. (What does 'educated' mean? Among other attributes, able to speak standard English.) This definition also rather masks the fact that educated people in different parts of the British Isles (England, Wales, Ireland and Scotland) observe slightly different standards in both grammar and vocabulary. According to Ron Carter and others, only negative definition is possible – 'You can only say what Standard English *isn't* not what it is.' That is to say, certain forms, such as 'done' for 'did' and 'seen' for 'saw', are excluded from standard English and designated 'non-standard', not, it needs to be added, because there is anything linguistically wrong with them but because that is what they are perceived to be by 'educated people throughout the British Isles'.

What can, however, be said, by way of positive definition, is that standard English is closely connected, in most people's minds, with the written form of the language, and particularly with the grammar and vocabulary of carefully planned writing. Otherwise I think it is best thought of not as an entity but as an abstraction, a hypothesis perhaps, or as a convenient way of referring to the outcome of a very real historical process, associated with political unity, popular education and developments in mass communication, which has resulted in linguistic congruence around certain forms of spoken and written English (those of what was originally the East Midlands dialect of Middle English used by Chaucer) where previously there was considerable divergence.

There are similar problems with the cognate term 'dialect'. Sometimes it is used, as in the statutory provisions and the definition of standard English above, to include standard English, because of the latter's regional origins. In popular parlance, however, it is more often used to refer exclusively to non-standard forms of English. Occasionally it is restricted still further to only those non-standard forms which (unlike 'done' for 'did' and 'seen' for 'saw') are regionally based. Forms (like 'done' for 'did' and 'seen' for 'saw') which are widely distributed and more markers of social class than anything else are usually then labelled 'sociolect'. There is also disagreement over whether particular grammatical forms or lexical items (for example, 'dead' for 'very') are to be classified as dialect, sociolect or register. Another confusing difference in usage concerns the relationship of dialect to accent. Some linguists regard dialect and accent as separate phenomena, on the ground that native speakers of English from different parts of the British Isles can be heard using standard grammar and vocabulary in a variety of accents. Other linguists, however, regard English accents (rightly in my view) as part, indeed the most important part, of English dialects, on the ground that no one uses non-standard grammar and vocabulary with the non-regional accent (technically known as Received Pronunciation) which, according to the commonest estimate, is used by less than 5 per cent of the population.

If 'dialect' is limited to grammar and vocabulary, the use of the term to characterise regional and class variation in the British Isles is, in a sense, misleading. For it gives the impression that in these islands there are as identifiably different dialects in grammar and vocabulary as there are in Italy or German-speaking countries. A more accurate characterisation would be to say that there exists, on the one hand, an overarching and dominant class dialect or sociolect, usually known as standard English, which is spoken fully by a quarter of the population, and, on the other, a range of dialect 'rumps' (remnants of regional rural dialects that survived the process of standardisation and nineteenth century urban dialects, like Scouse, that never really established separate identities) none of which differ significantly from standard English in either grammar or vocabulary.

These problems of identification and definition are well illustrated by the extracts from the transcripts of Liverpool children telling stories and discussing *Hamlet* in the previous section. The majority of the children came from working-class backgrounds, and many from homes which would normally be labelled poorly educated and socially disadvantaged. Do they or do they not speak standard English? Do they or do they not speak dialect? If you look back at what they say, you will find very few examples of non-standard grammar, in either the teacher's presence or the teacher's absence. In the case of the primary school children, there are none in the stories by Natasha and Vincent or in the small-group discussion of Ophelia in the brook. In the case of the secondary school children, the story by Kevin is also free of non-standard forms.

For the rest, the few examples of non-standard grammar can be classified as follows: personal and possessive pronouns – 'me and Katie' for 'Katie and I', 'me' for 'my' (easily the most common of all the non-standard forms); past tenses and participles ('come' for 'came', 'seen' for 'saw', 'done' for 'did', 'fell' for 'fallen'); choice and omission of prepositions ('I'm telling your mother on you,' 'out the window', 'went the shops'); and subject–verb agreement ('My mum and dad was there'). In addition to those exemplified by the Liverpool children, the other instances of non-standard grammar you are likely to come across (depending to some extent on where you are teaching) are: multiple negation ('I never had none'); present tense forms ('s' omitted or added); relative, reflexive and demonstrative pronouns ('what' for 'who', 'hisself' for 'himself', 'them' for 'those'); and adverb forms ('good' for 'well', 'slow' for 'slowly'). In the case of several of the Liverpool children's usages it is hard to know whether to classify a form as non-standard or as characteristic of the grammar of speech among 11 and 12 year olds ('Paula just like was screaming and everything'). The problem is even more marked in some of their lexical choices. What, for example, did you make of Stacey's 'jibbed the taxi'? Is it dialect, generational argot or idiolect (i.e. peculiar to her)? And how would you classify 'never' for 'didn't', 'went' for 'said', 'footy', 'felts', 'legged it up the path' and 'screamed the whole road down'?

The conclusion suggested to me by the transcripts is not that these children, who in my experience are, in this respect, very representative of the broad mass of working class children in our schools, do not speak standard English 'as a native dialect', rather that they do indeed speak it except for a handful of non-standard grammatical forms, which are not used by all of them or not to the same extent, and a variety of lexical items which may be as much matters of style or register as regional or class dialect. Were you to have heard the tapes of the Liverpool children telling stories and discussing *Hamlet*, you would undoubtedly have identified them as speakers of Liverpudlian or Scouse. The transcript extracts, on the other hand, do not enable you to do so. This is consistent with what is known about English dialects. It is essentially the way people talk, their accent, rather than the words or grammar they use, which distinguishes one group of English-speakers from another.

The pedagogic questions this leaves you with in regard to the statutory provisions for Attainment Target 1 (quoted at the beginning of this section) are: (1) what justification can there be for trying to persuade those pupils who use non-standard forms to drop them in 'public or formal settings' and (2) how is this goal to be achieved? My own answer to the second question is that I have no idea (nor has anyone else) and to the first that linguistically and educationally there is none. As the Cox report points out and then proceeds to forget, the way we talk is fundamental to our sense of identity. Whether to retain non-standard usages, in formal or informal situations, is for pupils themselves to decide; any attempt at persuasion on your part could be resented.

The contrary argument, implicit in the statutory provisions, turns on the highly problematic concept of 'appropriateness'. Although most people certainly do try to observe this criterion in their daily linguistic behaviour, matching language to context, interpretations of what is appropriate in a particular situation often vary considerably, and there are occasions when other considerations may override it. The statutory provisions expect English teachers to agree both that non-standard grammar and vocabulary are generally inappropriate 'in public or formal settings' and that this view should be imposed on pupils. But is it actually so? My impression is that they are increasingly acceptable – for example, on local radio and certain kinds of television programme. It is also noticeable how many ordinary people, interviewed on television, choose not to alter their natural speech despite the 'public setting'. Interestingly, the statutory provisions make no comment on those occasions, much more frequent and prominent in the lives of many of our pupils and their families, in which standard English and Received Pronunciation would seem inappropriate and might even be an embarrassment.

Nor does non-standard grammar or vocabulary pose significant communication problems, as the statutory provisions appear to suggest ('Standard English is the language of wide social communication'). Communicative competence is as much about developing a repertoire of listening skills as a repertoire of speaking skills. Our pupils, because of the centrality of television, radio and video and audio tapes to their lives, are at ease with a range of Englishes, including American and Australian versions. Where there can be a problem, as pupils do need to recognise (otherwise it can come as quite a shock if they leave home to work elsewhere) is over accent, of which Kingman, Cox and the statutory provisions nevertheless take a more permissive view.

Your main responsibility is to provide the educational forum for pupils to discuss such matters as rationally as possible. The statutory provisions you do need to abide by in the first profile component, therefore, are those for knowledge about language. These require that you discuss clearly and openly with your pupils: differences between standard and non-standard grammar; regional accents and vocabulary; social attitudes towards these differences; the question of correctness and appropriateness; and formal and informal styles of speech. It is almost never too early to start on this kind of work. Much of it is certainly within the competence of top juniors, as I shall attempt to show in Chapter 9. You may already have noticed how several of the Liverpool primary school children changed non-standard to standard forms ('me' to 'my', 'was' to 'were') in the written versions of their stories quoted earlier in the chapter; that Joanne identified these changes as an aspect of the difference between talking and writing; that Vincent changed 'entry' to 'side-road'; and that Catherine in her transcription tried to convey something of the Liverpool accent ('de' for 'the').

ASSESSMENT

The invidious aspect of the statutory provisions on spoken standard English is the clear implication that any pupil who declines to discard non-standard features in his or her native speech 'in public or formal situations' cannot be assessed higher than level 6. This really is a retrograde step, taking us back to the early days of CSE, when some examination boards systematically discriminated against speakers of non-standard English. My recent experience of GCSE is that non-standard English is not even an issue. I have been involved in two moderations and no one mentioned it, despite the fact that in one case, referred to in a journal extract in Chapter 1, the candidate awarded the top grade on the board's video, a Muslim girl of Asian origin, regularly used northern dialect forms such as 'It were right nice' for 'It was very nice'. Whether you will be able to adopt a similar permissive view in National Curriculum assessment, ignoring what the statutory provisions say about standard English, remains to be seen. At least I hope you agree with me that it is absurd for a pupil to be debarred from the highest levels simply because he or she persists with the likes of 'seen' for 'saw' or 'me' for 'my'.

I must confess I have always had my doubts about oral assessment. This is partly because I am not convinced that it is possible to identify and assess 'oracy', a term coined by Andrew Wilkinson in 1965, in the sense that it certainly is possible to identify and assess literacy, though that too has its problems, as we shall see in the next chapter. My scepticism is borne out by the complete failure to operationalise criterion-referenced assessment in GCSE. The criteria so far devised are so vague as to be virtually meaningless, and at neither of the moderations I attended were any of them cited. Instead the teachers present fell back on a mixture of 'informed impression marking' and norm-referenced assessment – 'If he's a three, she's at least a two'. My main concern, however, is that what is really being assessed in a pupil's performance in oral English is their personality and, in some instances, a sensitive element in their sense of identity. The early forms of CSE assessment, at least where I was teaching, implicitly recognised that this was a problem by making the basic tests reading aloud and giving a prepared talk – traditional product exercises, in which some kind of objective assessment is possible and a candidate's personality plays a relatively unimportant part.

I believe it is traditional product activities such as these that should form the basis of oral assessment, though CSE was also right to allow pupils a measure of choice. Unfortunately for me the orthodoxy has moved in exactly the opposite direction, taking GCSE and the National Curriculum with it. An important influence here was the Assessment of Performance Unit (APU) at the DES, now the Evaluation and Monitoring Unit of the School Examinations and Assessment Council. During the 1970s and 1980s it experimented widely with forms of oral assessment, even going so far as assessing paralinguistic features like eye contact. It actively discouraged face-to-face pupil–assessor testing, favouring instead the tape-recording of pupils engaged in a range of communicative tasks in pairs and small groups. In GCSE the formal oral examination has been replaced by continuous assessment within course work, and you will have noted examples, in Chapters 1 and 3, of me attempting assessment of this kind, for example as part of the work with the fourth year class on *Of Mice and Men*. My objection to it is partly the sheer practical difficulty, with or without schedules and checklists, but mainly the way it disadvantages pupils who can speak perfectly well but do not shine in group discussions because they are, by nature, taciturn or diffident or simply do not value working in that way.

FURTHER READING

I do not know a single book on oral work to recommend. Several of the books already mentioned or recommended – *Language, the Learner and the School* by Douglas Barnes *et al.*, Barnes's *From Communication to Curriculum* and David Jackson's *Continuity in Secondary English* – include interesting examples and examinations of small-group discussion. On the question of non-standard English I have always thought that Peter Trudgill set the issues out well in 1975 in *Accent, Dialect and the School*, although the separation of accent from dialect made by him and other sociolinguists seems to me to misrepresent the facts of regional and social variation in English.

Chapter 5

Reading

To instruct children in the Rudiments of Reading is doubtless one of the most arduous, the most irksome, and perhaps the most unthankful offices in which any person can be engaged. Many children have naturally an aversion to books; and others are so dull and inattentive that it is scarcely possible to teach them anything . . .

(John Hornsey, *The First Guide to Reading*, 1815)

Have we not always been aware of two kinds of reading done by school children: of the book that went into the desk when the teacher came into the room, and the book that came out of it ready for the lesson?

(Marjorie Hourd, *The Education of the Poetic Spirit*, 1949)

I think we have got a nation of literate illiterates. There are too many people who do not read any more, including teachers. . . . Parents do not read to their children as much. . . . Children do not see a model of reading any more. Reading in a way has been devalued.

(Betty Root, in evidence to the House of Commons select committee on education, 1991)

TEACHING LITERACY

Being able to read and write is still generally regarded as the most fundamental trait of an educated person and the most precious skill a school can impart to its pupils. Yet a very real question mark hangs over whether or to what degree literacy is or can be taught. Dogberry, the village constable in *Much Ado About Nothing*, is not normally remembered for the wisdom of his utterances. But was he not more right than wrong in observing that 'to write and read comes by nature'? Certainly the Newbolt report, which quotes his remark, is somewhat less than persuasive in arguing the opposite view, and nowadays there is an influential school of thought, whose founding father he could claim to be, which maintains that, in a literate society, children learn to read and write in much the same way that they learn to walk and talk – by reading and writing. If you have, or have had, children of your own, you may already hold an opinion on this issue. You might also like to ask your parents whether they remember how you learned to read and write. My mother always insisted that I could read by the time I started school and that she did not 'teach' me in the ordinary sense of that word. I simply started as a consequence of being read to in a house full of books. Nor was my experience in any way exceptional. Many children begin to read and write quite independently of instruction at school, although a recent survey by the National Association of Headteachers concluded that fewer than 5 per cent fall into this category.

The obvious weakness in the Dogberry position is the fact of illiteracy. Whereas all children, excluding those with a physical disability, learn to walk and talk, a significant minority leave school functionally illiterate. Estimates of the size of this minority vary because of the absence of an uncontested definition or criterion of what it is to be functionally literate, but the commonest suggest that between 5 million and 6 million adults, or 10 per cent to 15 per cent of the population, either cannot read and write or do so only poorly. An interview-based survey of 1,000 16–20 year olds, carried out by the Adult Literacy and Basic Skills Unit in 1990, found that, although only a very small number were totally illiterate, a quarter admitted to difficulties with reading and a third to difficulties with spelling. More strikingly, two out of three of those admitting to reading problems were not interested in receiving help and almost half the whole sample never or rarely read a book.

In theory children are supposed to be able to read and write by the time they leave infant school at the age of 7; their education thereafter is premised on this assumption. However, all primary school teachers are well aware that some children do not meet this expectation. How many no one knows. Although a majority of LEAs test at around this age for the purpose of identifying weak readers, the results are not normally made public. In 1990 a group of educational psychologists representing nine LEAs helped to create one of the periodic panics about illiteracy and reading standards by revealing that the percentage of 7 year olds in their areas classified as non-readers or very poor readers had increased from 10 per cent in 1985 to 15 per cent (some 360,000 children), and that there had been a corresponding decrease in the percentage of good readers over the same five-year period. The Secretary of State for Education at the time, John MacGregor, asked HMIs and the National Foundation for Educational Research (NFER) to investigate. Their reports, published early in 1991, painted a mixed picture, with many gaps in the evidence, but provided some corroboration of the psychologists' findings. Of the twenty-six LEAs who were able to furnish the NFER with analysable data, nineteen reported a decline in the reading scores of 7 year olds during the 1980s. Further corroboration was provided by other NFER findings published later in 1991 which suggested that the reading age of 7 year olds had declined by twelve months since 1985. The results of the first National Curriculum tests for children completing Key Stage 1 in 1991 indicated that the problem might be more acute: 28 per cent of 7 year olds had not progressed beyond level 1 in reading (in other words, were effectively non-readers).

After 7, as all primary school teachers also know, it is very difficult to make up lost ground. One reading expert, Joyce Morris, has calculated that the chance of a pupil doing so before leaving school at 16 is only one in eight. The Bullock report estimated that between a third and a quarter of older pupils could be in need of remedial attention; and most of the comprehensive schools I have known have operated on a similar estimate. The HMIs' report of 1991 concluded that one 11 year old in four was unable to read fluently and one in twenty 'hardly able to read at all'. On the other hand, the APU surveys of 11 and 15 year olds, carried out in 1979, 1983 and 1988, seemed to point to less gloomy conclusions. They found no decline in standards over that period and that very few 11 year olds were illiterate 'in the sense that they are not able to read many of the words and sentences they can understand in speech', although many did have problems with reading 'between the lines', drawing inferences from what they read, and selecting and synthesising information.

Which of these estimates most accords with your perception of your first year (year 7) mixed ability classes will, of course, depend on the school and area you teach in. If the bulk of your experience has been, like mine, in the inner city or on disadvantaged estates, you will probably find the estimates of the Bullock report and the HMIs closer to the truth as you see it. The reading age scores sent on by the primary schools may range from as low as 6 or 7 to as high as 14; and the overall profile of the class may be heavily tilted towards the bottom end, with the number of inexperienced and reluctant readers greatly exceeding the enthusiasts. This was certainly the case in the Knowsley school in 1989. In the latter I also came across Jamie, the like of whom I had never encountered before, simply because in the 1960s and 1970s a pupil with his level of problems would have been in a special school. So far as I could make out, he could neither read a sentence he could say nor write one about something he had done which I could understand.

Where the APU findings do chime in with the schools and pupils I have known is in the suggestion that reading difficulties are, in most instances, more a reflection of inexperience (hence the problem with higher-order skills) or lack of motivation than mechanical deficiency. It is not so much that poor readers cannot read as that they do not or will not. I tried something like the two APU reading tests for 15 year olds – Graham Greene's story 'I Spy' and a newspaper article on the social aspect of unemployment – on the bottom fifth year group in the Greater Manchester school in 1987. It was soon apparent that about half the group were incapable of working their way independently through either, even though the two texts were quite short. The other half coped reasonably well with both the independent reading and the comprehension questions I had set. On a subsequent occasion I separated out the poor readers and started to read the Greene story to them. All appeared to follow the first paragraph but thereafter eyes and attention started to wander. When I asked them to read the beginning of the story individually to me, a handful declined on the ground that this was an infant school activity and beneath their dignity, whereas those who complied only really stumbled over unfamiliar words. Talking to the whole class later about the exercise, it was their experience of, and attitude to, reading which most impressed itself on me. With two notable exceptions, they were just not in the habit of sustained reading of consecutive prose; nor could they see any good reason why they should be.

Some poor readers do, of course, have other problems as well which may be linked, either causing, exacerbating or arising from the failure to master literacy. Jamie, for example, had been through major heart surgery, was an irregular attender and something of a social outcast. Other poor readers may have unsupportive parents, low intelligence, weak visual memory, inadequate aural discrimination, or be so hyperactive or disruptive that the idea of them sitting down to read a book is inconceivable. But in general, I would say, the problem represented by that third or quarter of a school's population estimated by the Bullock report to be in need of remedial attention is best understood as low motivation to succeed in reading or too narrow an experience of it. Looking back, I can think of many individuals, groups of friends and whole classes who fell into this category of inexperienced and reluctant readers.

Preparing for a GCSE wider reading assignment with the fourth year class at the Knowsley school in 1989, I discovered that none of the boys and only half the girls ever read books at all. There is nothing new about this. When I was on teaching practice at a Liverpool secondary modern school in 1962, the English teacher I was attached to said his main problem was getting his pupils to read; and I particularly remember chatting to a group of fourth year girls in the 1970s and their astonishment at discovering I did not watch television. When they asked me how I filled the long winter evenings and I replied, 'Reading,' they were momentarily dumbfounded. 'What, books?' one of them finally asked incredulously. We also have John Hornsey's evidence from 1815, quoted as an epigraph to this chapter, that 'many children have naturally an aversion to books'. These are the pupils Betty Root calls the 'literate illiterates' and Liz Waterland 'the true non-readers', those who can read but for one reason or another choose not to. In his autobiographical short story 'Baa Baa, Black Sheep', Rudyard Kipling creates in the character of Punch a boy who temporarily falls into this category because of the dull and punitive teaching he receives: ' "Now I can truly read," said Punch, "and now I will never read anything in the world." '

To return to Dogberry's remark, he was, in my view, more right than wrong; for most of us, 'to read and write' does come 'by nature'. But for a significant minority it does not, or only with difficulty. To compare the acquisition of literacy, therefore, with learning to talk or walk, which everyone manages comfortably apart from the handicapped, is somewhat to misrepresent the facts. A better analogy would be a skill like swimming. It is a natural human activity, and most people learn to do it well enough to enjoy a holiday at the seaside, though perhaps not well enough for life-saving purposes. Only an enthusiastic minority, however, develop into really good swimmers, while another minority seem destined to paddle in the shallows for the rest of their lives if they even venture into the water at all.

This analogy is particularly pertinent to me, for, whereas I quickly became a good reader, I was for much of my childhood a non-swimmer, about which I was very embarrassed. When I was a small boy, my father maintained that swimming lessons were unnecessary for my brothers and myself on the ground that, provided we went to the baths and the seaside, we would learn naturally. Unfortunately, it did not happen, because, I think, our desire to learn was less intense than our fear of drowning; so my mother sent us to private lessons when I was 11 or 12, and we all learned to swim in a matter of weeks. What stands out in my memory from those lessons is that the difference between being a swimmer and a non-swimmer was not knowledge about strokes or leg movements or breathing, although instruction in these matters certainly helped, but confidence in my natural ability to float and the part my teacher played in instilling that confidence. Once I believed in myself, I did indeed learn to swim 'by nature', by swimming.

The teacher's role, and particularly the role of the secondary school teacher of English, in children's mastery of literacy is the subject of the rest of this chapter and of the next. Although the teaching of reading and writing are properly thought of as going on side by side, mutually reinforcing one another, I shall, for convenience, take them separately. Both are also, of course, constant features of this book, which explains the limited space specifically devoted to them. In the case of reading I share the view of the Newbolt report that, 'when the mere technique, the recognition and use of the symbols, has been mastered', which it has in the case of most secondary school pupils, 'the lesson should be called "Literature" rather than "Reading" '; and literature has two chapters of its own.

APPROACHES TO THE TEACHING OF READING

When I started teaching, all I knew about the teaching of reading was what I could remember from being at primary school – that in the infants children worked their way through a graded reading scheme until they were good enough to be allowed their own choice of books from the library. It simply did not occur to me, even though I was starting in a comprehensive school and one of the classes on my timetable was called 2F, that I might have to teach children whose reading ability was no better than that of an average top infant and whose attitude towards reading was a good deal worse. As it turned out, I was somewhat shielded from the full brunt of the problem because of the practice, normal in the 1960s, of segregating 'remedial' children into special schools or into special classes within ordinary schools. 2F were more of an F in behaviour than reading ability, and I remember that we read *The Silver Sword* together in the autumn term of 1963 without any noticeable difficulty. Two years later I taught many of them again when they were fourth year leavers and even more badly behaved, and we read six books together during the year, including *Cider with Rosie* and *Lord of the Flies*.

It was not really until the mid-1970s, when I was confronted with bottom-heavy mixed ability first year classes, that I began to investigate seriously the teaching of reading. Today the situation facing you may be even more acute. Not only are the likes of Jamie increasingly to be found in ordinary schools because of the 1981 Education Act, they are also more likely to be found in ordinary classes because of the abandonment of remedial departments in favour of floating 'special needs' teachers. If you find yourself as ignorant as I was, the most important thing you can do – more important than reading about the teaching of reading or attending courses on the subject, though these have their place – is to visit your feeder primary schools. They will almost certainly have a policy document and a graded reading scheme for you to look at, as well as teaching aids such as flash cards, phonic charts and sentence makers, and a library and book corners for you to explore. Talk to the teachers about their ideas and practice and, if possible, observe them in action with a class and with individual children.

In the course of discussion you will very probably come up against some of the controversial issues – Are standards of reading declining? What are the best teaching methods? Why do some children succeed and others fail? – which you may already have heard or seen debated on your initial training course or in the media. The crucial issue is that of teaching method. Sixteen years ago the Bullock report concluded that 'there is no one method, medium, approach, device, or philosophy that holds the key to the process of learning to read'. Although nothing has happened or been discovered since to overturn that conclusion, some teachers, parents, psychologists and teacher trainers continue to argue as though the opposite was the case, passionately championing one particular method or approach as the route to success and sometimes blaming its rivals for children's failure.

The main reason for the confusion and dissension is that no one really understands what happens when people read or exactly how children acquire the capacity. Kenneth Goodman's description of reading in 1967 as 'a psycholinguistic guessing game' remains the most popular summary, although recent American research has concluded that it seriously underestimates the importance of memory and attention to detail in the strategies used by good readers. Given this lack of understanding of the process, it is hardly surprising that teachers and others involved in reading should be so divided over why children fail and how best to ensure that they do not. The Bullock report identified the nature of the problem in learning to read as the poor relationship between sound and symbol in English – forty-four phonemes to be represented by twenty-six letters. This view is widely shared, although Sir James Pitman's ingenious invention of the 1960s, the Initial Teaching Alphabet, in which the relationship is perfect – forty-four graphemes for forty-four phonemes – did not in the end appear to secure significantly better results. The nature of the debate about solving the problem can be represented as being between advocates of reading by ear, such as Sir James Pitman, and advocates of reading by eye or, as it is more commonly expressed, between phonics and look-and-say.

This debate reaches back well into the nineteenth century and has now, I think, been more or less resolved. There are very few pure advocates of one or the other, and most teachers sensibly amalgamate the two, teaching phonics or 'word attack skills' for the estimated 70 per cent of the English vocabulary which is regular, and using word recognition or building up a 'sight vocabulary' for the 30 per cent which is irregular. An exclusively phonic approach would not make much sense simply because (Margaret Meek has pointed out) the relationship of sounds to letters in English requires 166 rules, to which there are 661 exceptions, whereas a purely visual approach would make sense only in a language, like Chinese, whose writing system was based on pictograms rather than an alphabet. What perhaps can be said is that, as a child's competence and confidence as a reader increase and the problem becomes less the deciphering of isolated letters and words and more the comprehension of consecutive prose, reading by eye takes over almost completely from reading by ear.

This older debate has in the last decade been rather pushed into the background by a new one – between those who argue that children should be taught to read in the traditional way through a graded reading scheme and those who argue in favour of a 'real' books or 'apprenticeship' approach which stresses reading for meaning and for pleasure. The latter are, of course, followers of Dogberry. For them, learning to read is a natural process which requires little direct instruction but plenty of sensitive encouragement and gentle guidance on the part of the teacher; and they are predictably well represented within the orthodoxy on English teaching. Although the debate often takes the form, like the phonics versus look-and-say debate before it, of a technical disagreement between specialists, with both sides claiming higher success rates and implicating their opponents in children's failure, it strikes me, a detached outsider, as more ideological in character than anything.

The 'real' books advocates have, I think, implicitly recognised this by labelling their opponents behaviourists and themselves psycholinguists, and by representing the choice, even if light-heartedly, as between organic and inorganic, free-range and battery, and wholefood and junk books. Referring back to the discussion of ideology in Chapter 2, I would say that the traditionalists were utilitarian instrumentalists while the 'real' books advocates fell somewhere between a child-centred philosophy and liberal humanism. The primary concern of the former is with children's ability to decode written texts for the practical purposes of everyday life, because that is what society and their parents expect, whereas the preoccupation of the latter is that children should come to value and enjoy the habit of reading.

As an English teacher you will almost certainly feel ideologically inclined towards the 'real' books argument, and *prima facie* it has much to recommend it. If so many children do, like me, learn to read as a natural consequence of being read to from a picture book on a parent's knee, it would appear reasonable to apply the same 'apprenticeship' approach, learning from an adult how to 'behave like a reader', in school. Equally, it does seem odd, looking back, that my primary school should have insisted I worked my way though a reading scheme, whose dismal cover I can still visualise, when I had arrived in infant reception already able to read books like Jean de Brunhoff's stories of Babar the elephant. No one can deny that the more famous of the dicta promulgated by supporters of the 'real' books movement such as Frank Smith, Margaret Meek and Liz Waterland – 'Reading to children teaches reading,' 'Authors teach children to read,' 'Reading is learned by reading,' 'Children learn phonics by reading, not reading by phonics' – have a certain pithy plausibility about them; they sound as though they ought to be true even if they are not.

The question is whether the 'real' books approach can work for all or most children, particularly those who do not come from bookish homes and for whom reading in adulthood is likely to be limited to strictly utilitarian functions, the local newspaper and magazines. The 'real' books advocates have perhaps been guilty of confusing two aims: the unexceptionable one they share with everyone else of trying to ensure that children can read for all the practical purposes of daily life, and the more questionable one, peculiar to them, of converting the population into a nation of 'real' readers or, as some would say, bookworms.

The available evidence suggests that most primary school teachers, something like 90 per cent, favour 'a mix of methods', although a few schools in certain areas are reported to have abandoned reading schemes and gone over entirely to 'real' books. The teachers I know still rely on a scheme but supplement it generously with a variety of books, and also make some use of what is usually called the 'whole language' or 'language experience' approach, which the advocates of 'real' books some-times claim for their own but which antedates their campaign by a good ten years. In this the stress falls on the interrelations between the different modes of language, so that the teaching of reading is integrated into the broader aim of all-round language development. For example, what children can say – an oral story perhaps – might be converted, with the teacher's help, into a written text, a 'real' book if you prefer, for them and others to read. A clever invention within this approach was the sentence maker, first introduced as part of the *Breakthrough to Literacy* materials in 1970 and still widely used today, which requires children to manipulate printed word cards to make their own stories.

On one thing infant teachers of most persuasions do seem agreed – that the crucial factor in children learning to read is not the application of this technique or that but (after, of course, the degree of interest and encouragement shown by their parents) the attitude of their teachers, both to them and to books, and the quality of the quadrangular relationship between child, parent, teacher and books deriving therefrom. The HMIs, in their 1991 report, go further and identify the quality of the teaching (especially 'systematic phonic teaching'), together with the effectiveness of school organisation and classroom management, as the crucial factors. LEAs and headteachers, on the other hand, are inclined to blame factors outside the school's control for poor reading standards – disadvantaged home backgrounds, staffing difficulties, underfunding, industrial action, class size and the introduction of the National Curriculum. If the teachers themselves are right (that it is the quality of the quadrangular relationship which counts), you may be disposed to conclude that there can be little reason for continuing to think of the teaching of reading as a recondite art into which the novice needs to be initiated and to trust to the maxim that teaching reading is learned by teaching reading. If, on the other hand, the HMIs are right (that the quality of the teaching is even more important), you will need, at the very least, to find out about phonics.

Taking my own advice (offered above), I recently decided to check out what I had read and heard by interviewing the head of the infant department at the Liverpool primary school. The school serves a Roman Catholic and predominantly working class catchment area on the outskirts of the city centre, which scores high on indices of social disadvantage, such as the numbers of parents out of work, of one-parent families and of children entitled to free school meals. On the positive side, there is a flourishing PTA and the great majority of parents are keen for their children, almost all of whom start in the nursery, to succeed. The head of infants, a teacher for thirty years, took me through the language policy document, showed me the books and resources available and explained the practice of the department. This clearly fell into the mixed method category adopted by most schools. After pre-reading activities designed to develop visual discrimination and auditory skills, as well as a favourable attitude towards books, in the nursery (where I met one boy able to read who was not yet four), the children move on to a mixture of phonics, word recognition and real books, including those they make themselves, in the infants.

The basic reading scheme used – or language development scheme, to be more precise – is Ginn 360, which is multi-method and is followed throughout the school up to and including top juniors. Because they attach importance to phonics, the infant department have supplemented it with other schemes. Besides Ginn 360's own reading books there are a variety of others, colour-coded for difficulty, in book corners and the library. The help of parents is actively sought. Parents are given advice on what to do and not to do when hearing children read and play their part in record keeping. When children move on to the juniors, only a handful are normally in need of remedial attention. For the school year 1990–1, however, tests revealed that almost a third of the group were. The head of department offered no simple explanation for such an exceptional occurrence; nor did she for why some children were good readers and others poor – there could be so many factors involved in both. On whether standards had or had not declined over the years she had been a teacher she was equally cautious. The change she did comment on was the change in teaching methods. Whereas in 1960 reading was taught more narrowly, as a necessary skill in itself, nowadays it was seen as part of overall language development, topic-based and more richly resourced. A consequence of this, and one likely to be reinforced by the requirements of the National Curriculum, could be that today infant children spend less time on learning to read in the traditional sense.

READING IN SECONDARY SCHOOL

The most obvious relevance of the primary school experience to you as a secondary school teacher of English is in your work with poor or reluctant readers. In 1987–8 many of my students became preoccupied with the problems of what are now generally referred to as 'special needs' pupils after meeting them for the first time on teaching practice, and were keen to devote their main method assignment to some aspect of 'remedial' work. In advising them I found it hard, bearing in mind Joyce Morris's one-in-eight calculation, to steer a line between idealism and realism and to decide what practical suggestions I could usefully give.

In the 1960s, when 'remedial' readers were hived off from the mainstream in special classes or withdrawal groups, I often wondered what they actually did there. Whatever it was, it did not seem to do them much good; being placed in a 'remedial' class or group in first year was usually a life sentence. Only slowly did it dawn on me that there was, in the words of the Bullock report, 'no mystique about remedial education' and expertise in it was something of a sham. Now that 'special needs' teachers normally, and rightly, work alongside mainstream teachers in the classroom, it has become clear that the assistance they can give is essentially that of an extra teacher – hearing children read, talking to them about what they have read and written and helping them with difficulties. Sometimes teachers are able to use other pupils – older ones in vertically grouped classes, better readers in mixed ability classes, native speakers in multilingual contexts – to perform a similar function, although paired reading, as it is usually called, has a wider applicability than this.

In the 1970s some teachers of mixed ability classes or lower sets had recourse to reading laboratories, of which that produced by SRA was the most popular, although these too were designed for the whole ability range rather than just for poor readers. Basically they continued where primary school reading and language development schemes left off and shared with them the advantage, from the harassed teacher's point of view, of running themselves on an individualised basis. Children worked at their own pace, marked their own work and charted their own progress. They were liked by the teachers who used them because they guaranteed peace and quiet and seemingly purposeful activity on Friday afternoons and by the children because they could cheat with impunity. To the English teaching orthodoxy, on the other hand, such schemes have always been suspect because of their association with behaviourism and programmed learning. The particular objections to the SRA reading laboratory have been that most of the texts are of indifferent quality and the reliance on multiple-choice questions encourages neither reading for meaning nor reading for pleasure.

Although I must plead guilty to having occasionally made use of such schemes myself, because of the overwhelming need for

peace and quiet on Friday afternoons, my preferred approach to
the problem of the poor and reluctant reader has been to combine
something resembling the primary school 'language experience'
approach with individualised reading and accessible (if necessary,
simplified) adult literature. The first thing you will need to do,
however, and it is not as easy as I may make it sound, is try and
establish what each pupil can and cannot do in reading and does
and does not want to read, even if that leaves him or her with a
diet of nothing but fishing or fashion magazines. For enrichment
I follow David Holbrook, whose book *English for the Rejected* was,
and remains, so inspirational for teaching 'remedial' children, in
recommending a programme of traditional and classical fare –
ballads and folk songs, myths and legends, straightforward
modern novels such as *Animal Farm* or stories by authors like
Roald Dahl and Graham Greene, and simplified versions of
Shakespeare and other pre-twentieth century authors.

I tried all these on the bottom fifth year set in the Greater
Manchester school in 1987. They became obsesssed with the folk
song 'The Foggy Dew' and periodically asked me to sing it, never
perhaps having heard a teacher sing anything except hymns
before. They also sat and listened to my retellings of *Macbeth*,
Romeo and Juliet, *Hamlet* and *King Lear* 'rapt withal', as I reported
in Chapter 1. Occasionally I dramatised parts of the Shakespeare
plays, using the techniques described in Chapter 8, and
afterwards gave them my own versions of the plots to read. At no
point did I turn to books specifically written for older 'reluctant'
readers. This is because I share the view of the Newbolt report that
'we should act up to our own tastes and offer to the young nothing
which is not in some degree a work of art' and have constantly at
the back of my mind David Holbrook's charge that English
teachers who offer pupils reading material which falls well below
his touchstone *Huckleberry Finn* are guilty of 'a kind of betrayal'.
One of the few positive features of the statutory provisions in
English is that they require that all secondary school pupils,
including remedial readers, should be introduced to Shakespeare
and 'some of the works which have been most influential in
shaping and refining the English language and its literature'.

Most books specifically written for 'reluctant' readers in
secondary schools are characterised by the 'formulaic vulgarity' I
referred to in my essay 'A classical education' reproduced in
Chapter 1. Covering for the teacher of a bottom band fourth year

set in the Greater Manchester school, I was asked to carry on with their class reader. I forget what it was called but the title included the name Sharon, from which something of its abysmal content and style can be deduced. The dialogue contained much gratuitous vilification and swearing, and the narrative clicked through supposedly relevant issues – abortion, drug abuse, leaving home, and so forth – as though the novel had been written to a publisher's checklist, which it probably had. Its literary merit I rated at zero.

What, then, should the reading curriculum in English comprise? Seventy years ago the Newbolt report summarised its ingredients as a mixture of what would now be called intensive and extensive reading and information skills. A very similar summary can be extracted from the Bullock and Cox reports and from the statutory provisions of the National Curriculum. The problem of instituting extensive reading – that is to say, pupils reading widely and in accordance with their own wishes – has already been touched on. Something like half the teenage school population appears to have little or no wish to read books at all. To teachers who love and value literature, for whom reading may be, in the words of the Newbolt report, 'the most varied and fruitful [experience] in the whole of life', this situation is hard to come to terms with, and we continue to hope that all our 'reluctant' readers will one day experience that moment of epiphany Rudyard Kipling describes in his autobiography, when it came to him that reading was 'a means to everything that would make me happy'. Even more fondly we perhaps also hope that the moment may be partly brought about by something we do as teachers. In 1921 George Sampson visualised such a moment like this: 'One day a man read something to you. He didn't tell you anything, or teach you anything, he just read something, and you suddenly found that straight in front of you was a door that led to paradise.'

Over sixty years later an undergraduate student of mine, reflecting on his school days, recalled an actual moment of this kind in his own childhood, but without Sampson's figurative flourish:

The first recollection of an English lesson that I have took place in the third year of primary school. The memory is of the teacher reading from Gerald Durrell's 'My Family and Other

Animals'. The reason that I can remember this experience rather than any other is that the story, concerned with the capture and observation of animals by the author as a young boy, was the first that I had heard read or read myself that was concerned with real adventure, rather than the make-believe world of Enid Blyton and the like. And this discovery of how interesting people's lives could be, out there in the real world, has led me to read voraciously ever since.

(Dale)

I hardly need to stress that reading aloud to children is perhaps the most important thing you can do as an English teacher to encourage their own reading, and arguably also the most important skill in the English teacher's repertoire that you can seek to cultivate.

There are a number of other strategies for fostering 'extensive' reading available to the school or English department as well. Several have been much commended in recent years: school bookshops, writers in school, book weeks, reading evenings, and silent reading sessions during school time which involve all pupils and everyone on the staff from the headteacher to the school secretary (though I have yet to hear of one including the caretaker or the dinner ladies). But you may feel, as a probationer or relatively powerless classroom teacher, that most of these fall rather outside your area of discretion, and it is certainly true that being in a position of authority considerably enlarges the range of what you can do to encourage the habit of voluntary reading. When I was head of department in the mid-1970s, I not only taught in the school library but installed in it a school bookshop – and effectively controlled the budgets of department, library and bookshop.

All English teachers, however, can convert their classrooms into libraries and attempt to institute silent reading sessions. I have always had something like an infant school book corner in my room where pupils were free to browse and pick and choose and from which they were able to borrow. Building up a collection is much less of a problem than you might imagine. If you ask around, you will easily find people prepared to offload paperbacks on you, while visits to junk shops, second-hand bookshops, book sales and so forth can yield a rich harvest at very little cost. I recently picked up good hardback copies of novels by

Willa Cather and Joyce Cary from my local junk shop for only 20p each. About the same time one of the local supermarkets was selling brand-new paperback copies of classics of nineteenth century British and American fiction (approximately thirty different titles) for less than £1 each.

Your room should also include a selection of reference books for pupils to practise their study or information skills on. If your department has its priorities right, it will already contain sets of adult (not school) dictionaries and thesauruses. If you are very lucky, you may be able to get hold of a set of encyclopedias as well. To these you can start to add second-hand or your own copies of individual reference books. My short-list would be: the Authorised Version of the Bible, a complete Shakespeare, *The Oxford* or *Cambridge Companion to English Literature*, *The Cambridge Encyclopedia of Language*, Brewer's *Dictionary of Phrase and Fable*, an atlas, and dictionaries of quotations, place names, first names and surnames. Equally indispensable are newspapers (several now publish excellent junior editions or supplements) and magazines, for which your technology department may be kind enough to design racks or display stands.

In an ambience of this kind reading, consulting, exchanging and discussing books all happen more readily than in rooms where the only books are sets of school texts. Mention of Willa Cather reminds me of how a group of fifth year girls and I discovered this underrated novelist together in the 1960s (I had not even heard of her at that time) in precisely such an ambience. I also remember from the same decade, though in a different school, an Indian girl who read everything in the book corner I recommended to her, plus everything from my personal collection, including George Eliot and Tolstoy. Unfortunately, instituting a library lesson, in which everyone, including the teacher, gets their head down over a book for thirty minutes or so is no longer the straightforward proposition it was in that decade, although I may be guilty of remembering 'with advantages'.

Today, or so it seems to me, the bulk of reluctant or indifferent readers, who come to school essentially for social reasons, can see no reason why they should engage in a solitary activity they dislike when there are friends to chat to or lark about with. In the Knowsley school in 1989 only one of my five classes was capable of using the weekly lesson in the school library for the purpose for which it was intended – silent reading and the exchange of books, although a small minority of pupils in the other four were, just as a small minority in that one class were not. More or less the same was true in the Greater Manchester school two years before. There I also had a pupil who refused to do anything but read (writing was particularly hateful to him) and who occasionally asked whether he could retire to the stock cupboard to indulge his passion rather than participate in the lesson. If you do manage to institute silent reading sessions with your classes, and are not teaching in leafy suburbs or rural areas, I would say you can congratulate yourself on a notable achievement.

As to what pupils choose to read, I would leave that entirely up to them. 'Let a child first read *any* English book which happens to engage his attention,' opined Dr Johnson. '. . . . He'll get better books afterwards.' I have always adopted a permissive policy and never known a pupil abuse it by bringing in pornography or anything else that might scandalise the powers that be. Your pupils may seem to you to opt for rubbish or material below their reading or chronological age, but adolescents do need to go through an omnivorous and indiscriminate phase before settling on what suits them. Coleridge, reflecting on his experience as a young reader, described himself as 'a library cormorant . . . I read everything that came in my way without distinction. . . . My whole being was . . . to crumple myself up in a sunny corner and read, read, read.' When I was 15 and 16 I read all my mother's collection of fiction, as well as the stories in her women's magazines, for descriptions of sexual passion and thereby made the acquaintance of Tolstoy. Although I found *War and Peace* hard going in parts, I did at least finish it. *Anna Karenina* I thought the most wonderful novel ever written. No novel I have read since has caused me to revise that adolescent judgment.

I.A. Richards once famously observed that 'we are all of us learning to read all the time'. Some such belief must explain why 'intensive' reading in the form of comprehension, one of the oldest elements in the English curriculum, continues to occupy a central position despite being loathed, according to the evidence of APU surveys, by many pupils, most of whom can probably read, in a technical sense, perfectly well. It remains fundamental to GCSE, for example, albeit in rather different form to that of its GCE O Level predecessor, being as much a test of writing as of reading. Its survival, and its new form, are very largely due to the Bullock report and its 1970s contemporary, the Schools Council

Effective Use of Reading project. These were premised on the belief that pupils need to develop 'higher-order reading skills' so that they can engage in more 'active interrogation' of the denser texts they encounter as they progress through school. This idea had been present in the Newbolt report but without any illustration of what it might mean in practice or how it might differ from the traditional comprehension exercise in which pupils explained the meaning of words and phrases and wrote short answers to show that they had understood the passage. The Bullock report and the Schools Council project tried to clarify the aims of comprehension and to expand and vary the kind of responses pupils could make.

Between them they identified five kinds of question pupils could be asked about a passage: literal (what does it actually say?), inferential (what is implied?), reorganisational (how would you summarise the main points?), evaluative (is it true or false?), and aesthetic (is it well written?). This does not exhaust all the questions one might want to ask. You may well feel, for example, that distinguishing fact from opinion and literal from metaphorical meaning deserve categories of their own. You may also feel that the simple continuum from 'closed' to 'open' questions, which I have often used with my pupils and is perhaps implicit in the classification to some extent, would have made it more lucid. But there can be no doubt that it has provided teachers with a useful intellectual framework for working in.

The Schools Council project was also largely responsible, through its DARTS (directed activities related to texts), for giving currency to many of the imaginative and enjoyable ideas for making comprehension more fun which have since become a standard part of the English teacher's repertoire: cloze procedure (asking pupils to fill the gaps in a text), prediction (asking them to speculate on what might happen next), sequencing (jumbling up the parts of a text and asking pupils to rearrange them), transformation (asking them to change the form or content of the text), question setting (asking pupils to devise the questions), problem setting (asking them to solve a problem posed but not answered by the text), and non-verbal (getting pupils to respond to a text through mime, diagrams, cartoons, etc.).

The justification for all this activity is that it helps pupils to read more reflectively as they come up against more complex material. Whether this is so or not I leave for you to decide. Two things I would try and dissuade you from, however, are using extracts from texts for comprehension, which was the norm when I started out, and using inferior material like holiday brochures, unheard of then but all too common now. Always use complete texts, whether poems, newspaper articles, essays, stories or whatever, and texts of some intrinsic value. During my GCE O Level year my English teacher did no comprehension practice with us, arguing that the study of literature gave us practice enough, and surely he was right. I would also urge you to devise your own questions and exercises instead of relying on other people's books or past examination papers. It may be time-consuming but it is also rewarding.

Examples of mine are to be found in Chapters 8 and 9. As these deal exclusively with the main literary genres of fiction, drama and poetry, I thought I would mention here two examples of work on other genres which seemed to me reasonably successful. The text in the first example was a local newspaper article on a famous criminal case in Liverpool, the Maybrick murder, if murder it was, in 1889. The class involved was the upper band second year (now year 8) in the Knowsley school. After we had sorted out problems of literal comprehension, I set them the task of summarising the prosecution and defence arguments, as well as the judge's summing up, within tight word limits (precis remains, I would say, the most important of all comprehension skills), before asking them to debate the two critical questions raised by the case: did Mrs Maybrick murder her husband and did she get a fair trial? Comprehension in this instance also naturally included dramatisation and equally naturally led on to a written assignment – 'Write your own story of a baffling murder case'.

In the second example I gave the top fifth year set (now year 11) at the Greater Manchester school D.H. Lawrence's essay 'Nottingham and the Mining Countryside' to read. Their task was twofold. First of all, they had to draw a plan of Eastwood, using a road map to help them if they wished, mark in on it all the places mentioned by Lawrence, and on that basis conclude whether he had or had not described his home town well. Second, they had to devise a diagrammatic way of representing Lawrence's argument, dividing it into stages which had to be labelled with a catchy caption. From this several members of the class wrote what was to prove the best assignment in their completed course folders – an essay entitled 'Middleton [the name of their town] and the

Surrounding Countryside'. The similarity between the situations of Middleton and Eastwood – villages industrialised in the nineteenth century but still affording easy access to beautiful countryside – invited such an assignment; and the best essays followed Lawrence, on my suggestion, in freely mixing autobiography, factual description and critical comment.

Another legacy of the 1970s is the emphasis now laid on study, library and information skills – on reading to learn rather than learning to read – although the idea, once again, is traceable back to the Newbolt report. I am not convinced that the emphasis is necessary, and some of the schemes devised, notably SQ3R (survey, question, read, review and recite) on which SRA reading laboratories are based, seem excessively behaviouristic. If we take one of the study skills particularly stressed, learning to read at different speeds for different purposes (skimming and scanning and so forth), does not this develop perfectly naturally once a certain degree of technical competence has been achieved and a certain amount of familiarity with books, bookshops and libraries has been acquired? It requires no special instruction on the part of the teacher. About twenty years ago, however, I did get interested in the question of reading speed and whether fast readers also comprehend more ('read fast, think slow' was the paradoxical advice of Eric Lunzer of the Effective Use of Reading Project). I put a number of my classes through a programme designed to improve their reading speed, and discovered not only that the faster readers were better at comprehension than the slower ones and that a pupil's comprehension score improved as he or she learned to read faster, but also, and to my chagrin, that quite a few pupils as young as 13 and 14 read faster than I did.

If you have managed to create a book corner in your classroom and pupils have access to a library, and opportunity and encouragement to use reference books, they will soon acquire all the library or information skills they require. They do not need lessons on the contents page, subheadings or the index, nor do they on how to find their way round a library. I have never mastered the Dewey system of classification, for example (some libraries do not even use it), and, if I want to find a section, author or book in a library, I do the commonsense thing and ask a librarian. Occasionally he or she will send me to the catalogue or microfiche, neither of which poses any major problem to most people; and nowadays, of course, many libraries are equipped with simple computer programs, which are usually even more helpful than librarians and which almost any pupil could operate. The one library or study skill which it is worth spending time on, however, is that of note-making. It was the only skill required for the GCE O Level English Language paper, as part of learning how to summarise, which my own teacher actually taught. He drilled us ruthlessly in the art of extracting the key points from a text and condensing them within a prescribed number of words in consecutive prose of our own. Experience since has convinced me that note-making for the purposes of precis is, like precis itself, one of the most valuable skills school can teach.

ASSESSMENT

Finally, I need to say something about the assessment of reading, and in particular about reading tests, which the national assessment may, but seems unlikely to (being, like GCSE, criterion-referenced and unstandardised), render redundant. Standardised reading tests were developed between the two world wars as part of a more general programme of testing children's ability and attainment. They can be taken by individuals or groups and are usually norm-referenced. The results allocate each child a reading age or quotient somewhere within a normal distribution curve and, thereby, provide teachers and parents with some idea of how he or she performs in relation to other children of the same age. The skills tested are usually word recognition or sentence completion and rarely involve more than literal comprehension. Such tests have always been anathema to the English teaching orthodoxy and were criticised by the Bullock report as an inadequate way of trying to establish how well children read, which led to the APU's development of more rounded and humanistic forms of assessing reading in the 1970s and 1980s. However, I would not dismiss reading ages and quotients out of hand, if you inherit them from your feeder primary schools or find them imposed by your own school. They can give you some idea of where you stand, should you feel you need it. But they should be treated with caution. They can easily become self-fulfilling and should not therefore normally be divulged to parents and pupils, unlike your own personal assessments of a more rounded kind, made with or without tests, which you should certainly share with both.

The kind of rounded and humanistic assessment favoured by the orthodoxy is best represented by the diagnostic testing of individual children and, in particular, by the miscue analysis devised by Kenneth Goodman in the 1960s. If you are not already familiar with miscue analysis, you should certainly make every effort to become so and will find it exemplified in the first national tests taken by 7 year olds in 1991. What it essentially tries to do is, through tape-recording and interviews, to identify the sorts of mistakes poor readers make, the strategies they employ and how these affect their grasp of meaning. It also tries to reach beyond literal comprehension in order to make some assessment of children's capacity to draw inferences from, and express judgments about, what they read. Also very well worth examining as an example of formative assessment of an especially rich and rewarding kind is the much admired ILEA Primary Language Record.

FURTHER READING

I have read only a tiny fraction of the vast literature on reading, so I hesitate over recommendations. From the 1970s you should certainly read the Bullock report (DES, 1975) and *The Effective Use of Reading* by Eric Lunzer and Keith Gardner. A little book I found very useful while teaching in that decade was a BBC publication, *Reading after Ten* by Elizabeth Goodacre *et al.*. From the 1980s I have enjoyed the books of the 'apprenticeship' lobby – Margaret Meek, *Learning to Read*, Frank Smith, *Reading* and Liz Waterland, *Read with Me* – without being completely convinced by any of them. If you want to enliven your comprehension work, 'Twenty-two ideas for variety in comprehension work' by Mike Taylor and Bill Deller is useful, though it duplicates, to some extent, the ideas found in similar lists for teaching literature. You will find it reproduced in Anthony Adams (ed.), *New Directions in English Teaching*.

Chapter 6

Writing

She could write a little essay on any subject exactly a slate long, beginning at the left-hand top of one side and ending at the right-hand bottom of the other, and the essay should be strictly according to the rule.

(Charles Dickens, *Our Mutual Friend*, 1864–5)

The trouble went on, day after day. She had always piles of books to mark, myriads of errors to correct, a heart-wearying task that she loathed. And the work got worse and worse. When she tried to flatter herself that the composition grew more alive, more interesting, she had to see that the handwriting grew more and more slovenly, the books were filthy and disgraceful.

(D.H. Lawrence, *The Rainbow*, 1915)

TEACHING WRITING: IMITATION VERSUS CREATIVITY

Writing at school was originally (that is to say, in the period of the Renaissance) conducted in Latin or involved the translation, paraphrase or reproduction of a Latin passage in English. Even after the native tongue became acceptable in its own right the emphasis, as in Latin, was on the imitation of classical models and on writing according to prescribed guidelines, whether the end product was an essay, a letter or a poem. That such an emphasis should have produced Milton, who wrote prose and verse fluently in both languages, is understandable. That it might also have been partly responsible for the great upsurge in literary talent represented by Shakespeare, the Elizabethan and Jacobean dramatists, and the Metaphysical poets, seems remarkable, at least to us, brought up as we have been to take essentially Romantic ideas about artistic creation for granted.

For it was during the Romantic period that the imitation of models was first challenged as a basis of children's writing and in which children's personal reactions to topics that interested them were first encouraged. However, as we saw in Chapter 2, it was not really till the beginning of this century that 'creative' or 'free' writing posed a threat to the long reign of imitation and not really till after the Second World War that the latter was overthrown. Then, you will recall, a succession of English teachers, led by Marjorie Hourd, argued that children should be encouraged to write spontaneously and intuitively, quoting in their support Keats's famous observation in one of his letters: 'If poetry comes not as naturally as the leaves to a tree it had better not come at all.' Classroom preparation for writing, and teacherly interference in general, were frowned on; the importance of mechanics and formal properties was played down; and what emerged from the child's pen, including the mistakes, was treated as sacrosanct. The only pedagogical artifice admitted was the use of multi-sensory stimuli to get writing under way – pictures, music, objects to feel, and so forth.

Since then the excesses of this 'free spontaneous expression' approach have been recognised, and a number of otherwise child-centred educationalists – Peter Abbs, for example – have maintained that, if children are to become serious writers, they must learn to see writing as an 'artistic process' or 'craft' whose formal properties they need to master, whether they are working on fact or fiction, verse or prose. Instead of Keats, R.L. Stevenson might be quoted. All writers, he once observed, have to play 'the sedulous ape' before finding voices of their own. During the last twenty years a consensus on the teaching of children's writing has emerged which to some extent constitutes an accommodation between imitation and creativity. It was partly anticipated (yet again) by the Newbolt report, owes something to the National Writing Project of 1985–9 and is now firmly inscribed in the National Curriculum. Setting aside, for the moment, concern over handwriting, spelling and the other so-called 'basic skills', which naturally find a place in the statutory provisions, I think the main elements in the consensus can be listed as follows:

1 Children should be encouraged to take greater responsibility

for their work. This means choosing their own topics and having more say in how their writing is presented and assessed.

2 Children should be encouraged to develop a repertoire of writing skills for a range of genres, audiences and purposes.

3 Children should see writing as a 'craft' or 'long, painstaking, patient process' (to quote Donald Graves, one of the main architects of the consensus) and themselves as 'real' writers for 'real' audiences. Final pieces of work should emerge only after considered attention has been given to the preliminary activities of planning, drafting, redrafting, editing and proof-reading – which may well result in fewer pieces of work being completed.

4 The classroom should become a writing workshop in which children co-operate in discussing and improving one another's work and their teacher writes alongside them while also carrying out the duties of editor-in-chief.

5 At the end of the school year each pupil should have a file or folder containing his or her best work in a range of genres.

Like all consensuses, and the larger orthodoxy on English teaching of which it is part, this one is in jeopardy of ossifying into uncritical assertion. One even occasionally catches the whiff of doctrinal intolerance. 'Surely everyone teaches drafting now,' said a head of department at a meeting I attended in the late 1970s. I would strongly recommend you approach the orthodoxy's claims in a spirit of open-minded agnosticism. Some elements – I would say (1), (2) and (5) – are, of course, no more than common sense, at least to teachers, though I can imagine many parents dissenting from (1). The others – (3) and (4) – however, seem to me to deserve more critical attention than they have so far received.

WRITING IN A RANGE OF GENRES

I want to start with (2) – the idea that children should write in a range of genres from an early age – not, in this case, because I disagree with it, but because it needs elaborating. There have been a number of attempts since the Newbolt report to classify the genres children can be expected to try their hand at. The report itself drew a broad distinction between writing as 'factual statement' and writing as 'artistic expression', which George Sampson rephrased, in *English for the English*, as respectively 'statement or record' and 'creation or invention'. Most teachers and educationalists have been satisfied with a similar twofold categorisation, though sometimes with a different distinction in mind. The Cox report, for example, distinguishes between 'private' and 'public' and the National Curriculum between 'chronological' and 'non-chronological' writing. The most influential of all recent classifications has been the threefold one devised by the Schools Council's Writing across the Curriculum Project, under James Britton's direction, in the 1970s. This distinguishes between 'poetic' (corresponding to Newbolt's 'artistic expression'), 'transactional' (corresponding, more or less, to Newbolt's 'factual statement') and 'expressive' (or what many people would call 'personal') writing. The project also devised a classification of the audiences for whom school writing is intended, which has been much used – the pupil him or herself, the teacher (either as assessor or partner in a dialogue), another trusted adult, other pupils and the public in general.

The project's research revealed that most writing in secondary school in the mid-1970s was transactional and written for the teacher as assessor, and led it to recommend an increased use of 'expressive' writing ('poetic' writing being well established in, and mainly only appropriate to, English) and of writing for a greater variety of audiences. George Sampson in the 1920s took a rather different view. He argued that it was right for schools to concentrate on writing as 'statement or record' rather than writing as 'creation or invention', because the latter was unteachable and only a minority of pupils had a talent for it or were likely to become professional writers: 'Our business is with the sparrows, not the skylarks.' Although no English teacher would probably want to put it quite like that now, it is being increasingly acknowledged that primary school children, and younger pupils in secondary school English lessons, have perhaps been spending too much time on 'expressive' and 'poetic' writing and not enough on the 'transactional' writing – reporting, expounding, explaining and arguing – on which their educational and professional future is more likely to depend.

It is clear that a range of writing, including the supposedly more difficult 'transactional' genres like the discursive essay, is well within the capacity of older primary school pupils, whether 'skylarks' or 'sparrows'. After only five weeks of the autumn term 1990 10 year old Leanne from the Liverpool primary school (something of a 'skylark' in a school like hers) already had in her file of best work in English two interview-based biographies, a book review, the framework for a debate, a shape poem and a front page news story done on the computer. Here are the first biography (the second, a 12 page account of her mother's life, is unfortunately too long to include), the book review and the debate framework, in Leanne's final version:

Michelle is a very nice girl her parents are hard-working citizens called Val and Chris they have no pets but they are a happy family with 4 daughters and 1 son Michelle's hobby is dancing, her favourite popstar is Madona, but in her free time she likes to watch Kate & Allie which is her favourite TV programme and play out with her best friend Linda. Michelle is 10 year's old. In December 5th Michelle will be 11. Michelle's favourite boy's name is Steven & her favourite girl's name is Niomi. Next year Michelle will be going to Broughton Hall and when she's older she would like to be a bus driver she hope's her bus is yellow because this is her favourite colour. Michelle's worst colour is pink but she hates Darren M and always calls him crackabangbang because it's her favourite saying. Her worst hobby is netball and her favourite football team is Liverpool. But she wouldn't say no to some hot curry because this is her favourite food.

My favourite book is 'Matilda' by Roald Dahl. I like this book because it is funny, excited & quite cheap. My favourite and funniest chapter was the 'Hat and the superglue' were Matilda wanted to get her own back on her dad. So one night when they were all out Matilda got some superglue and squeezed an extra large blob in her dad's hat and left it to set. The next day as usually her dad put on his hat and went to work but when he got to work he went to take his hat off & he found that his hat would not come off he pulled and pulled but it wouldent even budge, it was quite embarrassing and when he came home every one had a pull but it wouldent move so in the end Mrs Wormwood had to cut it off and Mr Wormwood looked so funny. 'Matilda' is a new book it has just come out I have read lot's of Roald Dahl's book's but I think Matilda is the best.

Motion: Animals in captivity

For

The zoo keeps animals so that we can see the animals & be able to know what they look like. The circus keeps animals for entertainment and to show people what animal's are capable of.

Some of the animal catchers catch animals because they are becoming extinct & they want to save them.

Against

Cruelty to animals is when people are on horses and they whip the horse's.

Some animal's in the zoo or the the circus loose their pride when comander's tell them to do silly things & people laugh at them.

I think animals should have the right to be free just like human beings because they have a life just like you & me.

Over the same period (five weeks) in the second half of the spring term 1991 Leanne and her classmates (both 'skylarks' and'sparrows') produced a mini-folder of work for the topic on Dickens and *Great Expectations* referred to in Chapter 3. This included a biography of Dickens, a discussion of the way Pip's character changes during the course of the story, a comparison of the simplified written version they had read with David Lean's film version, another character's version of an episode (e.g. Estella's account of first meeting Pip) and the transformation of an episode (e.g. the return of Magwitch) into a play scene for acting out.

As proof that transactional writing is within the capacity of 'sparrows' too, here is Katie from the previous year's top juniors writing towards the end of the school year, first of all on a topic straddling the 'personal' and the 'factual', which had been preceded by class discussion of what it might include, and then on a discussion topic, for which she had been given a framework and some facts and figures:

My city

Liverpool is a city which has famous places and people its is famous for are football teams, the Beatles, and our two cathedrals which are called Metropolitan and Anglican cathedral We are the only city in Europe with two cathedrals We are also are known for the very famous Beatles who sing strawberry feilds, yestday, yellow sumberine, and help. We are trying to clean up are city a bit more and start campaigns and we are caring about our environment more. I would'nt move anywhere else. All the local parks in Liverpool are getting millions of pounds spent on them they are clearing out all the rubbish and sewage and restocking it with new fish in the ponds and cleaning up all the rubbish in the parks and making new swings and play grounds round there. I might go and live in Austraila or france but other wise I would not move out of Liverpool in early May we had a concert in the Pier head in memory of John Lennon millions of people came to watch and lots of pop singers sings Town and the pier head was packed I did'nt go but my cousin went and really enjoyed herself. I hope Liverpool keeps cleaning rubbish up and I hope to live here all my life.

The problem of truancy
Truancy is a very serious problem in British secondary school. Over 200, 000 children truant off school. This is 65 per cent of school children of all the people I know there is only one who truants all the time and he has been caught about five times, but he still misses school. 36 per cent take the odd day or lesson off, 10 per cent particuler days or lesson and 6 per cent take several days. Overall 16 per cent are playing truant. But the inner city schools are worse.

There are several reasons why children truant. One is because they get bullied by other children in the class or teachers pick on them. Sometimes they have difficulty understanding the lessons, another reason is because they are dyslexic.

How can the problem be solve may be we can solve the problem by getting inspectors around the streets more. The teachers could be more understanding and help truants to do their work. I think that more children would come in to school if they had a choice of lessons or did more fun work.

(Katie)

What, then, should a range of writing in English encompass, and where should the emphases fall? You may feel that these questions are adequately answered in the statutory provisions. My view is that they are not, because of the crucial failure to sort out English from language development and the responsibilities of English teachers from those of teachers of other subjects. This is not such a problem in primary schools because most class teachers, like the one in the Liverpool primary school, teach all the academic subjects and are best left to sort it out for themselves. However, in secondary schools it certainly is a problem. An English department needs to begin, in my view, by trying to establish which kinds of writing are already adequately catered for elsewhere in the curriculum. The Writing across the Curriculum Project reported in the mid-1970s that a very high level of 'transactional' writing was undertaken in science, history, geography and religious education. Although there may have been some movement in those subjects in recent years towards 'poetic' and 'expressive' writing, especially in the form of empathetic role-play, my impression is that this major bias persists, because of the nature of the subjects involved. From this it follows, I think, that, to avoid duplication in a crowded curriculum, English should retain its own bias towards the 'poetic' and the 'expressive' and concern itself only with forms of 'transactional' writing like biographies, reviews and argumentative essays which are insufficiently represented elsewhere.

The importance of maintaining the traditional bias with older pupils should be stressed too. If younger ones need to be introduced to 'transactional' genres sooner rather than later, then older ones need to be encouraged to persevere with writing which is 'expressive' or 'poetic'. This is one respect in which GCSE is a better exam than the discarded GCE O Level and most forms of A Level. Many of my undergraduate and postgraduate students in 1987–8, reflecting on their schooldays, commented critically on how they were discouraged from writing personally and imaginatively once they entered the sixth, or in some cases even the fifth, form, and on the very narrow range of writing expected of them during their degree course in English. I responded by following the example of other teacher trainers, notably Peter Abbs, in giving them opportunities to compensate for this neglect by writing personal and imaginative assignments as part of their method work.

The other important question concerns whether all genres need to be formally taught. There have always been those who claim that, if children are provided with enough examples – enough good models – of the genres they are to write in, they will learn 'by nature' what is demanded. In other words, they will learn how to write by wide reading. There is something to be said for this view but it fully applies only to the ablest of pupils, particularly in the case of transactional writing. That is why, in teaching the essay, I have always supplemented the use of models (such as Lawrence's 'Nottingham and the Mining Countryside', referred to in the previous chapter) with advice on possible frameworks (like arguments for and against as used by Leanne) and on matters of organisation and style – opening sentences and conclusions, main points and illustrations, paragraphing and subordination. As children have developed, so I have withdrawn the props and their own practice has become their only mentor. Eventually they learn to write essays – to organise and substantiate an argument, link paragraphs, diversify syntax and vocabulary – by writing essays, which is not to say that a word of advice here and there will not continue to be required.

Transactional writing with younger children obviously requires classroom preparation and teacher guidance. I mentioned above that Katie's writing of her essay on Liverpool had been preceded by classroom discussion and that for her truancy essay she had been given a framework and some facts and figures. This second essay was, in fact, part of the same language awareness course (see Chapter 9) as the stories quoted in Chapter 3. The aim, as with the story-telling, was to bring out the differences between talking and writing – in this case, between oral and written discussion. The class teacher recognised that the class would need more help than they had received in the case of story-telling, particularly when it came to writing. First of all, they were shown a television documentary on truancy and encouraged to take any notes they thought necessary; then there was a full-class discussion to establish the main facts, sort out confusions and exchange opinions on causes and remedies; finally, for the essay, the teacher suggested a three paragraph framework (How serious is the problem of truancy? What are its causes? How might it be solved?) and an opening sentence (Katie begins with a variation on it). She also encouraged the children to introduce their own opinions and experiences (which Katie does).

Katie and some of her classmates undoubtedly found the task difficult. Juggling facts and figures did not come easily, nor did the use of the unfamiliar words 'truancy' and 'truant', which the teacher insisted should, in an essay, replace their own expressions 'sagging' and 'bunking off'. But in the end they all coped. Subsequently she offered them a choice of titles for a further essay.

This they wrote for homework with hardly any assistance from her. Here are the efforts of three children of very different abilities:

Should English clubs be allow back in Europe?
English clubs were first banned from Europe when Liverpool play Juventus there was alot of fighting and alot of people died. In my opinion English clubs should be allowed back into Europe another strong opinion I have is it should'nt just be English clubs that were banned in the first place because Juventus fans behaved just as badly so Italian clubs should have been banned as well as English clubs. And I think if it comes to it that fans should be banned from Europe instead of clubs. The FA did try I.d cards but they never worked. And I think it's a disgrace that the Leeds and Bournemouth fans invaded the pitch while the UEFA were watching English clubs behaviour. Maybe England could regain the reaspect by behaveing well at football matches.

(Mark)

Is a woman's place in the home?
Long live Mary Pankhurst! Well thats my cry, is it yours? And Lady Godiva who in defiance and protest rode on a horse through the town, naked, with only her long hair hanging down to hide her. She was most probably one of the first active Suffragettes. Lots of people are sexist nowadays, and that not just men! Not to say the men arent sexist, what about Judge Pickles the judge whos barmier than a barmcake, I bet when hes served salad he screams 'Aha! A provocatively dressed salad it deserves all it gets'. If he was walking down a dark side-street wearing a see through top Highheels fishnet tights and mini skirt and was attacked by a big hunky woman (or man) HE wouldnt say 'I got all I deserved' would he? Women should be safe to wear a plastic bag on the streets at midnight, why not? A sexist society asks Is a womans place in the home?

(Marie)

Should we have school uniform?
The reason why we have to wear uniform is because it makes you look smart and people can tell what school you go to. And people can say oh look at that girl she gos to St Sebastians and dos'nt she look smart. And if some one robs and they have there

uniform on the shopkeeper will now what school thay go to and he can phone up the school. And if some one is helping some one and thay have there uniform on thay can say what a love girl and she gos to St Sebastians. Some people don't like wearing uniform because thay want to look pretty in stead of smart and people wont now what school they belong to. And some people just want to show off there clothes and instead of all looking the same. Thay don't look like a school at all thay just look like a bunch of colours. But some dont like the uniform because of the colours instead of like it. But some people thing there own clothes are better because thay look better on them. I think that we should wear uniform because the police and firemen and nurses have uniforms and you can spot them out from each other so schools should just be the same as them so the people can spot which school we go to. And school uniform looks smarter than your own clothes and evry body is the same as each other. Instead of a big room of differnt colours and shades.

(Jill)

Formal teaching may also be necessary for younger children in respect of the other main non-poetic genres English teachers can be expected to concern themselves with – biography and auto-biography (including letters, diaries, journals and travelogues), which straddle the 'transactional' and the 'expressive'. Primary school children may well not know what either a biography or an autobiography is. This was the case with many in Leanne's class. So the teacher, having explained the meaning of the terms, prepared them for their introduction to the first by arranging them in pairs so that children who were not close friends sat together. Their first task was to devise a questionnaire for finding out more about one another's lives. They then took it in turn to ask the questions and note down the answers, before trying to translate what they had found out into consecutive prose. This was a trial run – learning what kind of questions to ask and how to convert answers into an interesting piece of work – for the major assignment of writing the biography of an adult relative or acquaintance.

The old imitation view of writing held that models and frameworks were required for 'poetic' writing too. This view has now been revived and applied to fiction as well as to poetry itself.

Although it has generally been accepted, except during the post-1939–45 war euphoria over 'free spontaneous expression', that to write poetry successfully children need to be taught about its formal properties (about rhyme scheme and metre, ballads and sonnets, metaphors and similes, alliteration and assonance), it has, until quite recently, been assumed that for the writing of stories and plays children need no particular assistance except on relatively minor matters such as the setting out and punctuation of dialogue. Today, however, children are often invited to reflect explicitly on the formal properties of fiction too – characterisation, plot, setting, the narrative point of view – as well as the specific characteristics of sub-genres like fairy tales and detective stories, before embarking on their own efforts. They may even be asked to undertake assignments designed to enhance their understanding of form which resemble the competitions in a literary journal – rewriting fairy tales, completing poems whose rhyming words alone are provided, writing stories of fifty words with a recognisable beginning, middle and end, composing dramatic scenes in the manner of English, American and Australian soap operas, and so on.

I have no strong opinions on these recent departures and my own practice has varied considerably over the years, even in the case of poetry. For example, I have taught its formal properties to some classes but ignored them with others. Other genres, with the exception of the essay, I have tended to leave to teach themselves, so long as pupils know what they mean. By the time they start their GCSE course all pupils should be so familiar with the range of genres required – should, in effect, be independent authors in all of them – that no direct teaching of any of them on your part is necessary.

BECOMING A 'REAL' WRITER

The children's work quoted so far, being somewhat less than perfect, raises a number of other questions to do with the teaching of writing or – if one's view is that writing cannot be taught, only learned – to do with how the teacher of English can best facilitate its development. It is here that I find myself most at odds with the consensus on writing in school. According to the orthodoxy pupils should be encouraged to see themselves as 'real' writers (proposition 3 on p. 129) or at any rate as apprentices in the process of becoming 'real' writers, rather in the same way as they should be encouraged to behave like 'real' readers. Although the widespread acceptance of this view has had several beneficial consequences, such as the publication of children's work in attractive formats and the search for 'real' audiences (younger children, pupils in other schools, the local community), there are also problems with accepting it.

In the first place, the model of writing proposed by the orthodoxy bears little resemblance to the way many 'real' authors actually write. For example, it favours the busy hum of a collaborative workshop (proposition 4 on p. 129), in which pupils are constantly discussing the different stages of their writing, as the ideal setting. This would be defensible if the writing actually was collaborative and the intended outcome a joint or group production of some kind, such as a class newspaper or a radio play. However, such is rarely the case. Collaborative writing is the exception, not the norm, in school as in adult life, and its results are invariably inferior to works of individual authorship. English literature has produced only one work of genius written by more than one person, the Authorised Version of the Bible, and the beauty of that is very largely due to the genius of one man, William Tyndale. Writing is essentially a solitary activity demanding a high degree of self-motivation and self-discipline. As Sylvia Plath once observed, 'the thing about writing is not to talk about it but to do it'. The ideal setting for writing in school, therefore, is single desks and silence.

I do not wish to imply that there are no occasions when you should encourage your pupils to help one another with their writing or share what they are doing or have done. But these only really occur before writing gets under way, for example, if a pupil is genuinely stuck ('Have a look at Leanne's biography in her file'), or when it is more or less over, during the editorial and proof-reading stages. In any case, far more important than these are the greater number of occasions when you and your pupils should have your heads down over your individual pieces of writing. For these a buzz of talk is a distraction and an irritation. It is precisely what one does not want and an almost certain guarantee that less writing will be done. If there are to be prescribed times for silent reading, why should there not also be times for silent writing? The problem is, as with silent reading, actually instituting something which other pupils – those for whom school is essentially a social arena and social chat its main activity – find alien. Darren, one of my top set fifth year pupils in the Greater Manchester school in 1987, took my attempt at imposing silent writing lessons, to get course work finished, as a personal insult and did his utmost to undermine it, even though he was one of the furthest behind. I knew many pupils in the 1970s and 1980s who said they could not write at school because it was too noisy. As their homes were not exactly havens of peace either, they got precious little done. If you manage to institute silent writing lessons to complement those in silent reading, you will have good grounds for self-congratulation.

If one negative result of the collaborative workshop model, or, perhaps I should say, of the absence of silent writing sessions, is that less writing gets done, another is that pupils become so dependent on the help of their teacher and peers that they never become fully independent writers, even though they may successfully complete their GCSE course work folders. Indeed, one of the weaknesses of GCSE, at least in its 100 per cent course work form (soon, rightly, to be abolished), is precisely this: that a pupil can gain a good grade despite the fact that his or her folder is unofficially well known to be a joint effort in which teacher, relatives and friends may all have played a part. When I returned to the classroom in 1987 after an absence of nine years, the extent to which older pupils had failed to achieve independence, especially in writing, was one of the things which most shocked me. Even pupils in the top fourth and fifth year sets seemed to want me to do everything except hold the pen for them. They were constantly badgering me for plans for their written assignments or for corrections to their rough version so that they could copy out the final version from it. When I pointed out that it was supposed to be their assignment, not mine, they retorted that other teachers helped their classes in these ways, which, I was subsequently even more shocked to discover, was indeed the case, even though the second form of help was and is contrary to GCSE regulations.

The other aspect of the orthodox view which seems to me to have inhibited children's evolution into independent authorship, and considerably reduced their productivity, is its odd insistence on a long gestation period – planning, drafting, redrafting, revising – between the conception and birth of a piece of writing. According to the orthodoxy the final piece of work which goes in a pupil's file should be arrived at only after it has passed through a series of approximations, perhaps differing markedly from one another in form, content and style, which almost certainly means fewer rather than more final pieces. The justification given is that this is how 'real' writers work, and different versions of prose or verse by well known writers are sometimes presented to pupils to prove the point. But, in fact, there is considerable variation in how 'real' writers work, and only some fit the orthodoxy's stereotype. Thomas Hardy, for example, often revised the periodical versions of his novels heavily before they were published in volume form (usually to reinstate potentially inflammatory material) and regularly revised his poems even after they had been published. But he once told Robert Graves that he never made more than four drafts of a poem, for fear of 'its losing its freshness'. Whilst W.B. Yeats said his idea of happiness was to spend the rest of his life rewriting the poems he had already written, the Russian poet Osip Mendelstam got a poem perfect in his head before committing it once and for all to paper.

Some authors do not appear to do much revising at all. If Heminges and Condell, editors of the First Folio edition of Shakespeare's plays (published in 1623), are to be believed, his 'mind and hand' 'went' so successfully 'together' that 'we have scarce received from him a blot in his papers' – leading Ben Jonson to comment 'Would he had blotted a thousand'. In a recent interview the novelist Muriel Spark, whom no one could accuse of not being a perfectionist, gave a vivid account of how she writes her novels – 'in longhand with a fountain pen, straight on to the page' of a '72-page spiral-bound' exercise book, 'rarely correcting anything'. Nor is she untypical. When I asked my students in 1987–8 about their practice for writing assignments, a very mixed picture emerged. Only a small minority were great planners, drafters or revisers. The majority wrote straight off the top of their head. I would never have guessed from the assignments themselves who fell into which category.

An important fact about 'real' writers, which the orthodoxy's stereotype seems to ignore, is that many of them write fast and furiously and are extremely prolific. This is no more than one would expect, given that they must earn a living by the pen and are probably driven by an inner daemon as well. According to the editors of the new Oxford edition Shakespeare wrote five plays – *Much Ado About Nothing*, *Henry V*, *Julius Caesar*, *As You Like It* and

Hamlet – straight after one another and in less than two years. In the case of the great nineteenth century novelists, the Flauberts, agonising over *le mot juste* and spending between five and twenty-five years on a novel, are greatly outnumbered by the non-Flauberts. Flaubert's compatriots Balzac and Zola wrote novel sequences of respectively ninety-one and twenty volumes each in a twenty-year period, while Stendhal dashed off his masterpiece *La Chartreuse de Parme* in an impassioned seven weeks. Among British novelists, Scott wrote eighteen novels in ten years and Trollope forty-seven in less than forty, while Dickens started *Oliver Twist* before he had finished *Pickwick Papers* and *Nicholas Nickleby* before he had finished *Oliver Twist* – leading the *Quarterly Review* to complain, 'Mr Dickens writes too often and too fast.' It is hard to believe the three of them found time for drafting, let alone redrafting, especially as they wrote much else besides fiction and also led full social lives. Even the perfectionist Hardy produced fifteen novels in the first thirty years of his creative life and over 900 poems in the second thirty, to say nothing of short stories, a vast prose and verse drama and two volumes of autobiography.

Drafting is neither a necessary part of writing nor, as the orthodoxy rather implies, a sure way of improving it. There can easily be cases where the original version is superior to the revised version. For example, in my choice of Lawrence's poem 'The Last Lesson' as an epigraph for Chapter 1 I have followed Keith Sagar, the editor of the Penguin selection of his poetry, in preferring the version he wrote as a young man to the better known revised version included in the *Collected Poems* of 1928. And did not Hardy make a mistake in omitting from the final version of *Tess of the Durbervilles* that Tess spoke dialect (see the epigraphs to Chapter 4) 'only when excited by joy, surprise, or grief', as the original periodical version had reported. Was the revised *Dunciad* of 1743 an improvement on the 1730 version or *The Prelude* better for the many changes Wordsworth made to the original draft completed in 1805 between then and 1850? What of literary works left incomplete or unrevised like Coleridge's 'Kubla Khan' or Wilfred Owen's 'Strange Meeting'? In the introduction to his selection of First World War poetry, *Up the Line to Death*, Brian Gardner points out: 'Many of the poems in this book were jotted on to the backs of envelopes and messages, or sent home in letters. Many enjoyed no revision; some were found after death among personal papers and in battledress pockets.' Were they any worse for that? One poet killed in the war, Julian Grenfell, said that all the war poets knew every line they wrote had to be good because it might be their last.

There is also the question of whether drafting and revision are applicable to all genres. Coleridge distinguished between two kinds of writing, 'one for immediate and wide impression, tho' transitory – the other for permanence . . . the best we can do'. Falling into the first category might be his own notebooks and (among the writing of his contemporaries) the letters of Byron and the journals of Dorothy Wordsworth. None of them was written with publication in view, even though their status has subsequently proved to be permanent rather than transitory, and we value them precisely because of the immediacy and vividness resulting from their having been dashed off rather than carefully composed. Personal letters, diaries, journals and notebooks are, almost by definition, not for drafting or revision; we are rightly suspicious of those which have undergone either. Nor do these processes seem wholly appropriate for poetry. The poet James Fenton once said you cannot revise a poem, only tinker with it. 'Tinkering with' is a much more accurate way of describing what Hardy, Yeats and Lawrence did to their poems than 'revising' or 'redrafting', both of which suggest major alterations in form, style or content.

Generally speaking, for school purposes, I would say that drafting and redrafting are more appropriate to 'transactional' than to 'expressive' or 'poetic' writing. Even in 'transactional' genres, you would be well advised not to try and impose drafting and redrafting on your classes. If your aim really is to provide an apprenticeship course in writing, it would make more sense to encourage them to write fast and often. As very few of your pupils will ever become 'real' writers, however, I would be inclined to leave the decision as to whether to draft or not to them. It suits the personality and style of some but not others. With younger pupils I tend not to put pressure on, even when a redraft really does seem desirable. You may have felt, for example, that Katie's piece on Liverpool above would have benefited from being rewritten, to sort out the jumble of environmental improvement, the Beatles and where she would like to live. But she was happy with the way it was, and a jumble like that is fairly typical of young children's writing, part of its charm, and sorts itself out in due course.

In my view, the model of the writing process which held sway before drafting to death became fashionable – that of 'rough' and 'fair' copies – is both superior in itself, because closer to how professional authors actually write, and more appropriate for school. According to this model there will normally be few substantive differences between the two versions. Most changes that are made will be editorial revisions and corrections at the proof-reading stage. The importance of these two skills – editing and proof-reading – has long been acknowledged, and some schools and teachers (including my own in the 1950s) have even gone so far as to teach the symbols and terminology used by professional editors and proof-readers. They also provide perfect opportunities for co-operative work. Most authors are not the best editors or proof-readers of their own efforts, which is no doubt why publishing houses employ others to do it for them.

This is perhaps the moment to mention the word processor, since its most obvious benefit is in the final phases of preparing what one has written before it is printed. I have written this book on a word processor, having always written by hand for a typist before. Its advantages are obvious, well known and need no rehearsal from me here. I am not convinced, however, that it is the educational godsend some would have us believe. Besides the assessment problems posed by the presence of spelling and style checkers, there is also the overriding difficulty, in all the schools I know, of adequate access to keyboards, monitors and printers. More important than these pragmatic considerations, however, is the simple fact that some children do not like using them for their writing. This is not just because they write faster and more efficiently than they type; it is also because they prefer the individuality of their own writing to the anonymity of screen and print-out. I must say I share this feeling and do not find it surprising that some professional authors, like Muriel Spark, should still prefer to write by hand.

RESPONDING TO CHILDREN'S WRITING

In considering how one should respond to children's writing, I do not propose to say anything on marking and assessment. Your department almost certainly already has a policy on these in line with the expectations of GCSE and the National Curriculum. On the positive things that can and should be done with children's writing advice also seems superfluous. No English teacher needs to be told that pupils' work should be published, displayed, shared and generally welcomed and approved whenever possible. Instead I want to concentrate on what are variously known, depending on one's ideological position, as the basic skills, secretarial aspects or surface features of writing – on, in other words, the mistakes and weaknesses in children's work and what can be done to remedy them.

That a significant minority of children have problems with this aspect of writing was confirmed by the APU surveys between 1979 and 1988. The results were mildly encouraging to the extent that the surveys concluded that only a very small proportion of 11 year olds are non-writers (like Jamie in the Knowsley school) in the sense of being unable to construct legible and comprehensible sentences; and that the great majority (something like 95 per cent) have 'a reasonable mastery of the grammatical conventions of written English, and some awareness of the need to provide stylistically appropriate writing'. However, they also revealed that three 11 year olds in a hundred have difficulty composing an intelligible sentence, while the work of one in ten contains numerous errors (on average one orthographic or spelling mistake in each line and one grammatical mistake in every third line).

The first thing you need to do with your pupils' work is to categorise the errors they make and the weaknesses they display. You might like to try this now by looking back to the primary children's writing quoted earlier in the chapter, listing and labelling the mistakes and noting which are common to all and which particular to individuals. The main common weakness to strike you is probably in punctuation. All the children have a problem in identifying sentence breaks and with the use of the apostrophe. In addition, Marie and Jill are weak on commas while Katie is weak on capital letters. In spelling there are predictable difficulties over words like 'embarrassing' and 'submarine' but you may have been surprised to find Jill misspelling everyday words like 'they' and 'goes'. Here you may have come up against a classification impasse too. Is it that Jill does not know how to spell these words or simply carelessness on her part? Poor proof-reading could also explain a number of other errors and failings – the weak sentence structure in the writing by Mark, for example, or Leanne's confusion of 'loose' and 'lose' and 'were' and 'where'. In the case of Leanne, an ambitious young writer with already a style of her own, you may also have noted what might be called semantic or lexical errors – her odd use of 'but' and 'worst' and of words like 'usually', 'excited' and 'commander'.

With my students in 1987–8 I found that a very useful focus for discussing mistakes and weaknesses was a piece written for me by a third year (now year 9) Sikh girl ten years earlier and reproduced in my book *Positive Image*. The context of her writing was a topic on gangs she and her class were working on, and its immediate inspiration seemed to be a mixture of racist activity in the locality and a recent school strike in which most pupils had refused to return for lessons one afternoon because industrial action by teachers had deprived them of school lunch. This is what she wrote:

The Punjabi Gang
The school was on strike because of colour differences. In this school there was only about 350 kids. There was 200 Punjabi people in this school and about 150 black people. And then after a time more white people came, about 100 of them. Nearly every Punjabi boy wore a turban on his head and nearly all the girls wore trousers. Everybody picked on brown people just because they were different religioned and wore different clothes. And everybody said, 'Pakis out', because we speaked in our own language. I really got fed up and I said to every Punjabi people in school that don't come to school on the following day. On the next day there wasn't no Punjabi people in school. There was only white people and black and the teachers got shocked about this. On that day the teachers tried to go round everybody houses who was away, but they couldn't because there was so many. But Mr D knew that I was the leader of the gang so he came round to my house. And he said to me, 'Tell all the gang to come back to school,' but I said, 'NO! NO! NO! and that's that.' But Mr D kept on saying, 'If anybody say anything else you come and tell me and I'll do something about it.' So I said, 'Okay'. So I told all my gang to come back to school. When we was in school nobody said a word about it. This time the Punjabi people start saying to white people, 'White honkeys and bloody white shit.' No one said nothing so I think the Punjabi people won. HA! HA! HA!. Finish.

(Baljit)

After they had read the piece, I asked my students to note down the corrections they would make, how they would classify them and what advice they would give to Baljit for the improvement of her writing. You might like to do the same before reading on. The biggest category of error (virtually unrepresented among the Liverpool primary school children) is grammatical, although my students disagreed sharply over whether 'error' was the right word for every instance. Obviously, in the first place, Baljit makes a number of mistakes which are those of someone whose first language is not English – 'religioned', 'speaked', 'every Punjabi people' – though one or two of these (e.g. 'say' for 'says', 'start' for 'started') may be careless slips. She has also acquired non-standard forms – in negation and subject–verb agreement – which some students wanted to call errors and others not. The only other obvious weakness is the confusion of direct and indirect speech in 'that don't come' which is sometimes to be found in the writing of younger native speakers too. All the students liked the piece and said approval would be the gist of what they would communicate to Baljit. One said she would encourage her to cut down on the use of 'and' but, although several felt the piece demanded some kind of discussion of racism with either Baljit or the class as a whole, none, surprisingly perhaps, objected to her use of the phrase 'bloody white shit'.

From these discussions I drew up the following short classification of mistakes and weaknesses which I hoped the students would find useful on teaching practice. I called it, after William Empson, 'Seven types of incorrectness':

1 Careless slips, confusions and omissions (i.e. the pupil's proof-reading, not his or her knowledge, is at fault).
2 Spelling mistakes.
3 Punctuation mistakes.
4 Grammatical incorrectness:
   (a) Mistakes due to the fact that the pupil is not a native speaker.
5 (b) Ill-formed sentences (i.e. they are truncated, endless or otherwise do not cohere).
6 Grammatical inappropriateness (i.e. use of non-standard forms).
7 Semantic or lexical incorrectness (e.g. Leanne's 'excited' for 'exciting' and 'commander' for 'ringmaster' on pp. 131–2).

To this classification several important qualifications need to be made – first, as we shall see later, punctuation is not wholly a matter of right and wrong; second, non-standard forms are not linguistically wrong but sometimes in writing are nevertheless not quite right; third, corrections can legitimately be made on social rather than linguistic grounds to other usages too (e.g. 'bloody white shit'); and, fourth, in longer pieces by older pupils new categories may be required to cover stylistic weaknesses (e.g. overuse of 'and') and structural errors (e.g. *non sequiturs*).

As for remedies, it has, for as long as I can remember, been the conventional wisdom among English teachers that, in the words of the Cox report, 'a measure of tolerance of errors . . . is essential'. Does the policy of being economical with corrections make sense? I think it does, at least with younger children and those who make a great many mistakes, if only to avoid discouraging them and saddling their teachers with an unbearable burden in marking. As they move up through the secondary years, however, increased stringency needs to be applied, and once they embark on the GCSE course they should know that all mistakes will be picked up. This policy must obviously be explained to pupils and parents, especially if it involves, as it should, work in the 'best' file being untouched by the teacher's pen or pencil apart perhaps from some positive comment at the end. Both groups are inclined to assume that what is not corrected must be all right.

My active policy for correction has been to work on a pupil's or class's 'favourite' mistakes – their regular errors and failings. I encourage individual pupils to be responsible for their own by keeping a list of them – divided into the categories of a simplified version of the classification above – in their 'rough' books or jotters, while I keep a running record of those which are common to a number of pupils. Then every few weeks or so, depending on the class, I have a remedial session. With a good class this can take the form of pairs of pupils devising tests for one another based on their personal lists of 'favourite' mistakes. More often it is a whole-class affair. This begins with a dictation (an old-fashioned exercise whose usefulness has been underrated) in the shape of a humorous story written by me to include as many of the spelling mistakes collected in the previous weeks as possible. For the second part of the session I distribute a duplicated sheet which includes the correct version of the dictation (so that each pupil can mark his or her own) followed by verbatim (and, of course, anonymous) extracts from the work of different individuals in which something is amiss. The class's task is to identify the errors (they can be of any type in the classification except for spelling), correct them and, if necessary, as in the case of poor sentence structure, rewrite the extract. I do not make any great claims for this method in terms of its remedial effectiveness, but I have never known a class not enjoy it and it does impress upon them that you are concerned for the accuracy of their work.

Spelling, because of its central position in public concern, merits particular attention, although it is important not to get it out of perspective. Misspellings rarely confuse the reader. The centuries prior to the standardisation of spelling in the eighteenth were not conspicuous for breakdowns in communication. Neither Chaucer nor Shakespeare was a consistent speller, yet the fact is of no consequence in our efforts to appreciate their work. However, it would be foolhardy to give pupils the impression that they can afford to be equally cavalier in their writing. I do not think it really matters which remedial policy you favour – whether it is mine (dictation based on errors made, coupled with individual collections of 'favourite' mistakes), rules, published lists, games (such as Hangman or Scrabble), the Newbolt report's recommendation of wide reading rather than specific lessons, or any combination of these. The vital factor is that pupils see you care about spelling and expect them to care too.

It is also necessary that you should know about spelling and share the knowledge with your pupils. For example, a succession of would-be reformers have based their case on the allegation that English spelling is arbitrary and illogical. But it is not as chaotic as they sometimes pretend. The most famous of them, George Bernard Shaw, once said that the word 'fish' could be spelled 'ghoti' because of the way the relevant letters were sounded in 'rough', 'women' and 'ration'. He was, as usual, only half right, since 'gh' never makes an 'f' sound at the beginning of a word nor 'ti' an 'sh' sound at the end. There is a pattern or grammar to English spelling (70 per cent of words are regular, remember) and pupils can benefit from learning what the regularities and irregularities are and how, historically, it all came about. There are several useful rules to memorise (such as the well known but not always fully given 'i before e except after c when the sound is ee'), to which pupils can add their own mnemonics for their own 'favourite' mistakes. It also helps to be able to dismantle a word into its constituent parts – for instance, into prefix, stem and suffix – and to comment on the relationships between words (e.g. between 'full' and 'fill' and 'fulfil'). Spelling checkers on word processsors are, on the other hand, of very limited value. They do not enhance understanding, require (like dictionaries) initial proficiency, fail to pick up homophone confusions (e.g. 'wear' for 'where'), are inapplicable to proper nouns and sometimes do not admit alternatives (e.g. 'connection' and 'connexion') or differences in British and American usage.

In the case of punctuation you need to explain to pupils the difference between where it is necessary (e.g. a question mark) and where it is optional (e.g. the semi-colon, which George Orwell claimed to have avoided altogether in *Coming Up For Air*), and also between the different functions it can serve – to underline sentence structure, indicate intonation and ease the reader's passage through the text. Breaks within and between sentences often cause younger writers problems, as we saw in the primary school children's work quoted earlier in the chapter. Sentence analysis, such as one might expect to find, but rarely does, in language awareness courses, can help here, as can the old primary school rule: 'comma, a pause to the count of 1, semi-colon to the count of 2, colon to the count of 3 and full-stop to the count of 4'. The other big problem area is punctuation of direct speech in stories, since it requires pupils to bear in mind half a dozen different regulations at once. Like other English teachers I try to use cartoon strips to sort this one out (as in the Yobs example at the Knowsley school in Chapter 1). The pupils' task is to convert the cartoon into a story and the speech in balloons into direct speech. With older pupils, their attention should be drawn to two often neglected forms of punctuation, dashes and brackets, which can both be very useful in discursive essays.

Finally, I need to complement what I had to say about non-standard forms of speech in Chapter 4 with something on their place in writing. The Kingman and Cox reports and the statutory regulations all take the view that they are appropriate only when realism dictates, that is to say, in dialogue in stories and plays. The Newbolt report, surprising as it may seem, was more generous, quoting approvingly the remarks of a committee on adult education: 'Students should be encouraged to write . . . in their local language and with the material offered by the scenes and life which are familiar to them. . . . The provincial culture of England, Wales and Scotland, whether it be rural or industrial, is as nourishing a food for poetry as the Irish peasant life portrayed by Synge.' The reference to poetry and Synge is striking; neither of the two recent reports makes any reference to the role non-standard English has played in our literature. It is almost as though the members of the Kingman and Cox committees, notwithstanding the presence of literary figures in their ranks, were unaware of the multi-dialectal nature of literature in Middle English, literature in Scots, English dialect poets like John Clare and William Barnes, the dialect poems of Tennyson, Hardy, Kipling and D.H. Lawrence, the serious interest in dialect taken by novelists like Scott, Emily Brontë, Mrs Gaskell and George Eliot and had never read *Huckleberry Finn*. Turn to any page of the latter and you will find examples of precisely the non-standard forms so common among our working class pupils today – multiple negation, non-standard subject–verb agreement and non-standard past tense and participle forms.

Huckleberry Finn is, of course, the first person narrative of an ill-educated and homeless boy. The use of non-standard forms is, therefore, justifiable on grounds of realism. Its predecessor *Tom Sawyer*, being a third person narrative, confines the non-standard forms to the dialogue. Similarly, in Lawrence's case, he uses dialect in the dialogue of his Nottinghamshire-based novels, stories and plays, and in a few of the early poems, but otherwise always writes in standard English. This suggests to me that the advice we give to our pupils ought to be that, although non-standard forms are normally judged 'inappropriate' – by parents, employers, society at large – in 'transactional' writing, there can be occasions when they are perfectly 'appropriate' in both 'expressive' and 'poetic' writing and not just in fictional dialogue.

Such advice is necessary with some children but not with others. Several of the top juniors quoted in Chapter 4, for example, changed to standard forms automatically when translating their story into its written version and Joanne, for one, made explicit reference to having done so. Others, however, removed them from the rough versions of their truancy essays only when the teacher pointed them out. This is about the right age – third or fourth year juniors (years 5 and 6) – to intervene, so that by the time they start secondary school children know that non-standard forms are acceptable in some types of writing but not in others. In my experience, provided the advice, and the justification given for it, are clear, it will be followed by virtually all non-standard speakers, without them feeling they are being 'got at' or discriminated against. In a very real sense, of course, they are being discriminated against. From a linguistic point of view there is no reason why pupils should not write whatever they like in non-standard English. So it is important you make it plain that it is history and convention they are up against, not the views of English teachers. Conceivably social attitudes might change. In the spring term of 1991 the *Education Guardian* invited young readers to submit reviews in their local dialect of a television programme; over 300, from all over the British Isles, responded.

FURTHER READING

An excellent book on writing from the 1970s, which I found very useful as a teacher, is William Harpin's *The Second 'R'*. Much recommended from the 1980s, and one of the best books on English teaching written in that decade, is *Writing* by the American educationalist Donald Graves, although it is more directly relevant to primary than to secondary schools and inclined, like many books on the subject, to treat young children's writing with undue piety. As for the mechanics of writing, Don Smedley's *Teaching the Basic Skills* is full of common sense and helpful advice.

Chapter 7

Teaching literature

> Most tedious was the close study of English Literature. . . . Only
> in odd streaks did she get a poignant sense of acquisition and
> enrichment and enlarging from her studies . . .
>
> (D.H. Lawrence, *The Rainbow*, 1915)

> Literature, not being a knowledge subject, cannot and should
> not be *taught*.
>
> (The Newbolt report, 1921)

EXPLANATORY AND EXPERIENTIAL APPROACHES

In 1921 George Sampson and the Newbolt report registered
strong opposition to the idea that English literature should be
taught as though it were a branch of knowledge and warned of the
danger of its being subsumed within history or sociology. Eleven
years earlier, in 1910, the Board of Education circular on teaching
English in secondary schools took a very similar line when it
observed that the real teachers of literature were the great writers
themselves and warned teachers against coming between them
and young readers. All three were reacting against an academic
factually based tradition which was by then well entrenched in the
classroom, reinforced by the public examination system, and has
been ousted from the 11–16 curriculum only relatively recently.

The origins of this academic approach lay, paradoxically, in the
educational work of two of Rousseau's English-speaking disciples,
the Irish novelist and teacher Maria Edgeworth and her father. In
a series of books published between 1798 and 1817 they argued
that literature had to be explained to children if they were to
appreciate it properly. By the middle of the nineteenth century,

when the first examinations were introduced, pupils were being subjected to a barrage of exercises on meaning, etymology, allusions, imagery, logic and grammar, intended to increase their understanding of the literature they read, as well as being required to undertake longer writing tasks like summary, paraphrase and character description.

The Newbolt report rejected this approach in favour of one which emphasised children's active experience of the text. What in practice it meant by this – reading aloud, learning by heart and dramatic performance – had always complemented the explanatory approach in many schools. The report, however, reached beyond customary practice in a passage, actually in its section on adult education, which seventy years later continues to represent many English teachers' conception of enlightened literature teaching:

> The vital thing is to make it obvious from the outset that literature is alive . . . the aim should not be knowledge or even 'appreciation', but creation. The students are not to be passive recipients, but active participators; they must be fired to do things, to write poems, and perhaps plays or at the very least to act the plays of others.

Yet, for most of the past seventy years, it has been the academic approach which has dominated the literature curriculum, at least in the upper reaches of secondary schools, quite simply because of the subservience of GCE O Level and A Level boards to the requirements of university English departments. Generations of English teachers have protested that this approach, based on the textual analysis and critical discussion of often quite complex set texts, was inappropriate for all but an academic elite of children. Even in their case, it was argued, the intellectualism of the approach (murdering to dissect, in Wordsworth's famous phrase) converted the study of literature into a glorified comprehension test, while the need to prepare for a sit-down examination encouraged the parroting of ill-digested facts and factitious views.

At the first school I taught at the headteacher, a lover of literature but a scientist by training, concluded that GCE O Level English Literature was, therefore, more likely to impede than enhance literary appreciation and removed it from the curriculum. You have no doubt also heard many people say that they could not contemplate reading Shakespeare, Dickens, Jane

Austen or whomever for pleasure because of the soul-destroying way they were made to study them at school. However, the first effective institutional challenge to the academic approach was not mounted until the introduction of CSE in the mid-1960s; it was another twenty years before it was swept away in the GCSE revolution, though by then several GCE boards were responding to teacher demands at O Level, as they now are at A Level, by admitting CSE-inspired innovations like oral assessment, course work and open-book examinations.

The thinking behind the more recent impulse towards an active and experiential approach remains a combination of dissatisfaction with the explanatory approach, especially for mixed ability classes in comprehensive schools, and belief in one of the oldest tenets of child-centred progressivism – the heuristic theory that children learn best by doing. More recent exponents of the application of the theory to literature teaching have added to the range of activities familiar to liberal-minded English teachers at the time of the Newbolt report (reading aloud, recitation, creative writing, dramatic performance) a whole range of new ones, many derived from the work of the Schools Council Effective Use of Reading project in the late 1970s (described in Chapter 5).

The theory was given a novel twist in the 1960s when the notion of a child's 'felt response' to literature became current. Nowadays, perhaps because that particular phrase seems to imply commitment to the 'affective' fallacy of judging literature exclusively by its emotional effects, you are more likely to read or hear of 'informed personal response' or what in GCSE documents is known as 'real engagements with texts'. The general idea is to foster more authentic reactions to literature among pupils by encouraging them to trust their native instincts and speech, rather than adopting the views and diction of their teachers and of literary critics, and to set their own world and experience of life against those of the text. More recently there has been some attempt to dignify the theory and practice of experiential approaches with references to German 'reception' and 'reader response' theory – a good example of *post hoc* rationalisation in the application of critical theory, to which I referred in Chapter 2.

For my part I have always thought that the defects of the academic approach, as represented by the traditional versions of GCE O and A Level, were exaggerated by its critics and, in most cases, more a reflection of poor teaching than of anything inherent in the approach. My own teacher at these levels at school was the embodiment of rigid academicism. His aim was to introduce us to the canon from Chaucer to T.S. Eliot and to teach literary scholarship and appreciation. In the case of Shakespeare, for example, whose plays were central to his curriculum, he took us through the text line by line, explaining references and difficulties and drawing our attention to linguistic and rhythmic felicities. He also told us about Shakespeare's life and times, his use of sources, the iambic pentameter and the production, printing and editing of his plays. We were expected to learn speeches by heart, do textual analyses of short extracts out of context and write discursive essays making reference to the views of major critics from Dr Johnson to Dover Wilson. His method was highly didactic, even autocratic, and would nowadays be called transmissionist in the sense that our role as learners was largely limited to receiving, and later regurgitating, what he told us. Yet he was an inspirational teacher. The weaknesses in his pedagogy did not detract from his capacity to communicate his knowledge of, and passion for, great literature.

Equally I believe the virtues of the modern version of the experiential approach, and of GCSE courses based on them, to be fewer than its exponents maintain and that some of the popular activities associated with it (board games, flow charts, designing book covers, and so forth), several of which are represented in this book, run the risk of deflecting children from the text rather than enhancing it. 'Trivial pursuits' they have been called by one critic, Roger Knight, and not unfairly. What, in my view, is now required is some kind of amalgamation of the best in both traditions – a reconciliation perhaps between knowledge and creativity, explanation and experience, understanding and action – so that the teacher of English is able to initiate as many pupils as possible into something of their literary heritage.

The easiest way of allowing you to judge for yourself whether this is either practicable or desirable is to set before you examples of how I have recently taught a poem, a short story and two novels (plays are dealt with in the next chapter). These are intended as exemplars – that is to say, as indications of how any poem, short story or novel might be taught. As such they are not perfect, nor could any single example be. For the poem I have chosen a short lyric, whereas a longer narrative poem would require different treatment; the short story I have selected because it is so dramatisable, which is not the case with all short stories; and the two novels are relatively short twentieth century classics which can be taught faster and more easily than their Victorian predecessors. But, on the whole, I think they serve their purpose. Because I share Jerome Bruner's belief that 'any subject can be taught effectively in some intellectually honest form to any child at any stage of development', I attach relatively little importance to differences in age and ability between children and classes. I have taught the poem and the short story, though not the novels, to secondary school pupils of all ages and abilities, and also to adults.

THE POEM: 'JANUARY' BY R.S. THOMAS

Poetry is both the most revered element in literature teaching and the one many English teachers feel most anxious about. The reasons for teachers' anxiety are, I think, threefold. In the first place, whereas the majority of English teachers habitually read novels and go to the theatre, poetry reading is as much a minority pursuit among them as in the population at large. It is hard to feel self-confident about teaching children to appreciate poetry when you do not normally read it for pleasure or edification yourself. Second, there is the problem of what to discuss. In novels and plays plot, character and theme usually yield fertile matter for debate, whilst very few poems have a plot or characters and, although most do have a meaning of a kind, simply eliciting that does not somehow seem quite enough. As for evaluation, educated adults have difficulty explaining at any length why they do or do not like a particular poem; children are unlikely to fare any better. Finally, there is the vexed issue of the formal properties of verse and the terminology required to examine them. Most of the words needed for talking about fiction and drama, such as plot and character, are familiar from everyday usage. This is not the case with poetry, although you can usually expect classes to understand what you mean by line, verse (in the sense of stanza) and rhyme. Children have to be taught about prosody and some teachers are unsure how to do this and even of their own state of knowledge.

A useful principle to bear in mind is that the experience of reading and listening to poems should precede, and in the case of young children take precedence over, explaining, analysing and evaluating them. If you have no idea where to begin with a class,

I suggest you start by using odd moments (the end of lessons is ideal) to read, or play records or tapes of, some of your favourite poems. Then you can ask the pupils to join in by browsing in anthologies to find poems they like. These they can read to one another, copy out, illustrate, learn by heart or use to make an anthology, taped perhaps, of their own. Once you have established poetry reading in this way as an ordinary and enjoyable classroom activity, you should feel confident enough to launch into more systematic and overt teaching.

You could not do better than try the poem I have chosen, 'January' by R.S. Thomas. I first read it during my probationary year in A. Alvarez's influential anthology *The New Poetry*, published by Penguin in 1962, since when it has been one of my favourite poems and Thomas one of my favourite poets. I have used it with every conceivable kind of class and never known it fail to make an impact. Yet I have not met another teacher who has used it or come across it in a school poetry anthology. So here it is:

> The fox drags its wounded belly
> Over the snow, the crimson seeds
> Of blood burst with a mild explosion,
> Soft as excrement, bold as roses.
>
> Over the snow that feels no pity,
> Whose white hands can give no healing,
> The fox drags its wounded belly.

What might one do with such a poem? A popular initial ploy these days is to dismantle it, give the pupils the bits and ask them to reassemble it. When I last used 'January' with a class, the upper band second year (now year 8) in the Knowsley school, appropriately in the month of its name 1989, I began by scattering the words, all in lower case, over the blackboard, then asked them, without revealing that the words made up a poem, to see if, working in pairs, they could extract a line or possibly two lines of verse out of them. Several pairs quickly produced the actual opening line and a half. Next, having admitted the words were those of a poem, I joined the pairs of pupils into groups of four, gave each group the seven lines of the poem on separate pieces of paper and asked them to arrange them in order, bearing in mind that there were two verses of four and three lines respectively. This proved quite difficult. Although most groups soon agreed that the repeated line came best first and last, there was lively disagreement over the order of the remainder; the fifth line, for example, could, both syntactically and semantically, come second.

The advantage of starting like this is that it is fun, gets the class involved straight away and provides a nice balance between creativity and rigour. It takes them immediately into the meaning of the poem and makes them think hard about the part grammar and punctuation play in conveying it. Other popular ways in are omission exercises based on cloze procedure. In these the class are given the poem with every seventh (or whatever) word, or certain categories of word, left out, depending on the poem and the aim behind the exercise. If it is a rhyming poem, you might leave some of the rhyming words out and ask the pupils to supply them. If it is written in strict metre, you might want to see whether they can find words which both make sense and fit in metrically. If it is a poem rich in imagery, like 'January', you might omit the metaphors and similes. You could, of course, omit much more. I could, for example, have given them only the last word in each line, with or without the title, and asked them to produce a poem around them, using Thomas's line lengths or their own. The title was, on this occasion, all that I omitted and, after the poem had been successfully reassembled by all groups, I invited suggestions. 'The Wounded Fox' was voted the best and generally reckoned to be superior to the poet's.

Once a poem has been reassembled (pupils can Sellotape their lines together or a rolldown board can be used to reveal it), and any comprehension difficulties have been sorted out ('excrement' usually needs explaining – I say 's – h – i – t', which gets a laugh), it is important to celebrate the reunification with a reading aloud. This should emphasise, above all, the way the poem's movement turns on the counterpoint between the syntax and the metre. You may, therefore, want to do the reading yourself, but you can involve the whole class, too, by using one of Cicely Berry's group speaking exercises, devised for Shakespeare drama workshops and discussed in the next chapter. Divide the poem into parts according to punctuation breaks and the class into that number of groups (i.e. seven in the case of 'January'), and give each group a phrase or clause. So group one has 'The fox . . . snow', group two has 'the crimson . . . explosion' and so on. The result is a choral reading which you can vary for pace, tone and volume (whispering is a useful technique). Finally, ask each group to prepare a choral reading of the whole poem. By the time they are ready, you should find that they know it by heart, so you can ask a group to volunteer to come out to the front and perform without looking at the text. First and second years (years 7 and 8) will be happy to do this, older classes less so.

A good deal of exploration will inevitably have taken place by now of the poem's meaning, language and rhythm, but you may want to sharpen or deepen it by asking the groups to concentrate on one or more of these aspects and jot down the gist of their deliberations for a whole-class discussion. GCSE classes might consider all three, but with younger ones I would recommend you limit them to the most striking feature of 'January', its use of language. It is an ideal poem for introducing children to the concepts of metaphor and simile, having such marvellous examples of both, as indeed it also has of personification, though you need to be wary of burdening them with too many technical terms at once, as your science colleagues will confirm to you.

My explanation of metaphor and simile to first years runs something like this: 'In both cases X is compared to Y because they have Z in common; the difference is that the comparison is made obvious in the case of a simile through the use of "as" or "like", whereas in a metaphor it is merely implied.' Similes cause few problems and pupils will readily furnish highly imaginative examples of their own for describing foxes, blood and snow (assuming you want to stay close to the poem). Metaphors, however, can prove, to use a common one, a real stumbling block for some classes and pupils. Accumulating as many examples as possible from everyday life, 'dead' metaphors as they are sometimes called, is a useful preparatory activity, because it allows you to underline that what a poet is searching for is an image which is both 'alive' and apt. For this Thomas's 'crimson seeds of blood' is the perfect illustration.

With older classes you may want to take the matter further by analysing particular images in detail. Even with my second years I was keen to bring out what was so striking about Thomas's choice of metaphor, namely what you might want to call in teaching a sixth form group its oxymoronic quality – seeds are associated with new life whereas the picture portrayed is of a wounded, perhaps dying, fox. There are examples of something similar in the equally striking similes 'Soft as excrement, bold as roses', and 'mild explosion' is perhaps a third. The whole poem, in fact, could be said to pivot on the antithesis between images of life and images of death. With older classes you will probably also want to discuss the poem's meaning at greater length. For this I.A. Richards's famous acronym 'sift' – sense, intention, feeling, tone – which I was taught to use at school, remains an invaluable framework. In the case of 'January' it brings out the key issue of whether Thomas is a neutral observer of nature 'red in tooth and claw' or actively trying to engage our sympathies for the fox.

As for prosody, this is not the poem to use to teach it to those who know nothing. You need poems written in strict metre, and preferably iambic pentameters, for that. But for those who know something – the difference between metre and free verse, how to count syllables and stresses – they could be asked, as the second years were by me, to work out, in pairs, what the pattern in 'January' is (eight or nine syllables, four stresses). The choral speaking exercise should also have brought out how important enjambement and caesura are to the rhythm, although you may not want to use these terms with most classes. Deciding how much technical information and terminology on prosody to teach really is a tricky issue, on which you will need to feel your own way cautiously. Trying to impart too much too fast is obviously a mistake, but then so is imparting nothing at all. If you shirk your responsibility completely with younger classes, you will end up with the situation I faced in the Greater Manchester school, when I was asked to revise *Comus* and *Samson Agonistes* with the Upper Sixth. I had anticipated the lack of any classical or biblical background, but not that they would not know what a metaphor was or anything at all about Milton's prosody.

After so much analysis it is good to finish off with a choice of creative activities. I offered the second years three, of which they could do one or more. The first is based on the fact that the poem resembles a picture. I suggested they might like to copy it out neatly and illustrate it in the way that William Blake did with his poems ('The Tiger' would make an illuminating comparison, in fact). 'January' also resembles a story without a beginning or an end – we do not know how the fox got wounded nor whether it survived – so the second possibility was to write the story behind the poem. Finally, they could write a poem of their own as a response; for those who needed a framework I recommended they make it an acrostic poem on January or some related word. This suggestion proved popular. Here are some of the class's efforts:

Snow falls upon the ground,
Not a murmur or a sound.
Out of the window we take a look –
White as the pages in the book.

(Mark)

Silky snow passes over the village,
No creatures dare to come out.
Over the town the snow goes,
Winter is over and spring begins.

(Nick)

Blood is so red
Like the petals on a poppy.
One more time,
One more time,
Dying people die no more.

(Suzanne)

White snow falls through the branches
Of the bare oak tree in the winter months.
Umbrellas decorate the skyline,
Numerous colours each contains.
Daytime is not much lighter than night,
Evening falls out early: four o'clock,
Daytime now to cease.

(Sarah)

The bare trees and the white hills,
January, the cold icy month,
The time when everyone is indoors.
But if you do venture outside,
You would see something . . .
The robin, the fox and the blackbird too.
So now you see January can be very friendly.

(David)

I have not exhausted the possibilities of what might be done with
a poem like 'January'. If the class have enjoyed it, an obvious
follow-up would be to read other poems by R.S. Thomas – not just
the nature poems but those dealing with religious issues. He is one
of our finest religious poets and pupils are often surprised to
discover that the author of 'January' is a clergyman. It is vital, in
my view, for them to have this sense of a real person and a real

context behind a poem. In Thomas's case you might
use of the fact that he attracted media attention f
support the shadowy Welsh nationalist group Meibion ,
in their campaign of fire-bombing English-owned holiday
cottages in Wales.

Another possibility for follow-up I have already hinted at –
comparison with other nature poems and nature poets or, more
narrowly, with other poems about foxes, for example, Ted
Hughes's 'The Thought-Fox'. From this a class might assemble,
and perhaps perform, an illustrated anthology of their favourite
animal poems. Children are much exercised about animal rights
at present and if, like my second years, they are adamant that
Thomas's fox must have been wounded by humans, they may well
want to discuss, or even dramatise, some aspect of the relationship
between animals and humans, particularly the question of blood
sports. How much you decide to do will depend on how popular
the poem proves and what you want to get out of reading it. I have
spent as little as five minutes (the end of a lesson) and as much as
a week's lessons on 'January'.

THE SHORT STORY: 'I SPY' BY GRAHAM GREENE

I enjoy teaching short stories because they can usually be
managed within a lesson and a homework – especially those short
stories, and they are in the majority, which are dramatisable.
Graham Greene is not, I think, in the first rank of English short
story writers, but he has written several outstanding examples of
the genre which appeal to pupils in school – 'The Destructors',
'The Case for the Defence', 'The Basement Room', 'I Spy', 'Proof
Positive', 'The End of the Party' – and are all to be found in
Twenty-one Stories, published by Penguin. My favourite is 'I Spy',
which packs so much into its three pages whilst opening up a
number of interesting avenues for the teacher and class to
explore. Like 'January' it goes down well with all ages from first
year secondary to adults. If you do not know it, you will need to
read it before proceeding. Once you have done so, you might also
like to note down, now that you are familiar with some of the
things that can be done with literature, how you would tackle it in
the classroom, before you look at my ideas.

One starting-point is anticipation activities. Draw the class's
attention to the story's title and ask them what they think it might

be about. They should all recognise the reference to the children's game of the same name and some will also guess that it is about the more serious business of spying. An exercise like this is particularly important with younger classes, who can find the story difficult and easily miss the point. Older classes familiar with Greene's work could be asked to base their predictions on what they have already read by him. Religion, sex, sin, crime and guilt are some of the themes they are likely to mention. The next stage is comprehension, using one or more of the variations on this traditional activity described in Chapter 5. First of all, during a silent reading of the story, ask the class to list all the words whose meaning they are unsure of and see if a combination of the dictionary and the context helps them deduce what it might be. You should be prepared for quite long lists, including not only words like 'wraith' but words like 'boisterous' and 'spasmodically', of which even GCSE classes can claim total ignorance. Most classes will also need some historical background on the First World War – Zeppelins, Huns and what happened to those convicted of spying.

You could leave some of this to emerge from the popular device of asking the pupils to frame the questions. After a second reading of the story, preferably aloud by yourself, explain to them that you are interested in three types of question (derived from the classifications of the Bullock report and Schools Council Effective Use of Reading project referred to in Chapter 5): first, factual or 'black and white' questions to which answers are to be found on the printed page, e.g. 'Why did Charlie want to smoke a cigarette?'; second, 'reading between the lines' questions, e.g. 'Who were the men in bowler hats and mackintoshes?'; and, third, open-ended questions to which there are no right answers, e.g. 'Will Charlie tell his mother what happened next day at breakfast?'. The pupils' task is then, in pairs, to devise two questions of each type to pose to the rest of the class. When they have done this, the first pair, chosen by you, choose another pair to put a question to, having first said which category it belongs to. If they answer satisfactorily, they become the questioners (if not, the question goes on offer to the class), and so on until each pair have both asked and answered a question. To ensure that this does indeed happen, and that weak pairs are not picked on, you will need to insist that, once asked, a pair cannot be asked again. This approach usually succeeds in bringing out the essence of the story, for even young children are as fascinated by Charlie's relationship with his father – How did he resemble him? Did he love him or not? – as they are by the business of spying.

My main pedagogic interest in this story is in how to dramatise it. A PGCE student of mine in 1987–8 suggested an alternative way into it, using drama, which I have subsequently refined. This again involves the pupils working in pairs of A and B (if there is an odd number in the class you will have to join in yourself), but this time on three separate bits of dialogue extracted, and slightly adapted, from the story before they have actually read it:

A: Have a cigarette.
B: No thanks, not while I'm on duty.

A: I'll get my coat.
B: I'll come with you if you don't mind.

A: Don't you want to speak to your wife?
B: Not me. She'll have her chance later.

There are a number of Cicely Berry's activities one can apply to these bits of dialogue so that pupils both memorise them and enter to some degree into the characters and the situation, though they may not be the same as those of the story. If you are not able to use the drama room or a similar open space, push desks and chairs to the walls of the classroom and ask everyone to face their partners. They then have to repeat their lines after you and in unison, until they know them, whereupon they exchange roles and learn their partners' lines in the same way. Once they are all thoroughly familiar with the whole dialogue, try unusual ways of saying it – whispering, singing, vowel sounds only, mouthing silently their partners' lines as they voice them – and, afterwards, add some action – inconsequential action to begin with (sitting back-to-back on the floor, standing on one leg, etc.), then realistic action. For this ask the pairs to find a simple movement (a gesture will do) to complement each bit of dialogue and freeze each one in a tableau (if you are unfamiliar with terms used in drama teaching, you will find them explained in the next chapter.) Finally, they can practise running the dialogue through, pausing briefly at each tableau, to clarify, but not make explicit, what they think the situation and relationship between A and B are.

You can now move to the story itself. After a dramatic reading, with yourself as narrator and pupils reading the dialogue, divide the class into groups of six so that everyone has a part (if there are five in a group, one of the bowler-hatted men can double as the policeman; if seven, one person can direct). The group's first task is to establish a set – front door of shop, counter, relationship of shop to bedroom, etc. – either mentally or using whatever props are to hand. Then ask them to prepare three tableaux – one for the moment when the policeman tries the door, one for the moment when Charlie's father goes to fetch his coat and one for the moment just after he and the men have left and Charlie is on his way to bed – and a mime of the whole story, pausing to freeze each tableau. When they are performing their finished version, either to another group or to the rest of the class, walk around and at the point of a tableau touch a character on the shoulder as a sign that he or she must say out loud, in role of course, what he or she is thinking (Charlie's mother can say what she is dreaming).

This is, more or less, the story as written. Many teachers prefer to work on the story as it might have been. One much-used technique is to change it at a critical juncture. The obvious change to make to 'I Spy' is to bring Mrs Stowe into the action. Go back to the second tableau and tell the class that Mrs Stowe is woken up by the voices below and goes downstairs to investigate. Ask them to devise a new third tableau to take this change into account and an improvisation to link it to the second. You can follow this up by inviting them to suggest how else the story as written might be developed. Some may want to go back to the moment of Mr Stowe's arrest before the story opens. More likely, however, are suggestions to do with developments after the story ends – next day at breakfast, next day at school, visiting Mr Stowe in prison, his trial and execution. From these you could try and build up a sequence of tableaux, mimes or improvisations around the room showing the story from the moment of Mr Stowe's arrest to the moment of his execution. It gives a class a tremendous sense of satisfaction to see Greene's original story framed by theirs.

This by no means exhausts the range of possibilities. There are, for example, the moral issues raised by the story which you or the class may want to discuss – stealing, peer group pressure and smoking, spying and the punishment of spies. Another interesting aspect of the story, drawn to my attention by a German teacher of English who bases his approach on it, is its use of proverbs – 'as well be hanged for a sheep as a lamb,' 'a stitch in time saves nine', 'never put off till tomorrow what you can do today', 'while there's life there's hope'. Finally, there are writing activities arising out of the reading, the drama or the discussion. One rather old-fashioned exercise I like to set younger classes is to summarise 'I Spy' in exactly fifty words, neither more nor less. Surprising as it may seem to those with bitter memories of precis work for GCE O Level, children love doing this, if only because it means writing something short rather than long. Here are two pieces of imaginative writing, carrying on from where Greene leaves off, from the Knowsley school, the first written by a first year (year 7) boy of average ability, the second by a second year (year 8) girl with some flair and sense of style:

> The next day Charlie woke up about 8 o'clock. He went down and had his breakfast, his mum said 'Have you been down before me'
>   'No,' Charlie replied.
>   Charlie's mum went to open the shop when she saw muddy footsteps going across the floor. He went to his mum and she said 'Wev had robbers in the shop
>   'No, father went to Norwich but he came back with two Stranges Charlie replied. His mother said 'Do you know were he is?
>   'Yes he is in the old bill with those two stranges' Charlie replied
>   His mother said 'Charlie you stay off school and help me to find your father.'
>   Charlie said 'Are thanks mum'
>   They got in the car and went to the police station, they found that he was in a differant station. They found the right one. As they walked in they hurd BANG! His mum ran to the field and their lying dead was Mr Stowe.
>
> (Steven)

Charlie woke up the next morning feeling uncomfortable. He did not know who the two men were, or were they had taken his father, but he felt scared and wondered whether to tell his mother. He decided not to yet. His father should be back today and if he wasn't then it would be no surprise, as his father was hardly ever where he said he would be. Charlie thought of his father. His expression last night had been strange, as if he didn't care about anything any more. His last glance around the shop had been as if he were saying goodbye for the last time. Charlie was scared. He knew that he had to tell his mother, but if he told her, he would have to tell about him stealing cigarettes. He slowly walked downstairs, dragging his feet. He went into the kitchen where his mother was making breakfast. 'Mum,' he said. 'Yes,' she replied. Charlie poured out the whole story. His mother was so shocked about the news of his father, that she didn't think about Charlie stealing the cigarettes. Charlie felt more unhappy and scared than ever before when his mother told him that his father was a spy and if he was found guilty then he would be executed. Charlie wanted more than anything else for his father to come home so that he could tell him he loved him ... It was a year later. Charlie was thirteen. It had been the worst year he had ever had. The boys at school were shocked about his father and avoided him. For weeks after the execution he cried himself to sleep. However the pain was fading and though he would always feel sad about his father, it didn't hurt so much now.

(Amanda)

With older students familiar with Greene's work you will want to discuss how far 'I Spy' is representative of his distinctive themes, as of course it is. Spying and betrayal are constant motifs in his writing, and in his life too, to judge by recent revelations – the Soviet spy Kim Philby was a friend – and by his autobiographical works. The first of these, *A Sort of Life*, contains the following admission, which would make a good starting-point for discussion with sixth-formers and some GCSE classes: 'every novelist has something in common with a spy: he watches, he overhears, he seeks motives and analyses character, and in his attempt to serve literature he is unscrupulous'.

THE CLASS NOVEL: *OF MICE AND MEN* AND *LORD OF THE FLIES*

On the whole I am opposed to what the Bullock report disparagingly refers to as the 'slow plod' of the class novel, preferring approaches based on indivualised or group reading. Not only does it bear no relation to reading fiction for pleasure outside school; it appears almost expressly designed to put pupils off spending their leisure in this way. For a start, it takes absolutely no account of individual preference or aptitude. Anthony Trollope observed in his autobiography, 'It is more true of novels than perhaps of anything else, that one man's food is another man's poison.' The chances of your selecting a novel the whole class will like are slim and, if they are a mixed ability group, it may be too easy for some pupils and too difficult for others. Imposing an unpopular choice for half a term, or even a term (which is what the 'slow plod' sometimes amounts to), is asking for trouble. In any case, this length of time is far too long to spend on a novel a literate pupil could be expected to read in a week or less. I can see how it might be justified with a GCSE set tackling a Victorian novel written for serial publication (although most pupils nowadays are deprived of that particular cultural experience), but not with the kind of novel often chosen for the first three years of secondary school, and occasionally GCSE sets as well – a work of children's literature of 200 pages at most, which neither needs nor repays such protracted attention. Some teachers actually exacerbate the problem by insisting that all pupils read the novel at the same pace, even to the extent of forbidding its being taken home in case anyone reads on ahead.

Where pressure to do a class novel can prove irresistible, however, is at GCSE level, simply because so many pupils in that age group either have not developed the habit of private reading or have abandoned it. The class novel is the easiest way of ensuring that fiction is adequately covered in their course work folders. The two novels I have taught most recently at this level are *Lord of the Flies,* to a fourth year class at the Greater Manchester school in 1987, and *Of Mice and Men,* to a fourth year class at the Knowsley school in 1989. Neither was chosen by me but I was perfectly happy to teach them. Both can claim to be mid-twentieth century classics of the genre, if perhaps minor rather than major, and both are usually thoroughly enjoyed by pupils, although in several classes I have taught, including the fourth year in Greater Manchester, *Lord of the Flies* exemplified Trollope's dictum, being 'food' to some and 'poison' to others.

The first, and frequently ignored, issue in the teaching of the class novel is how you and the class should actually read it – fast or slow, silently or aloud, in lesson time or for homework. So far as speed is concerned, I would say that in the case of all twentieth century novels you should push through the narrative as fast as you can; and you may have noted, from my descriptions of practice in Chapters 1 and 3, that both *Lord of the Flies* and *Of Mice and Men* were finished within two or three weeks. *Of Mice and Men* is so short that you could, if you wished, read it all in class without seeming profligate with lesson time. For *Lord of the Flies*, however, and most other novels, I would suggest you read only the beginning, end and key episodes you want to discuss in class, allocating the rest for homework. This approach has the advantage of allowing those who so wish to read on and finish in their own time.

My system for reading in class has not varied for twenty-five years: I read the narrative and pupils read the dialogue. Where there are only a few leading roles, as in *Of Mice and Men* and *Lord of the Flies*, it is a good idea to have two or three teams of readers taking turns, so as to involve as many of the class as possible. Apart from bringing the novel to life for those who have difficulty with silent reading, this method has the further advantage of making possible the role-play activities described later. Difficulties can occur when poor readers volunteer, in which case you will have to use your discretion, and when fewer pupils than you need do, in which case you will have to do more of the reading yourself. On no account should you fall back on reading round the class. I was warned against it during my PGCE course but the practice continues to flourish. It is a guaranteed way of killing any novel stone dead. You should also be wary of allowing class reading to go on too long; half an hour, or three-quarters in some circumstances, would be about right, leaving the rest of an hour's lesson for discussion or other activities.

The activities one might want to undertake on a novel are often usefully divided into before, during and after. If it is being studied for GCSE, you should ensure, course work pressure being what it is, that they all have some bearing on an eventual assignment. *Lord of the Flies* is particularly suitable for activities before the reading gets under way. There are, for example, several anticipation exercises one might use similar to those on 'I Spy'. You could start with the cover – my edition has a pig's head on it – and title, and invite suggestions on the likely content of the story in the light of these, while a first homework task could be to find out what the title refers to (the answer, if you do not already know, is in Brewer's *Dictionary of Phrase and Fable*), which should further stimulate pupils' speculation. You might also tell the class that it is a desert island story and ask whether they have read any other novels of this type (they are likely to mention *Robinson Crusoe*, *Gulliver's Travels*, *Treasure Island*, *Coral Island*, *Swiss Family Robinson* and *Swallows and Amazons*) and, if they have, what they take to be the hallmarks of the genre. I always draw a class's attention to the close relationship with *Coral Island* at the outset and encourage them to read it and/or one of the others (you will, of course, need to have copies of them available), because one of the possible assignments will be to discuss how far it is a typical desert island novel.

Islands, you may remember from Chapter 2, is one of the oldest of all topics or themes in English, having been used by Caldwell Cook before the First World War. It remains a popular one today, in both primary and secondary schools, and I like to use several activities developed in association with it when teaching *Lord of the Flies*. You could start by reading the class the account of what Robinson Crusoe salvaged from the wreck of his ship and then ask them to decide, in pairs, what ten things they would choose to take with them if they were castaways on a desert island. The pairs then form foursomes to compare lists and try to agree on a common one with the eventual aim, provided you think you can cope with the fierce arguments that inevitably arise, of arriving at a single list of ten items for the whole class. A similar activity, perhaps more relevant to the novel's theme, is to use the same pattern of progression (pairs, foursomes, whole class) for devising a list of ten rules which they believe would provide the best basis of a successful community of young people of their age marooned on a desert island.

Anticipation activities can continue to be used as the class works its way through the novel, to which you will need to add simple recapitulation just to keep absentees and defaulters on homework abreast of events. Much advocated also in recent years is the use of the reading log, in which pupils note down their thoughts on whatever they like – characters, plausibility of events, what might happen next, whether they are enjoying the story, anything. I prefer to give them more specific tasks, depending on the novel. In the case of *Of Mice and Men*, to bring out the neatness of its structure, I might ask a class to note down where and when each chapter takes place (in some editions they will have to make their own chapter divisions) and to give each chapter a title (e.g. 'The camp by the river' for chapter 1). I might also ask them to focus on the dialogue between Lennie and George, noting down what it tells us about them and their relationship as well as examples of their catch phrases, Americanisms and non-standard grammar. In the case of *Lord of the Flies*, a useful exercise is to take up Ralph's suggestion in the first chapter and draw a map of the island. As they read through the novel, pupils can then mark in the sites of landmarks and major events (e.g. Castle Rock, wreck of the plane, Simon's murder). Invaluable with lengthier and more complicated pre-twentieth century novels is some kind of device for keeping in touch with different strands of the plot and the relationships between the characters. A family tree for *Wuthering Heights* would be an obvious example, as would a visual representation of the relationship between its complex plot and the actual chronology of events.

Activities with a visual dimension – cover designs, posters for the film of the book, board games, strip cartoons – are commonly undertaken with younger classes once they have completed a novel. These can be fun but I have already expressed reservations about them so far as 'real engagement with texts' is concerned. At GCSE level I recommend you use the immediate follow-up period for oral work which can be assessed and lead on to written assignments as well. The first thing to do after finishing *Lord of the Flies* (I am tempted to say it should be obligatory) is to show the class Peter Brook's film version and ask them to collect as many differences between film and book as they can. All pupils are captivated by the stark beauty of the film, even those who have not much enjoyed the book, and they are remarkably observant about differences – everything from the famous improvisation by the boy playing Piggy on how Camberley got its name to the colour of Simon's hair. After that there are a number of issues, besides the rival merits of film and book, to explore in group or full-class discussion, which can be controlled by a conch, if anyone has one. Is it a typical desert island story? What is the significance of the title? Why do things go so badly wrong? Some episodes also lend themselves to dramatisation – the murder of Simon, for example, or the final scene on the beach – but you may prefer to work on episodes after the novel as written has finished – Ralph and Jack meeting their parents on their return home or a public inquiry in which those who read the parts of the surviving characters are 'hot-seated' in role.

Immediately after finishing *Of Mice and Men* in the Knowsley school I did some choral work on the dialogue similar to that described earlier in connection with 'January', with me taking the part of Lennie and the class as a collective George. They then had to prepare a passage of dialogue of their choice from the novel in groups and present it for oral assessment. On a later occasion I set them two further tasks for group work assessment: discussion of why George shot Lennie and whether he was right to do so; and translation of Burns's 'To a Mouse' (with the dialect words already glossed, of course), followed by discussion of why Steinbeck had taken his title from the poem and whether it adequately encapsulated the novel's theme. This particular oral activity was extremely revealing about the state of the class's cultural deprivation. Most of them were perplexed in the face of unfamiliar language and several even admitted to uncertainty over the meaning of 'thee' and 'thou' – 'Does it mean "we" or "you", sir?' Although such ignorance can partly be explained by factors outside teachers' control (notably the disappearance of the Authorised Version of the Bible from the popular culture), the almost exclusive concentration on modern literature in some schools must also take a share of the blame.

One of the respects in which GCSE English Literature is held by many to be superior to its GCE predecessor is that it permits a wider range of written responses – personal and creative as well as critical and discursive. Whilst in general sympathetic to this majority view, I think you need to ensure that the assignments you set towards the personal-creative end of the spectrum do demand 'real engagement with texts' and that the folders of all pupils, including those of low ability, include some writing of a critical and discursive kind. If in doubt, do not be afraid of inviting yet another generation of pupils to discuss the justice of Malcolm's concluding assessment of Macbeth and Lady Macbeth – 'this dead butcher and his fiend-like queen'; it necessitates far more 'real engagement' with the play than many of the popular 'trivial pursuits' on *Macbeth* – newspaper reports from the *Dunsinane Times*, letters between Malcolm and Donalbain, witches' spells, etc. – ever will.

Here are the assignments I set the two fourth year classes on *Lord of the Flies* and *Of Mice and Men* respectively, of which they had to choose to do one (I did say they could devise their own if they wished, but no one took me up on the offer):

Lord of the Flies
1 Write a letter to either William Golding or Peter Brook, giving your opinion of his work and raising any queries you would like answered.

2 Write a short story or play scene involving one or more of the survivors after the end of the novel.

3 Write an essay on the title of the novel. You should discuss what it means, why you think Golding chose it and whether you think it is a good choice.

4 Is the novel a typical desert island story? You should bring in comparison with other novels of this type which you have read.

5 'Children from a mixed state school of the same age (or 'Our class at the same age') would never have behaved as badly as the boys in the novel did.' Discuss.

Of Mice and Men

1 What does the dialogue between George and Lennie reveal about their characters and the relationship between them?

2 Write a review of the dramatised version of the novel at the Liverpool Playhouse as if for the Liverpool *Daily Post* or *Echo*.

3 In old age George decides to write his autobiography. Write the chapter which deals with his relationship with Lennie.

4 Write a newspaper report (e.g. for the *Soledad Times*) of the murder of Curley's wife and the shooting of Lennie.

5 Write a short story about events before the novel begins (e.g. the incident at Weed) or after it ends (e.g. George's trial for murder).

On reflection the assignments on *Of Mice and Men* seem to me less well balanced than those on *Lord of the Flies*, being rather skewed towards the creative end of the spectrum. This is partly, I think, a result of the intrinsic differences between the two novels (there is an intellectual dimension to *Lord of the Flies* lacking in the American novel), and partly a result of the difference between the two classes involved. The fourth year class at the Greater Manchester school were, on the whole, abler than their Knowsley counterparts. If you agree about the imbalance, feel that it matters and know *Of Mice and Men* reasonably well, perhaps you could consider how it might be rectified.

LIMITS TO THE ACTIVE APPROACH

In conclusion I want to revert briefly to the question raised by George Sampson and the Newbolt report – whether literature should be taught or at least whether teaching, in its most widely understood sense of imparting new knowledge and skills, is the best word to describe what is ideally done with literature in the classroom. Perhaps the main point to make is that, if you share my concern to induct children into part of their cultural heritage, English literature – and believe that it exists 'out there' as a collection of texts of proven aesthetic and moral value, connected through a history in which major and minor figures, movements and influences, genres and conventions can all be identified – then you will at least have something to teach. The problem arises with teachers who do not – who may, indeed, have no clear sense of purpose at all and end up teaching texts, both for GCSE and lower down the school, which neither need nor deserve to be taught. When this happens the activities may simply become ends in themselves or something to keep children busily engaged with. I do not wish to underestimate the value of children enjoying what they do at school, but it is equally important that they should understand, and accept, the educational basis of what they are asked to do. As to whether the activities exemplified in relation to 'January', 'I Spy' and the two novels are consonant with the aim of teaching literature, that is for you to judge, but I trust you can see that they are intended to enhance pupils' knowledge and understanding of what they read, besides helping to develop oral and writing skills.

The danger, however, which you do need to be alerted to is the threat posed to the integrity of the text and the author's intentions by activities of this kind. If the traditional critical approach to literature can be faulted for 'murdering to dissect', the modern active approach can be faulted for suffocating the author and the text in a riot of things to do. I would be very interested to know the reactions of R.S. Thomas, Graham Greene and William Golding to what I have suggested you might 'do' with their work, especially as the latter has already made known his objections to being treated as 'the raw material of an academic light industry'. English teachers cannot be reminded too often of the Board of Education's observation in 1910 that the real teachers of literature are the great writers themselves. You need to be wary of getting in the way between author and pupil and, if ever in doubt, should leave a literary text to speak for itself.

FURTHER READING

Easily the best book on teaching literature which I have read is *Teaching Literature 9–14* by Michael Benton and Geoff Fox. Useful starting-points, if you are unfamiliar with modern active approaches, are also provided by 'Twenty-four Things to do with a Book' by Geoff Fox and 'Thirty-six Things to do with a Poem' by Geoff Fox and Brian Merrick, both of which are reproduced in *New Directions in English Teaching*, edited by Anthony Adams. A similar list for teaching the novel is to be found at the end of the Cox report.

Chapter 8

Drama in English

Hamlet: . . . the purpose of playing . . . was and is to hold as 'twere the mirror up to nature.

(Shakespeare, *Hamlet*, c. 1601)

It is surely this paradox of losing oneself to gain oneself which has always made drama such a great moral as well as intellectual force.

(Marjorie Hourd, *The Education of the Poetic Spirit*, 1949)

A play is play.

(Peter Brook, *The Empty Space*, 1968)

DRAMA AS SUBJECT AND METHOD

In my experience those new to English teaching fall into three groups when the issue of drama is broached: the *aficionados*, who have often had extensive experience of amateur dramatics, may even be drama-trained and hope to dramatise as many lessons as possible; the drama-shy, who may be terrified by the prospect of facing the 'empty space', as well as the more physical and informal relationships, of the drama room; and, perhaps the largest group, the interested-but-uncertain, who probably did little or no drama at school or as part of their degree, recognise its classroom potential but have few ideas about how to start or proceed. All the auguries suggest that drama, notwithstanding the protests of the specialists, will increasingly be incorporated into English and therefore become one of your many responsibilities. So my first advice to you, if you place yourself within either the drama-shy or the interested-but-uncertain category, is that you should seek out every opportunity – workshops, day schools, conferences, courses

– to become a drama student. Books and articles can play a part in building up a repertoire of things to do, as well as a theory to underpin them (if you feel you need one), but only the experience can give you the confidence to launch out on your own. There is thus a limit to how far I can help you in this chapter. I have chosen to concentrate on drama as method or technique rather than drama as subject or content – and to illustrate method and technique through a discussion of teaching Shakespeare, simply because he remains, in Peter Brook's words, 'our model. . . . [His theatre] contains Brecht and Beckett, but goes beyond both'.

You will no doubt be familiar with the distinction between drama as subject and method from the Cox report, which equates the former with 'creative art form' and the latter with 'learning tool'. This is a convenient distinction but also an over-simple, and perhaps even confusing, one. For there are further distinctions to be made at some point in thinking about drama. First of all there is drama in the sense of a basic human activity as represented, for example, by much of children's play and by the variety of roles we are expected to assume in adult life. Second, there is drama as 'creative art form', which, however, can refer both to a literary genre and to theatrical performance. Third, there is drama as a school subject, whose relationship to drama as basic human activity, literary genre and theatrical performance can vary considerably from school to school and from teacher to teacher. In most schools it is closely allied to, even institutionally part of, English and may therefore tend to be seen primarily as a literary genre. In others, however, it is institutionally quite separate and linked with other performing arts like music and dance. Finally, within drama as a school subject, there is a distinction to be drawn between the content of lessons, whether it be literary material or other issues and themes, and the techniques or methods used to dramatise them, although you may find in practice they cannot be segregated so simply, since the techniques are as much what drama lessons are about, as much their content, as the material to which they are applied.

In theory it has always been self-evident what drama should be about. The two books which most helped me when I started teaching it in the 1970s (see the section on further reading) define it respectively as *'active* involvement and identification with a fictitious situation' and 'children, as participants, projecting into imagined or assumed roles or situations'. It has also always been accepted that to be 'dramatic' such 'fictitious' or 'imagined' situations must involve conflict or tension, as well as opportunities to resolve it and moments for reflection and discussion. In practice school drama has been interpreted to cover a diverse range of activities. Originally it mainly meant play-reading and theatrical performance, although there was, from earliest times, some application of drama techniques to other school subjects too. The Newbolt report's summary of possible content included the writing and performance of pupils' own plays, the reading and performance of plays by others, and the dramatisation of stories and poems.

Over the century there has been something of a shift away from the writing, reading and performance of plays in drama lessons, though these activities have by no means been wholly excluded, towards 'process' activities based on role-play and improvisation around topics, themes or issues chosen by the teacher or the pupils. This shift has been accompanied by some fierce disputes among drama teachers over both philosophy and pedagogy. Whilst it is still generally agreed that drama is about pupils 'projecting into imagined or assumed roles or situations', dissension has been sharp over how much weight is to be given to the different, and occasionally extravagant, aims and claims which have been advanced for the subject and over major pedagogic issues such as whether the emphasis should fall on drama or theatre, improvisation or performance; whether the teacher is most effective in or out of role; what balance to strike between small-group and whole-class work; and whether lessons are better tightly structured, with many teacher interventions, or more open-ended, with the teacher as unobtrusive facilitator.

I do not intend to arbitrate on these issues and would recommend you adopt an initial position which is both agnostic and catholic – undertaking your own explorations, putting all claims to the test and excluding no approach or technique on purely doctrinal grounds. Eventually you will settle on a pedagogy which best suits you, though it may take some time before you arrive and you should be prepared for your share of detours and mishaps *en route*. Do not allow yourself to be disheartened by these; what Peter Brook once defined as the special characteristic of the theatre – 'it is always possible to start again' – is equally applicable to drama teaching. Only now, after fifteen years of trial and error (not to say catastrophe), do I feel I know what and how

I want to teach in drama, whilst still being bedevilled by niggling uncertainties concerning both. For example, I do not really feel comfortable unless I am working on literary texts – plays, stories and poems – and in a tightly structured framework devised by myself. In this respect the work on 'I Spy' described in the previous chapter is typical of my practice. Within these self-imposed limits, however, I have tried to make use of a range of techniques, some of which are exemplified in the 'I Spy' work. Those I have found particularly valuable are:

Improvisation   Fundamental to drama teaching. Be warned that it does not necessarily 'come by nature'. To some pupils it does, whereas others are easily tongue-tied or struck dumb. Show them how they can help one another by avoiding remarks which close the dialogue down, and remember that it does not have to be spontaneous – it can be prepared and rehearsed just like scripted drama. If you are inexperienced in using it, I recommend you read *Impro* by Keith Johnstone.

Role-play   Also fundamental, but you should note that it is sometimes understood to include playing a specific character (e.g. Hamlet) and sometimes reserved for a narrower interpretation of the concept of role (e.g. servant, widow, football hooligan). Whether to adopt a role yourself, in either sense, is obviously for you to decide. It was a very fashionable technique in the 1970s and I would certainly encourage you to experiment with it. It is a good way of moving the action on and, if the role you assume is one in which you wield power or authority (King Lear, say, or a judge), of controlling it too.

Hot-seating   A popular form of role-play among English teachers because it can be used in the classroom without disturbing the furniture. Pupils, in role or character, are interrogated about their actions or behaviour by the rest of the class, who may or may not also be in role. Referring back to the example of *Lord of the Flies* in the previous chapter, Ralph, Jack and the other survivors could be asked to explain and justify their conduct, attribute blame, and so on. This technique can be developed into quite elaborate trials, meetings and committees of inquiry (into, for example, if you are teaching *The Merchant of Venice*, antisemitism in contemporary Venetian society).

Tableau Another popular technique among English teachers, though requiring the use of the drama room or at least an 'empty space'. It is sometimes referred to as photograph, sculpture or freeze-frame but I prefer the traditional theatrical term *tableau vivant*. Pupils adopt positions, gestures and facial expressions and hold them for, say, half a minute. The most obvious use of the technique is to suspend, and focus attention on, a significant moment of action in the narrative of a novel, short story or play, as in my work on 'I Spy', but it can also be used to represent relationships between characters, fictional themes and abstract ideas. If, for instance, you were teaching Marlowe's *Dr Faustus*, you could ask the class to devise tableaux representing the seven deadly sins. Tableaux can include language, both scripted and improvised, and normally involve role-play too.

Thought-tracking This is one way of using language in tableaux and is again exemplified by the 'I Spy' work. At a given signal (a touch on the shoulder by the teacher, perhaps) a character speaks his or her mind. The technique can also be applied to scripted and improvised dialogue. While one pupil delivers a character's lines an *alter ego* says what he or she really thinks.

Forum theatre Very valuable with older pupils and classes more experienced in drama. The class form a seated square round the actors, who may be improvising or performing a scene. They are not, however, a passive audience. They can stop the action to offer comments on how it might be improved or ask for the performance or improvisation of further scenes. In addition an individual from the audience can replace one of the actors through another technique known as 'tagging', whereby one of the former touches one of the latter on the shoulder (as in an 'excuse me' dance), or vice versa if one of the actors wants to be relieved.

Mime An excellent technique for keeping inexperienced and excitable classes under control and for making them think hard about what they are doing. With such classes it is also advisable, at least initially, to make the movement slow-motion and to limit, or even debar, any physical contact.

Defining the space, setting the scene It is important for pupils to make creative use of the area they are working in, whether drama studio or classroom, availing themselves of whatever props are to hand, even if only tables and chairs. The 'I Spy' work, for example, requires that they have a clear mental map of Charlie's house; anything they can do to represent it physically will help them considerably in performance. In the summer term do not be frightened of going outside when it seems appropriate.

Warm-ups and calm-downs   One version of drama doctrine says you should always start by warming the class up and finish by calming them down. I think it depends on the class, the kind of drama you are engaged on and the time of the lesson. I usually use warm-ups with older classes and adults but very rarely with younger ones, who are normally already warm enough. The warm-ups I use are a mixture of movement (with or without music), stretching and breathing exercises, most of which I have adapted from my experience of yoga, and drama games. Calming the class down is necessary only if they are going on to an academic lesson like Maths or Geography. The best way of doing it is to use the last five or ten minutes for discussion in a seated circle but I have also used concentration and relaxation exercises, again borrowed from yoga.

Drama games   The most popular and also the most contentious form of warm-up. Most of them are adaptations of traditional children's games, though a few – trust games, for instance – seem to have an adult provenance. They are ideal for groups of adults who do not know one another but should, in my view, be used only sparingly with children. The danger is that they can become an end in themselves and divorced from the actual drama. So I would recommend that, when you do use them, you try and integrate them into the subject of the lesson; you will find examples in the account of teaching Shakespeare below.

TEACHING SHAKESPEARE: AN ACTIVE APPROACH

Drama is by nature an active form of learning. It is, therefore, perhaps surprising that the prevailing approach to teaching plays in English lessons has concentrated on reading, writing and discussion. These, of course, have their place but plays, after all, are written primarily to be performed, an obvious enough fact whose only acknowledgment in many schools has been the annual school play. The school play is a fine institution, and I have seen many outstanding productions over the years, but the very real rewards it confers are rarely shared beyond a narrow circle of participants, leaving the rest of the school with the feeling that they have missed out on a wonderful party, besides severely disrupting the ordinary course of school life.

Caldwell Cook, George Sampson and the Newbolt report all argued seventy years ago that the performance (as opposed to study) of plays, including Shakespeare, should be part of everyday classroom experience. 'Class performances,' commented the Newbolt report, 'are joyous and instructive adventures. They may range from happy improvisation to a formal show on a special occasion. In their Elizabethan inadequacy of equipment they make an excellent introduction to the conditions of Shakespearian drama.' Yet most English teachers, including myself, could, until very recently, think of no way of teaching Shakespeare in the classroom which was not deskbound, limited to reading and writing and modelled on the requirements of GCE O and A Levels. Not only did this render him inaccessible to the bulk of the school population, it also instilled into many of those who were granted access to his plays an inveterate antipathy towards them.

Now, happily, a small classroom revolution is under way, very largely as a result of the work of the Shakespeare and Schools project at the Institute of Education, Cambridge, since 1986, which I would describe as the most hopeful and exciting development in English teaching in the last ten years, if not longer. What Rex Gibson, John Salway and the teachers seconded to the project have achieved is to pull together the work of a number of pioneers, develop the principles underlying a more active approach, test out a range of techniques (some deriving from the theatre, some from drama teaching, some from literature teaching) in a variety of school situations, and build up a bank of ideas for good practice which any teacher can now draw on.

At the heart of the project it is possible to identify four fundamental principles. The first is the one adumbrated by Caldwell Cook, George Sampson and the Newbolt report seventy years ago but little implemented since: namely, that Shakespeare's plays were written to be performed, not read. Indeed, so far as we can tell, Shakespeare seems to have taken no great interest in their publication in printed form; performance was their publication. A class's experience of a Shakespeare play should, therefore, be performance-focused, with pupils on their feet, moving with purpose and speaking the lines as though they meant them – in effect, acting.

The second fundamental principle is that Shakespeare is part of the national culture and must therefore be made available to all pupils. The statutory provisions of the National Curriculum now require that all secondary school pupils should have some experience of Shakespeare. The work of the project, and other pioneers, has shown that there is no reason why this requirement should not be extended to cover Key Stage 2 as well. For this to happen the teacher's approach has to emphasise not only performance-related rather than deskbound activities (if only because many younger pupils are incapable of following a traditional reading of the text) but also activities in which everyone participates.

Even plays previously reserved for GCE A Level, like *Hamlet* and *King Lear*, can then be taught to junior school children, as I shall attempt to demonstrate in the next section. Teaching the great tragedies to mixed ability classes of 7–11 year olds marks a clear break with traditional assumptions about which Shakespeare plays are suitable for which pupils, as do the project's experiments with extending the pre-A Level canon beyond *Macbeth* and *Romeo and Juliet* to encompass a greater variety of plays, including previously untaught ones such as *Pericles* and *Titus Andronicus*. The project's third principle is that, if active approaches are used, all the plays can be made accessible to all pupils. In practice, of course, some plays will continue to be preferred to others, because some are better, and more central to the national culture, than others.

Extending the Shakespeare canon in schools in these two ways may well mean teaching something less than the whole play and something other than the play as written or traditionally performed. The fourth principle is that, if classroom approaches are to be successfully child-centred, they must be exploratory. Teachers and pupils have to be prepared to take liberties with the text (rather as Shakespeare took liberties with his sources) – to revere him irreverently, in the manner of directors like Charles Marovitz in the 1970s and Michael Bogdanov in the 1980s. If you see yourself as a Shakespeare purist, you may well be sceptical about taking liberties with the text, being reminded perhaps of the expurgated versions included in Henrietta and Thomas Bowdler's *Family Shakespeare* (published in 1807), and about what you see as 'trendy' or 'gimmicky' productions of his plays.

But you will at least, I hope, concede that there is a place for simplified and abbreviated versions for younger and less able pupils. Charles and Mary Lamb's *Tales from Shakespeare* (also published in 1807 and, like the Bowdlers' versions, somewhat moralistically conceived) established an enduring model for what can be done. The best of their imitators, most recently Leon Garfield, have recognised, as the Lambs did not, the importance of retaining Shakespeare's text for the dialogue. Ideal, I would say, for the primary school, and for younger and less able secondary classes, is an approach in which the teacher tells the story, key scenes are dramatised using at least some of the text, relationships are discussed, and project work is undertaken on Shakespeare's life and theatre. The suitability of such an approach has long been recognised. I still have in my possession the book which introduced me to Shakespeare in school when I was 11 or 12. It is called *Approach to Shakespeare* and was published in 1925. Included in it are: information on Shakespeare's life and times; the Lambs' retellings of *A Midsummer Night's Dream*, *The Merchant of Venice*, *As You Like It*, *Twelfth Night* and *The Tempest*; extracts from Holinshed on Richard II and III, Plutarch on Julius Caesar and Sir Walter Scott on Macbeth; and scenes from nine of the plays.

I hope you are prepared to concede too that all Shakespeare plays are open to interpretation. There is no such thing as one correct reading, though there may be such a thing as an incorrect one. Moreover, a performance-focused approach has to accept that, as Rex Gibson insists, a play is, first and foremost a script, not a book, and resembles a musical score in the degree of latitude it permits, or active interpretation it requires of (depending on how you look at it), those responsible for its enactment, including decisions over the text. A production of *Hamlet*, for instance, necessarily entails decisions over which edition to use, what balance to strike between Quarto and Folio, textual problems and emendations ('sullied' or 'solid' in Hamlet's opening soliloquy, for example) and what cuts, if any, to make.

There is, of course, a difference between interpreting and editing a text and actually changing it, and that difference may well represent the limit to which you are prepared to go. The tradition of adapting, revising and transforming Shakespeare's plays goes back to the Restoration – to Davenant, Dryden and Nahum Tate's famous *King Lear* with a happy ending – and is seen by many teachers in a wholly negative light. I think this is unfortunate. Taking liberties with the text, playing with the plays, can be both insightful, opening up new ways of seeing them, and fun and has, after all, produced three of Verdi's finest operas, *Kiss me Kate* and *West Side Story*. Seeing Northern Ballet's superb production of Prokofiev's *Romeo and Juliet* with pupils from the Liverpool primary school, the sacrilegious thought occurred to me that the story makes a better ballet than a play. I would encourage you to take whatever liberties are likely to prove fruitful and enjoyable in your work on the plays, even to the point of engaging with Rex Gibson's test question – 'Can Iago be good?' As Peter Brook once observed, in taking liberties 'the texts do not get burned'.

For convenience I shall divide the kind of activities that can be undertaken on Shakespeare's plays (and anyone else's, for that matter) into three groups, without wishing to imply that the distinctions between them are absolute or that there is no overlap: work on the structure, playing with the play and work on language and verse. Because the subject of this chapter is drama, I have concentrated on those activities which are at least to some degree dramatic and have omitted those, such as creative writing and variations on comprehension exercises (projection, cloze, sequencing, etc.) which are essentially sedentary and have been dealt with in earlier chapters.

Structure

The first and most important problem facing you is how the class are to experience the story. If they are capable of reading it through in the conventional way, then I would recommend they do so as fast as possible, either individually or as a group. The most successful kind of class reading is, in my experience, silent while listening to the record or audio tape of a professional production, with minimum interruption from the teacher. Later on knowledge of the story can be reinforced by a visit to a live performance or class viewing of the video of a film or television version. With classes who are incapable of reading the story through in the conventional way the only possibility, really, is for you to tell it to them, though you may choose to rely wholly or partially on a simplified written version such as Charles and Mary Lamb's or Leon Garfield's. (The Lambs retold approximately half the plays, Garfield has retold approximately a third.) Rather than give the class the whole story at once, which is what older pupils prefer, you may choose to tell it episodically, pausing to dramatise certain scenes and for speculation on possible developments, which can work particularly well with primary school pupils.

Once a class are in possession of the story, there are a number of ways the knowledge can be dramatised. They can devise mimes, masques, burlesques and puppet shows; they can improvise on it while retaining the basic narrative thread (perhaps with a view to creating a late twentieth century update in the manner of *West Side Story*); they can create a sequence of tableaux of significant moments, with or without text; or they can produce a shortened version (lasting anywhere between five minutes and an hour). Reduction exercises can also be applied to speeches and passages of dialogue in order to bring out the underlying structure. For instance, you might ask the class, in pairs, to reduce all the exchanges between Barnardo and Francisco in the opening thirteen lines of *Hamlet* to single-word utterances of a piece with 'Barnardo?' 'He,' in order to elucidate its mood. The pairs then have to learn their version, making a different tableau or striking a different posture for each utterance. From this exercise performance of the dialogue as written, with movement and gesture added, follows naturally.

Pupils get great satisfaction out of performing an actual scene, or part of a scene, by Shakespeare, especially if it includes props, costumes, sound effects, and so on. Schools adopting this approach tend to fall back on famous comic moments – the robbery at Gadshill, Pyramus and Thisbe, the gulling of Malvolio, Caliban with Stephano and Trinculo. I would encourage you to experiment with serious moments as well. I have had excellent results from younger classes performing the murder of Banquo, the dumb show and the fencing match in *Hamlet* and the putting out of Gloucester's eyes. There is no need to worry about the distortion of structure that may be involved in separating out individual scenes in this way, nor about separating out the different narrative strands interwoven by Shakespeare (in *A Midsummer Night's Dream*, say) in order to clarify the structure, nor about discarding one or two of them if they do not seem suitable for a particular class. I am always tempted to stop *Julius Caesar* half-way through and have often thought *Cymbeline* would be a good play to do in school if it could be reduced to the Imogen–Posthumus–Iachimo plot.

Playing with the play

If you are interested in literary theory, you might like to think of some of the exercises in the previous section as 'structuralist', in the sense that they try to emphasise or elucidate a play's, or part of a play's, 'deep structure', and some of those in this section as 'post-structuralist' or 'deconstructive', in the sense that they point up ambiguities and gaps in the structure and seem to express more interest in the play as it might have been than in the play as it is. The best way of introducing the various possibilities to you is simply to categorise and list them. In each case any, or a mixture, of the drama techniques mentioned above can be used:

Missing scenes and characters   Pupils can create scenes which are described or referred to in the text but take place off stage (e.g. the death of Cordelia in *King Lear* or the apparent infidelity of Hero in *Much Ado About Nothing*) or scenes in which characters referred to in, but omitted from, the text (e.g. Rosaline in *Romeo and Juliet* or Sycorax in *The Tempest*) actually appear.

Pre-texts and sequels   Pupils can also create scenes before the play starts and after it finishes for which the text provides some evidence or suggestions (e.g. the expulsion of Prospero from Milan in *The Tempest* and Malvolio's revenge in *Twelfth Night*).

Changing the play   Pupils can be asked to change the play at a critical juncture (e.g. Hamlet kills Claudius while he is praying or Duncan survives the assassination attempt) in order to explore other dramatic possibilities. Alternatively they can be asked to keep the story but change the genre (*King Lear* as comedy, *The Taming of the Shrew* as tragedy).

Starting in the middle   To increase the speculation possibilities with younger pupils, you can start the story in the middle and work backwards and then forwards (e.g. Lear raving in the storm or the baby Perdita found on the shore in *The Winter's Tale*).

Transposing, juxtaposing and rearranging scenes and speeches
A good example of transposition and juxtaposition is John
Salway's suggestion that what Goneril and Regan say to their
father at the beginning of the first scene in *King Lear* can be
intercut with what they say to one another at the end. More radical
suggestions involve reallocating speeches, as in Charles Marovitz's
productions, and moving them around the play, as in Zeffirelli's
film of *Hamlet*, or even from one play to another. In case this idea
reminds you of the Duke's version of 'To be or not to be' in
Huckleberry Finn, in which words spoken by Hamlet get mixed up
with words spoken by Macbeth, I should stress that it is not so
dotty as it may sound. There are some striking similarities among
seemingly unrelated Shakespeare plays – between *Richard III* and
Macbeth, for example, and between *Hamlet* and *Measure for
Measure*. If you were teaching both of the latter for A Level, an
obvious activity would be to juxtapose and perhaps swap over
Hamlet's 'To be or not to be' and Claudio's 'Ay, but to die and go
we know not where.'

Alternative views of the play   Redramatising the story from the
point of view of minor characters, or characters who seem to us to
be hard done by, has been popular ever since Tom Stoppard's
Rosencrantz and Guildenstern are Dead became well known twenty
years ago. Candidates with a good claim to having their side of the
story more sympathetically presented are Caliban, Malvolio and
Shylock.

Setting the scene, creating the atmosphere   Most of the plays
provide plenty of opportunities for crowd scenes, hustle and
bustle, and sound effects which it would be a pity, particularly with
younger pupils, not to take advantage of. An increasingly popular
technique is to have the whole class in role as servants, soldiers,
courtiers, ladies-in-waiting, etc. setting the scene and creating the
atmosphere at Elsinore, Dunsinane or Lear's palace or as peasants
and slaves constructing military camps and fortifications in the
history plays or as mariners in one of the plays in which
shipwrecks occur – *The Tempest, Twelfth Night, The Comedy of Errors,
Pericles*. Shipwrecks also require sound effects, as do storms,
battles and moments of magic, in which music can be expected to
play a part, whether Elizabethan, classical, pop or composed by
the pupils themselves. In the summer other exciting possibilities

open up. That the comedies benefit from *al fresco* performance on lawns and among trees and bushes has long been recognised, but it has only recently occurred to teachers that it might be interesting to perform *Hamlet* or one of the other plays set in castles actually in one, even though there have been professional productions of Shakespeare in Elsinore and Ludlow castles for many years.

Drama games   All the plays lend themselves to the kind of drama games described in the books by Keith Johnstone and Clive Barker (see the section on further reading). For example, getting-to-know-you games like Jack to Jill and Stations (or Fruit Cocktail) can be used with younger pupils to familiarise them with the names of the characters, while Keith Johnstone's status games can be applied to the many greetings and farewells in the plays and used to convert other lines temporarily into greetings and farewells. A very popular game, for obvious reasons, which can be applied to several plays, is Keith Johnstone's Insults. I have used it successfully with both adults and primary school pupils on *Troilus and Cressida*, borrowing from Thersites' inventive lexicon of invective. Equally popular are the different variations on Murder in the Dark for the assassination of Duncan. Others I have experimented with are Pirate's Treasure (the rape of Helen in *Troilus and Cressida*), Grandmother's Footsteps (Lady Macbeth's sleepwalking and the gulling of Malvolio) and the wonderful game described by Clive Barker and called by him the Court of the Holy Dido (crimes and punishments in *The Tempest*).

Language and verse

For the many taxing and enjoyable activities now being undertaken on Shakespeare's language and verse in school we are all indebted, directly or indirectly, to the work of Cicely Berry, voice director of the Royal Shakespeare Company, though several originated with other great theatrical innovators such as Peter Brook. They were devised, of course, with actors principally in mind but have proved particularly suitable for school use too, partly because they involve the whole class, rather than dividing them into performers and audience, and partly because so many of them have a physical dimension. Cicely Berry has written eloquently of the need for an actor's intellectual understanding of the text to be complemented by a physical response to release impulses and imagination. For convenience I have once again been unable to resist the temptation to categorise them, this time into four groups:

Involving the whole class   Many of the exercises in this group apply the principles and techniques of choral work to speeches and dialogue. A soliloquy, for example, can be divided up thought by thought, phrase by phrase and even word by word and then allocated to pupils individually, in pairs or in small groups. Alternatively one pupil can read it while the rest of the class echo or query it or make some kind of physical response – miming, gesturing, encircling, jostling – without, one hopes, being subjected to the kind of audience participation Mr Wopsle received while playing Hamlet in *Great Expectations*. Similar activities can be undertaken on dialogue but with the class divided into large groups as appropriate – two for Macbeth and Lady Macbeth, three for the witches, etc. Another way of involving the whole class is to have them all on their feet, moving round the room and reading the text independently. At breaks in the text – change of thought, change of speaker, punctuation mark – they have to make a ninety-degree turn or some similar physical response.

Physicalising the speech   Other activities involve physicalising the speech, to use Cicely Berry's phrase. They include: asking the class to invent tableaux for particular lines or phrases; arranging pupils into shapes or patterns (circles, squares, pyramids, corridors, mazes) to represent or complement a passage of text; pupils speaking dialogue while playing a game (noughts and crosses, arm wrestling, etc.) or trying to solve a physical problem (e.g. getting up from a seated position in pairs while back-to-back, with their arms linked); and pupils reciting a speech after you as they carry out a group task like putting the chairs out or away.

Language games   Shakespeare's plays are full of language games – puns (3,000 of them, according to one critic, M.M. Mahood), puzzles, quips and quibbles – and hence particularly appropriate for the introduction of new ones. Some, for example Insults, have already been referred to. Two good ones for A Level and GCSE classes come from Peter Brook. In the first a line of text ('To be or not to be; that is the question,' say) is spoken round the circle, word by word, continuously and with increasing speed, but with a previously agreed word ('be', say) replaced each time round by whichever pupil it falls to with another which fits both grammatically and metrically. In the second you select a passage of dialogue or a speech which is metaphorically rich (Brook's example is an interchange between Romeo and Juliet) and ask the class to prepare a reading in pairs which excludes anything metaphorical. They then perform the dialogue or speech, speaking what is non-metaphorical and pausing silently over what they have omitted.

From these exercises it is an easy step to improvisation and translation games. You may recall from Chapter 1 how I gave a class a short extract from *Antony and Cleopatra* to improvise on without telling them anything about the story or the characters. Translation games can be improvised or scripted. You could, for example, ask a class in pairs to prepare a speech or passage of dialogue so that roughly half is Shakespeare and half translated into modern English. Alternatively bigger groups can work on a variation of the Insults game with dialogue in which some kind of verbal sparring occurs between two parties (Thersites and Patroclus, Malvolio and Sir Toby, Beatrice and Benedick, Helena and Hermia). Their task is to find the most appropriate modern idiom to replace the Shakespearian. The two parties agree on the translation of their half of the dialogue, write it down and learn it, and finally, in chorus, go to verbal war. Finally, and suitable for all classes, is to play with the way lines can be spoken – fast and slow, loud and quiet (including shouting and whispering), vowel sounds only and consonant sounds only, mouthing your partner's silently, singing.

Verse Cicely Berry rightly says, 'We have to know the mathematics of the lines so that we can tune into the quality of the thought.' The problem is, of course, how to teach the mathematics. A traditional chalk-and-talk explanation of the iambic pentameter was good enough for me, when I was at school, and still works well for many pupils today. For others, however, particularly those with a poor ear or sense of rhythm, explanation needs to be reinforced by activity in the drama room. The stressed syllables can be tapped, clapped, beaten and stamped as they are spoken. Other useful activities are speaking, with or without movement or gesture, from punctuation mark to punctuation mark (for enjambement) and half a line at a time (for caesura). If you are working on a play like *Romeo and Juliet*, you need to consider what you are going to do about its sonnets and use of rhyming couplets, and, if you are working on *A Midsummer Night's Dream*, about the latter's use of trochee and song. Learning the famous Shakespearian songs by heart ('Where the bee sucks', 'O mistress mine', 'When that I was and a little tiny boy', 'Who is Silvia?'), including the tunes, where they have survived, is perhaps the best way of all of reinforcing a feeling for metre.

TEACHING *HAMLET* TO 7–10 YEAR OLDS

In June 1989 I taught *Hamlet* to a vertically grouped class of 7–10 year olds at the Liverpool primary school, drawing on some of the techniques described above. The class teacher and I chose *Hamlet*, partly because we judged it to be a story primary school children would enjoy and partly because we wanted to see how a play normally reserved for A Level could be made accessible to pupils half the age of sixth-formers. In so doing we recognised, of course, that we would have to be cautious in exposing them to the text, besides making hefty cuts in the story. For the latter we took our cue from the 1988 production at the Liverpool Everyman Theatre. We converted it into a tale of two families, a kind of Danish *Romeo and Juliet* – omitting Fortinbras, Rosencrantz and Guildenstern and most of the political dimension. Because of the age of the children we also underplayed the sexuality. On the metaphysics or eschatology we took no decision; in the event, neither posed a problem, perhaps on account of the school's distinctive Catholic ethos.

The teaching essentially comprised four afternoon sessions of two hours mostly devoted to drama. Each session focused on one or two key episodes in the narrative – Hamlet and the Ghost, Hamlet and Ophelia, the dumb show, the death of Ophelia, Hamlet and the gravedigger, and the fencing match. In addition, the class teacher undertook preparatory and follow-up work with the class before and after each session. This included: research into Shakespeare's life and times; the construction of a model of the Globe Theatre plus simple props like crowns; illustrating scenes from the play; and creative writing. In effect, we followed the advice of everyone from the Newbolt report to the Shakespeare and Schools project in making the pupils' first experience of Shakespeare a mixture of traditional junior school topic work and the dramatised narration of a particular play. The following is my edited record of how the four sessions went.

Session 1   Hamlet and the Ghost

The class teacher had prepared for the opening session by getting the children to make name cards for all the characters, including those whom we had decided to omit, which started them speculating about the story and its relationships. Before we went out on the yard for drama, I gave the class a brief introduction to Shakespeare, his theatre and times. They had all heard of him ('the greatest writer in the world', one boy called him) and of *Hamlet*. Most knew the 'To be or not to be' line as well as 'Alas, poor Yorick,' because of its use in a television advertisement, but not the story. A few of the older ones were also aware of the debate over the future of the Rose Theatre on the South Bank. Once out on the yard I explained the initial situation at Elsinore and how everyone fitted in. To reinforce the names, we then played the getting-to-know-you game (usually called Jack to Jill) of crossing the circle with your name – 'Horatio to Claudius', 'Claudius to Gravedigger', etc.

I now turned to the main subject of the first session, the Ghost, and to the opening scene on the battlements. For this I had decided to teach the children how to drill – marching in step, coming to a halt, turning left and right – so that they could enact the changing of the guard at Elsinore, with half the class as Francisco and half as Barnardo, much as they might see it today at Buckingham Palace or Windsor Castle. Every child also had to learn a fraction of the dialogue, which might be as short as 'He,' or as long as 'You come most carefully upon your hour,' as well as who spoke immediately before them. After a few rehearsals they performed the scene, word-perfect, from the first line to the entry of Horatio and Marcellus. In the second scene I entered in role as the Ghost. The class were scattered in pairs back-to-back over the playground, so that I could move through them one way and afterwards retrace my steps. As I passed by they had to reach out to try and touch me, without moving from the spot, and say any one of the bits of text I had taught them – 'Speak to me,' 'Tis here,' etc.

After break we moved into the hall for the introduction of Hamlet. I remained in role as the Ghost, clearly indicated by the character card round my neck, and chose one small boy to play Hamlet. His task was to follow as I beckoned him to follow me across the hall, while the rest of the class had to try and block his progress without touching him. The action was to be slow-motion and accompanied by 'I'll follow it' for Hamlet and 'You shall not go, my Lord' for the rest of the class. We tried the exercise twice through and they performed with well controlled enthusiasm and spoke as loud and clearly as they had done in the first scene. I then converted them into a collective Hamlet, while I remainded the Ghost, and explained that I wanted to talk to them (him) privately. They gathered around and I told the story of my murder. Taking a bit of a liberty with the text, I asked them if they were prepared to avenge it and swear on the sword (I carried a toy one) to do so. They became engrossed in this situation – several of the younger ones seemed even overawed by it – and raised heartfelt doubts: 'What will happen if I don't?' 'What if Claudius isn't guilty?' 'What if he kills me first?' 'How should I kill him?' 'Shall I kill the Queen too?' Eventually, however, they all swore on the sword.

The role-play finished at this point. As teacher I asked the class how they thought the story might develop, drawing their attention in particular to the characters called Players and Gravediggers. How might they come in? The class got very close to the truth on the first and narrowed the latter down to the burial of Hamlet, Claudius or Ophelia. This concluding discussion revealed that they already had a good grasp of the initial dramatic situation and the relationship between the characters.

Session 2   Hamlet and Ophelia

I began by filling in the background to the relationship between Hamlet and Ophelia – her subordination to her father, his assumption of an 'antic disposition' – before we moved out on to the yard for drama. Our first scene was to be a mime of Hamlet coming to Ophelia in her closet as described by her to her father in Act II Scene 1. We divided the class into Hamlets and Ophelias, some of whom were boys because of the imbalance in the sexes. The Hamlets then arranged their clothes in the disorderly manner described in the text whilst the Ophelias sat on chairs facing outwards towards their partners and sewing. As I read the text – 'My Lord, as I was sewing in my closet' – they performed the mime prompted by the text, afterwards repeating it with roles reversed.

The second scene was the nunnery scene. I had extracted, and slightly adapted, a passage of dialogue, centring on Ophelia's attempt to return Hamlet's gift of jewels and beginning 'Soft you now, the fair Ophelia.' This time the pairs stood opposite each other in two lines separated by a row of chairs. The Ophelias started the action, kneeling in prayer in front of their chairs. As in the battlements scene, each child had his or her own bit of dialogue to memorise. When one of the Ophelias said, 'There, my Lord,' all the Ophelias had to place their jewels on their chairs; and when the last Hamlet said, 'Get thee to a nunnery,' all the Hamlets had to turn to point to the convent which happened by great good fortune to stand next to the school. Finally I chose one Hamlet and stood him in the circle of the rest of the class as Ophelia. Each Ophelia had one word of a reduced version of her 'O what a noble mind' speech to say and, as the speech rippled round the circle, the solitary Hamlet turned with it.

On our return to the classroom after break, we set the class the task of writing a letter – the boys from Hamlet to Ophelia, the girls vice versa – taking as starting-point Hamlet's as read to Claudius and Gertrude by Polonius in Act II Scene 2. The class teacher had already prepared the form of the letter on the word processor. The boys' began 'To the most beautiful Ophelia' and finished 'thine evermore, Hamlet', while the girls' began 'My dear Lord Hamlet' and finished 'thine evermore, Ophelia'. The children's job was to supply the content in the light of what they knew so far. The letters they wrote were thoughtful, touching and occasionally bizarre. Here are a sample:

From Hamlet to Ophelia

I am writing to tell you why I am acting strangely. I am acting strangely because when I came back from germany my mum had married my uncle so soon after my fathers death and my father said that Claudius killed him with the strongest bottle of poison but I have to find out if he is telling the treuth.

I am sorry that I have been acting strange in the last few days. I can't marry you. I can't see you any more. There was a murder in our family but only one. The only thing I can think about is the death of my father.

I am sorry about the way I've been acting. It is because I've seen the ghost of my father. I know you think I might be lying but I'm not. The ghost told me that Claudius murdered him but I don't know if it is true or not but I have to find out. I am acting mad so he wont suspect me. I am going to have to kill him. DON'T TELL ANYONE.

Im sorry about the way things have been going me being stupid not sensible and undependant you being kind and reliable. Im sorry about the way Ive been acting the way I have but my mind is not set on love but as soon as I've sorted out a few things our love life will be settled. But after my fathers death Ive been strange Ive got to go my love.

From Ophelia to Hamlet
I am writing to say Why! are you acting so strangely. Don't you love me any more? My father said that he doesn't want me to have anything to do with you but I love you so much what can I do?

I am writing to tell you that my father wants me to give you back all the gifts that you sent me and all of the letters. I am puzzled by the way that you are acting and would you tell me why you are acting strangely.

Why have you been acting so strangely these passed few days. You come to me with your buttons undone your stockings down to your ankles your knees hitting each other Just what has happened don't you like me you will have to write me a letter sweet hamlet.

My father said I can't go on seeing you because it's the tradition you're too important for me because you're a prince and I'm only a Prime Minister's daughter. I wanted to know why you are acting so strangely. You will have to write to explain. I really wanted to marry you because I love you.

The effect of Hamlet's letters was to change the story. The boys who wrote them all assumed he would confide in Ophelia, which meant that, if Claudius found out, she would be in as dangerous a position as Hamlet. This change goes some way to explaining what might otherwise simply seem wrongheaded speculation about Ophelia's death in the next session. By the end of this session I think it is true to say that the children's imagination had been captivated by the story. Several had brought in family copies of the play or complete Shakespeares (up to this point only the teacher and I had texts). One pupil had also brought in a commercial pack on Shakespeare from which a model of the Globe Theatre was subsequently made. The attention of other teachers and parents had been engaged by the work too. Some of the latter (and it should be remembered that the school's catchment area is predominantly working class) jokingly complained that they were being nagged by their children as to how the story ended when they did not know.

Session 3   The dumb show; the death of Ophelia

On my arrival for this session one boy recited to me unsolicited the first four lines of Sonnet 18, 'Shall I compare thee to a summer's day?', which he had taken the trouble to learn at home. In preparation for the first half of the session, whose subject was to be the dumb show in Act III Scene 2, the children had made crowns for the Player King and Queen. Some had also brought in gowns and imitation bottles of poison. We then divided the class into threes and gave each trio a simplified version of the dumb show's scenario. Out on the yard the children dispersed to rehearse. When they were ready, we collected them together for a grand performance for which the class teacher and I were in role as Gertrude and Claudius. They knew their objective was to make me react in such a way as to reveal my guilt. After the last group had performed, I rose angrily to my feet, saying I had had enough and demanding to know who had written these plays and why they were all the same. I then stormed off into the nearby bushes. To my astonishment virtually the whole class pursued me, shouting and bent on a lynching. This really was spontaneous theatre. After they had settled down I continued with the narrative, using individual children to dramatise events, up to and including the murder of Polonius. When it came to the moment where Hamlet stood poised to strike down his uncle at prayer, I asked the class what the boy playing the part should do. Most favoured a swift execution. A few, however, dissented – 'two wrongs don't make a right', 'he's showing he's sorry by praying'.

After break we returned to the classroom for group and plenary discussion of Millais's painting of Ophelia in the brook.

This work has already been described in Chapter 4. You will remember that it concluded with my reading of Gertrude's 'There is a willow grows aslant the brook'. We then asked the class to write down their reactions to Ophelia's death. Most chose to write poems. The older children tended to rely on Gertrude for inspiration, the younger ones on Millais. Here are a sample:

I am Ophelia as sweet as can be.
I love Lord Hamlet of Denmark.
I pick crowflowers, nettles, daisies and long purples,
To give to a peasant with rags on her feet
And a bag for a skirt to keep her warm from drizzle
And rain lashing down.
The river rises so deep.
When my death comes I'll sing to the deep.
When I picked my flowers,
How mad I felt,
I'll sink to the bottom with all my sad dreams.

(Paul)

Ophelia was lonely because she only had a brother,
She never had a father not even a mother.
She picked some flowers from the tree tops,
Then she slipped and down she drops.
There she sang with her hands in the air,
She didn't save herself because she didn't care.

(Jenny)

Picking flowers, sweet as can be,
The little robin whistling with glee.
Climbing high, nearly reaching the sky.
Suddenly slipping,
Falling into the brook.
Floating slowly, singing still.
There'll be a tomorrow, if you learn to swim.
Singing softly, down, down under the water,
There to drown.

(Joanne)

Far in the wood
Ophelia the most beautiful lady
Lies in the river
Sad

With flowers all over her
Down in the water
Floating
With her hair spread out like snakes.
(Michael)

Session 4   Hamlet and the Gravedigger; the fencing match; Judgment Day

We began the final session in the classroom with the graveyard scene. In preparation for it I had written up on the board a passage of slightly adapted dialogue between Hamlet and the Gravedigger, starting from Hamlet's 'Whose grave's this?' and finishing with the Gravedigger's 'but rest her soul she's dead', whose ghoulish wit we thought the class would appreciate, as indeed they did. After I had explained the background to the scene, and how 'poor Yorick' of television advert fame came into it, the class divided into pairs of Hamlets and Gravediggers. We then worked on the dialogue chorally before I asked them to see if they could memorise it. They all made a brave attempt, but no pair were word-perfect when their turn came to perform.

For the final scene of the play the class were rearranged into groups of five with one six – Claudius, Gertrude, Hamlet, Laertes, Horatio/Osric. After I had outlined the plan concocted by Claudius and Laertes for Hamlet's murder, each group was given, as for the dumb show, a simplified scenario of the action plus, in this case, bits of dialogue to remember – 'A hit, a very palpable hit,' 'I am poisoned,' 'The king's to blame,' etc. For the final performance, which took place on the lawn behind the convent in hot sunlight, the groups had access to basic props and costumes – crowns and gowns, swords, a drum and a goblet. Before they went off to rehearse, I emphasised that the sword fight had to be slow-motion and under control. In the event this aspect proved no problem; it was remembering the precise sequence of events, and the dialogue, which caused the difficulties, so during the performance I acted as narrator/prompter.

After break, back in the classroom, we did a final role-play called the Day of Judgment. Each child had to choose to become one of the dead characters, i.e. for the boys Hamlet, Claudius, Polonius or Laertes, and for the girls Ophelia or Gertrude. Each collective character was then interrogated in turn by the rest of the class as a collective St Peter whose responsibility was to decide whether he or she should go to heaven or hell. To me this was simply an amusing application of the 'hot-seating' technique. To the children, Catholics for whom heaven and hell were real destinations, it was serious stuff. They identified totally with the situation and asked some penetrating questions (of Gertrude, for example, 'Who came first, your son or Claudius?') – so much so that we ran out of time and the exercise was left incomplete.

Aftermath

After it was all over the class teacher assembled a wall display on the *Hamlet* topic. It consisted of the photographs she had taken, the materials and props we had used and the children's art and written work. Included in the latter was the outcome of a small project on Ophelia's flowers which two of the older girls had undertaken on their own initiative. The exhibition provided another focus for comment and discussion by teachers and parents on the open days later in the summer. Several parents commented on how much the children had enjoyed themselves and on how keen they had been to find out more about Shakespeare. One said her son had asked her what Shakespeare she had done at school. When she said, '*Macbeth*,' he replied, 'Well, I'm doing *Hamlet*.'

In addition, as a kind of evaluation exercise, I interviewed all the class in twos and threes to see what they had liked and disliked. An excerpt from these taped discussions has already been used in Chapter 4 to illustrate how teacher–pupil dialogue can escape from the original aim behind it into a life of its own. In general the interviews fully confirmed the impression of the topic's popularity with the class. When asked what they had liked so much, some children simply said, 'I liked it all.' 'There was nothing we couldn't be pleased about,' replied one boy, 'because we did something new every day.' Those who were more specific mostly mentioned 'the little plays we done' – 'the one where we were having a sword fight and the one where the poisoner killed the king' – but all the activities were mentioned by at least one child – 'on the battlements', 'when Hamlet was walking down to the Ghost and all the people tried to stop him', 'when we swore to revenge', 'when we were all sitting on Miss's desk and we were asking to see if they'd go to heaven or hell'. There were no substantive criticisms. Although several children admitted they had found learning their lines difficult because of the 'old English', they were all adamant that *Hamlet* was a good story – 'a bit sad and a bit happy', as one girl put it – and perfectly suitable for children of their age. The interviews also confirmed that many children had taken their enthusiasm home with them. 'My dad said, "very good," my mum said "very good," too', 'My mum said it was very good but I'm too young to act in plays,' 'I told my mum what I thought was going to happen and about the deaths and about my part.'

At the end of the summer term, when the class teacher came to dismantle the *Hamlet* exhibition, she decided to preserve as much of it as she could in a scrapbook. Whenever I run a workshop for teachers on active approaches to Shakespeare, I always take it with me to forestall remarks of the 'It couldn't be done in my school' ilk. If *Hamlet* can be taught successfully to a mixed ability class of 7–10 year olds in a working class area of Liverpool, it can be taught successfully to any class anywhere.

FURTHER READING

The two books on drama teaching which considerably influenced my early practice (referred to on p. 178) are *Drama Guidelines* by Cecily O'Neill *et al.* and *Learning through Drama* by Lynn McGregor *et al.*. Otherwise I have learned most from books written by theatre practitioners or intended for actors. Four I would particularly recommend are: Stanislavski *An Actor Prepares*, Peter Brook *The Empty Space*, Keith Johnstone *Impro* and Clive Barker *Theatre Games*. The one indispensable book for teaching Shakespeare is Cicely Berry's *The Actor and his Text*. Another excellent source of ideas is the journal *Shakespeare and Schools*, which is available from Rex Gibson at the Institute of Education, Cambridge, as is his compilation *Secondary School Shakespeare*. Both include up-to-date reading lists. If you are particularly interested in teaching *Hamlet*, you will find a stimulating account of a completely different approach from mine with secondary pupils in an article by Sarah Marshall, 'Behind the scenes', in the drama teaching journal *2D*.

Chapter 9

Teaching linguistic awareness

> To read the grammar alone by itself is tedious for the master, hard for the scholar, cold and uncomfortable for them both.
>
> (Roger Ascham, *The Scholemaster*, 1570)

> 'A horse is a quadruped,' [said Squeers], 'and quadruped's Latin for beast, as everybody that's gone through the grammar knows, or else where's the use of having grammars at all?' 'Where, indeed!' said Nicholas, abstractedly.
>
> (Charles Dickens, *Nicholas Nickleby*, 1838–9)

KNOWLEDGE ABOUT LANGUAGE

I have left to the last the most difficult of all issues in the English curriculum – what, if anything, pupils should be taught about language, at what age and how. As with other issues dealt with in this book, the Newbolt report laid the basis of what seems to me the position with the most to recommend it. Noting that hostility to 'traditional grammar' (especially to the imposition 'upon English of the forms of Latin' and the unwarranted prescriptions and proscriptions arising therefrom) had led 'many teachers to throw grammar entirely overboard', it insisted that it was 'highly desirable' for children to 'obtain some kind of general introduction to linguistic study' and that 'grammar of some kind' had to form 'the essential groundwork' of such study. This grammar, it argued, should be 'pure' (i.e. universal and therefore applicable across the range of languages taught at school) and 'functional' (i.e. related to pupils' own speech and language use). The report was aware that there were unresolved problems over precisely what to teach, when to start and whether there should be set lessons or a more indirect approach, but suggested that the higher elementary (i.e. upper junior and lower secondary) classes might be the best time to begin and that phonetics, the parts of speech and sentence analysis might constitute the basic content.

Notwithstanding the strength of the report's argument, fifty years later the teaching of grammar had disappeared almost without trace from most secondary schools. This was not just because of the increasing hostility among my generation of English teachers to what John Dixon, in *Growth through English*, called the 'folly' of imposing 'linguistic bodies of knowledge on pupils', but also because of the dramatic decline in the teaching of Latin and Greek and the shift in the teaching of modern languages from the grammar–translation–literature approach I experienced at school to one emphasising everyday oral communication and use. A further significant factor was the failure of modern linguistics to produce grammar books or other materials for school use which satisfied the Newbolt report's criteria in being both 'pure' and 'functional'. 'Our teachers', wrote Randolph Quirk in 1959, 'live in a no man's land between the discredited old grammar and the unwritten new.'

Then in 1971 came *Language in Use* (Doughty *et al.*), the one major development in teaching about language during my career as an English teacher and the starting-point of most subsequent innovations under the flag of 'teaching language awareness'. Rejecting a narrow 'grammar' approach based on formal analysis of words and sentences and on knowledge of technical vocabulary (though it does, in fact, assume familiarity with parts of speech and other basic terms), it reverted to the wider understanding of 'grammar' as the systematic study of language that prevailed in classical times and explored the possibilities of a 'functional' approach, in which the emphasis fell on 'how we use language to live' – on real utterances in everyday situations. Like the supporters of 'traditional grammar', the authors claimed, without, however, supplying evidence, that there was a link between its two main objectives of developing linguistic awareness and linguistic competence.

The Bullock report of 1975 had surprisingly little to say about grammar beyond the dictum, 'Explicit instruction out of context is in our view of little value,' which has since become an article of faith for the modern orthodoxy. The Kingman report of 1988 also contributed less than might have been expected, mainly as a result of having been given the very peculiar brief of recommending a model of the English language for teacher training purposes and indicating how much of this model might be made explicit to pupils. A more curious instance of putting the cart before the horse could scarcely be imagined. Before you can decide what teachers need to know, you have first to decide what pupils need to be taught, not the other way round. The brief was also remiss in limiting the committee's deliberations to a model of the English language when what secondary schools at least require is a model which is equally applicable to the other languages taught in school.

Nevertheless the Kingman model and the rest of the report do represent a useful starting-point for English teachers committed to teaching something about language to their pupils. Its overall position is a restatement of that of the Newbolt report. Latinate grammar is rejected but not 'conscious knowledge of the structure and working of the language' – 'It is just as important to teach about . . . the structure of English as about the structure of the atom.' The justification given is that this is worthwhile knowledge in itself and can facilitate and sharpen the discussion of literature and pupils' writing. The two reports also resemble one another in the importance attached to building on pupils' natural facility for, and curiosity about, language, so that, to use the terms of Kingman, 'implicit' awareness and 'explicit' knowledge can reinforce each other. This position was further restated and developed the following year by the Cox report, which, being unhampered by the limitations of the Kingman committee's brief, was able both to discard the monolingual bias and to direct more attention to matters of curriculum implementation. To the two reasons given by Kingman for teaching about language it adds a third – that it assists foreign language teaching, including the teaching of English as a foreign language – and also notes the extra need and potential for this kind of work in bilingual and multilingual situations.

So far as practice is concerned, Cox follows Bullock in arguing that such grammar as is taught should not be 'decontextualised' but integrated into discussions of pupils' writing and reading, and Kingman in arguing that it should be extended beyond its traditional confines of word and sentence to include two developing fields in modern linguistics, discourse and text analysis, as well as the wider area of language study mapped out by *Language in Use*. The Cox report clearly recognises that the two fundamental issues confronting teachers are what technical concepts and terms to teach pupils and how to teach them but falls disappointingly short of outlining anything that could be called a syllabus. Its statements of attainment and programmes of study do, however, appear to endorse the Newbolt report's view that the last year of primary or first year of secondary school might be the best time to start. Its recommendations for topics to study – language variety, language in literature and the history of language – are in line with the views of the modern orthodoxy, while its preferred methodology draws on the progressivist repertoire of active and inductive approaches.

The refusal of the Conservative government to publish the LINC project's materials in 1991 suggested that we are no closer than we were seventy years ago to resolving the problem of what to teach about language in school. Teachers appear trapped in the middle of a fierce ideological dispute between right-wing educationalists who would like to see a return to the 'traditional grammar' teaching rejected by the Newbolt report and left-wing sociolinguists who are hostile to any kind of grammar teaching and would like schools to take up issues such as language and power. Among English teachers, however, it is possible, I think, to discern a core of agreement at the centre of the debate, with a wider area of disagreement at the periphery and over details of practice. Most English teachers now accept that it is quite wrong for pupils to be deprived of necessary linguistic knowledge at school, as so many were in the 1970s and 1980s. It is also widely accepted that necessary linguistic knowledge should include, but not be limited to, grammar (in the narrower sense of the study of syntax and inflexion) and that its focus should, so far as possible, be comparative and multilingual rather than anglocentric, and multidialectal rather than exclusively on standard English.

Beyond this core of agreement, there persists considerable disagreement over content and method – over what to teach (how much grammar, for example), who to teach it to and when (all pupils in the first year of secondary school – year 7 – or only older and abler pupils), and how to teach it (directly through a specific course or indirectly through the context of writing or literature; and through explanatory or experiential approaches). My own view is that it should be firmly based on those traditional concepts and terms (such as the classical parts of speech) which remain fundamental to modern linguistics and pay some heed to phonology, semantics and wider aspects of language use (but relatively little to the academically fashionable, but essentially peripheral, pursuits of discourse and text analysis). I am well aware, however, from my own experience, that some traditional terms and concepts may prove beyond the capacity of many pupils. This is not an argument for not teaching them to anyone, as under one perverted interpretation of egalitarianism to be found in the English departments of some comprehensive schools using exclusively mixed ability teaching. It is an argument for trying to distinguish carefully between what is within the capacity of all, what is within the capacity only of some (like understanding the structure of the atom, to pick up the Kingman report's analogy) and what is probably best left for older pupils specialising in English or languages.

So far as methodology is concerned I strongly favour specific courses in knowledge about language, prepared and taught by an interdisciplinary team of teachers (representing English, the classical languages and whichever modern languages are taught in the school), and making use of a mixture of explanatory and experiential approaches. The orthodoxy's hostility to 'decontextualised' lessons is no more than doctrine for which I have yet to see a cogent justification and could theoretically result in thirty different lessons in a class with that number of pupils. Do lessons on the structure of the atom need to be 'contextualised'? Of course not. It is, like the structure of language, worthwhile knowledge, without which pupils' understanding of life is severely restricted. In the case of the structure of language, lack of such knowledge is likely, as the Newbolt, Kingman and Cox reports all in different ways point out, to limit both their competence in their native tongue and their ability to master the tongues of others. In the next section I want to attempt what all three reports to varying degrees shy away from – the outline of a possible syllabus for pupils – and, in the final one, to describe what happened when the class teacher and I taught a specific course in language awareness to her mixed ability group of thirty-six top juniors at the Liverpool primary school in the spring term of 1990.

THE OUTLINE OF A SYLLABUS

In his introductory book on linguistics John Lyons draws a useful distinction between microlinguistics and macrolinguistics. Microlinguistics refers to the study of the structure of language or languages as represented by the conventional subdivisions of grammar, phonology and semantics, whereas macrolinguistics covers psycholinguistics, sociolinguistics, historical linguistics and everything else pertaining to language and its use. I propose to avail myself of this distinction in outlining a possible school syllabus. The outline constitutes a summary of the concepts, terms and other aspects of linguistic content which I would expect pupils who had completed GCE A Level in English, classical or modern languages to be familiar with. Some of this content is certainly within the capacity of, and necessary for, both younger and less able pupils too, though personally I do not yet feel confident enough, despite many years of trial and error, to state categorically which content is and which is not. There is a general feeling, however, to which I subscribe to a degree, that work with younger classes across the ability range should concentrate on macrolinguistics, while much of microlinguistics is better reserved for older and abler groups.

Microlinguistics

Phonology

This is not normally thought of as a suitable topic for school pupils. However, I follow the Newbolt report in taking the opposite view. It seems sensible to build on the phonic knowledge which pupils have acquired in learning to read and which can assist them with spelling. I would expect them to be familiar enough with a simplified version of the International Phonetic Alphabet to understand how a word they do not know is to be pronounced by looking at the phonetic transcription in a good dictionary. I would also expect them to understand the meaning of the following phonological features: (i) Segmental – consonant, vowel, diphthong, syllable; (ii) Suprasegmental – intonation, stress. It is particularly important that pupils should understand the difference between consonant, vowel, diphthong and syllable as sound and as symbol.

Grammar

Some authors have dispensed with the term 'grammar' because of confusions in its use and rely instead on the terms used for its subdivisions, 'syntax' and 'morphology' (or what used to be called 'inflexion'). There is something to be said for following their example. However, I have persevered with 'grammar' because of its high profile in popular use.

Syntax Pupils need to be able to classify sentences into types, to analyse them into constituent elements and to identify parts of speech or 'word classes' (as they are often called nowadays). There is some disagreement about how sentences are best analysed and about the most suitable terminology to use. As far as English and most of the other languages pupils are likely to encounter are concerned, the points to stress are: that the structure of sentences (and of clauses and phrases) is hierarchical, which is why tree diagrams are often used to represent them; that the possible patterns into which the elements and words in a sentence can be organised are limited; and that the pattern or order selected decisively affects the meaning.

In 'traditional grammar' there were two main forms of sentence analysis, parsing and clause analysis, which were not without value but are rarely, if ever, encountered in today's classrooms. In modern linguistics there are also two, 'structural' and 'relational' analysis, which continue to depend on the terms and concepts of 'traditional grammar'. Both the latter can be illustrated through an example of what is often described as the most fundamental kind of English sentence (one that, in technical terms, is simple, active and declarative) – 'That woman in the blue hat has insulted the Lord Mayor'. Pupils can readily see that this consists of three elements – in technical terms, a noun phrase ('That woman in the blue hat') plus a verb phrase ('has insulted') plus a noun phrase ('the Lord Mayor'). In 'structural' analysis this can be represented as NP + VP + NP. Pupils can also readily see that this structure remains the same if the sentence is reduced to headline form – 'Woman insulted Mayor' – or considerably expanded ('That awful woman in the hideous blue hat, who used to live next to my mother, has insulted the nicest Lord Mayor any town could wish for') and that it therefore makes sense to refer to 'woman', 'insulted' and 'Mayor' as the 'head' of their respective phrases.

'Relational' sentence analysis attempts to go beyond the identification of constituent elements and characterise the relationship between them. In many simple, active, declarative

English sentences, as in this one, someone or something (a subject) does something (a verb) to someone or something else (a direct object), which is why it is represented as S + V + DO. The same pattern is discernible in many languages. Indeed, it is sometimes claimed that the division between subject and predicate (i.e. the rest of the sentence) is a feature of all languages. In some, however, the order of elements is different. In Welsh the verb comes first and in certain German subordinate clauses it comes last, while in Latin the order of words and elements is largely of stylistic significance only. The fact that the concept of 'verb' occurs in both structural and relational analysis is a possible source of confusion. However, although several alternative terms (e.g. 'predicator') have been suggested, none is generally accepted. A fourth concept which is widely used in relational analysis is that of the 'adjunct', which refers to the words, phrases and clauses 'modifying' (to use traditional terminology) the verb or sentence. For example, if the sentence 'That awful woman . . .' concluded with the clause 'despite the fact that he twice saved her life', this would be classified as an adjunct.

With regard to parts of speech, or 'word classes', they remain central to modern linguistic analysis as well as to general knowledge (being still used by the latest edition of the *Oxford English Dictionary*, for example), despite many attempts to reconceptualise and relabel them, and to increase or decrease their number, over the centuries. An important distinction for pupils to grasp is between those whose main contribution is to the 'content' of the sentence (nouns, pronouns, verbs, adjectives and adverbs) and those whose main contribution is to its 'form' or 'structure' (conjunctions, prepositions, articles).

My outline of necessary syntactical knowledge and terminology is as follows:

1   Sentence classification
   (a)   Simple, compound (co-ordination), complex (subordination).
   (b)   Declarative (statements), interrogative (questions), imperative (commands), exclamative (exclamations).
   (c)   Active, passive; transitive, intransitive; affirmative, negative.

2 Sentence analysis
   (a) Subject, predicate, direct and indirect object, complement, apposition, adjunct.
   (b) Clause, phrase (head, determiner, pre- and post-modification).

3 Word classes
   (a) Noun – proper, common; countable, uncountable; compound, collective.
   (b) Pronoun – personal, reflexive, possessive, relative, interrogative, demonstrative.
   (c) Verb – main, auxiliary, modal; stative, dynamic; regular; irregular; finite, non-finite (infinitive, present and past participle); phrasal and prepositional.
   (d) Adjective – attributive, predicative; comparative, superlative.
   (e) Adverb – of time, place, manner, etc.
   (f) Preposition.
   (g) Conjunction.
   (h) Article – definite and indefinite.

Morphology   The form of words is of relatively little importance in English grammar, there being very few inflexions (e.g. love, loves, loved, loving), though there are many derivations (e.g. unloved, beloved, loveless, loveable, lover). It is, however, of considerable importance in other languages – Latin, classical Greek and German, for instance – which is why I have included concepts important to them but not to English, such as case and gender, below:

1 Concord – noun and adjective, noun and pronoun, noun and verb; first, second, third person; singular, plural.
2 Gender – masculine, feminine, neuter.
3 Case – nominative, accusative, genitive, dative, etc.
4 Tense – present, past, future, etc.
5 Aspect – perfect, continuous.
6 Mood – indicative, subjunctive, imperative.
7 Word stem, syllable, prefix, suffix.

Semantics

Semantics is an expanding area in modern linguistics, having previously been rather neglected in favour of grammar and phonology. It is also a difficult area for school pupils because of the philosophical problems associated with meaning. Two aspects, however, have always been thought suitable for them, dictionary work and thesaurus work, to which I would add a third, translation.

In addition, there is something to be said for attempting work on different kinds of meaning. Lexical meaning (the meaning of words) needs to be differentiated from grammatical meaning, prosodic meaning and utterance (or pragmatic) meaning. If we compare the two sentences 'the boy loves the girl' and 'the girl loves the boy', we can say that the lexical meaning is the same (because the words are the same) but the grammatical meaning quite different (because in the first case 'the boy' is the subject and 'the girl' the object, whereas in the second case it is the other way round). An illustration of prosodic meaning would be the use of an ironic or sarcastic tone to convert the meaning of a sentence like 'That was nice of you' into its opposite. Utterance meaning involves a knowledge of the context for the sentence to be understood. While I was assessing students on teaching practice in the spring term 1988, one of them complained that some of the fourth year boys were 'very sexist'. When I asked what she meant, she gave the following illustration. She had gone into the classroom at the beginning of a lesson and said, 'It's terribly hot in here.' Syntactically this is a statement but in the context was clearly intended as a request that someone should open a window or turn down the heating. One of the boys, recognising the utterance meaning but twisting it to suit his own ends, shouted out, 'Take your top off then, Miss!'

My list of necessary semantic knowledge is as follows:

1   Dictionary work – literal and figurative meaning; denotation, connotation; multiple meaning (homonym e.g. 'bank' meaning area of ground, financial institution or row); homophone (e.g. 'flour', 'flower'); homograph (e.g. 'lead' as noun and verb); collocation (e.g. 'pretty' tends to be applied to females, 'handsome' to males); neologism, archaism; euphemism; malapropism; etymology.
2   Thesaurus work – synonym, antonym; classification and categorisation (e.g. names of family relationships; division of the colour spectrum; animal, vegetable and mineral; male, female and young in animals; the relationship between 'flower' and 'primrose').

3 Other reference work – proper names of people and places; proverbs, idioms; figures of speech (synecdoche, metonymy, etc.).

4 Translation – There are no specific terms or concepts to acquire but many interesting avenues to explore once pupils are sufficiently acquainted with at least one other language. The essential point for them to grasp is that no two languages are completely isomorphic. Even at an elementary level there are topics to investigate. Consider, for example, 'yes' and 'no'. In French and German pupils soon learn that there are two words for 'yes' – *oui* and *si*, *ja* and *doch*, respectively – and that they have to know when to use which. In Latin and Swahili, on the other hand, there are no strict equivalents for either 'yes' or 'no', agreement and disagreement being expressed in other ways. Pupils will also soon come across further distinctions and usages in other European languages which do not exist in English – for example, responses to, or anticipations of, 'thank you' such as the Italian *prego* and German *bitte*, or the distinction between formal and informal 'you', such as French *tu* and *vous*, or between 'know' a fact and 'know' a person, such as the German *wissen* and *kennen*.

At more advanced levels pupils can investigate the famous case of how different languages divide up the colour spectrum or examine literary translation into and out of English. Younger pupils, with little or no knowledge of a foreign language, could be asked to translate between dialects and registers of their mother tongue. A good example would be the translation of Burns's 'To a Mouse' into standard English, which the fourth year class at the Knowsley school undertook as part of their work on *Of Mice and Men* (referred to in Chapters 3 and 7).

Macrolinguistics

Macrolinguistics is a somewhat amorphous field of study. All I can do here is indicate some of the areas which other teachers and I have found interesting and productive in terms of developing linguistics awareness:

1 Historical linguistics – the history of English; language families (Indo-European).

2 Psycholinguistics – children's acquisition of language (from

cooing and babbling through two and three word sentences to 'good' mistakes such as 'goed' for 'went').

3 Sociolinguistics – different Englishes (American, Australian, etc.); standard and non-standard English; accent, Received Pronunciation; dialect, idiolect, sociolect, pidgin, creole; style (formal and informal, slang); register (the language of science, law, medicine), jargon; linguistic variation according to age, ethnic background and gender; mode (speaking and writing).

4 Comparative linguistics – other alphabets (e.g. Greek and Runic) and writing systems (e.g. Chinese characters); analytic (e.g. English), synthetic (e.g. Latin) and agglutinative (e.g. Swahili) languages; artificial languages (Esperanto).

5 Semiotics – other written codes (Braille, Morse, shorthand, etc.); visual communication (sign language, semaphore, street and road signs, etc.); animal communication.

Set out in this way, my syllabus may seem intimidating and likely to prove, in Roger Ascham's words, 'tedious . . . hard . . . cold and uncomfortable'. However, although there can be little doubt that any serious attempt at increasing pupils' knowledge of language will involve considerable amounts of presentation and explication on the part of the teacher, which many pupils may find difficult, lessons can still be made interesting. There will always be plenty of room, and opportunities, for pupils to carry out research, be creative and enjoy themselves. At the most obvious level several popular word games can contribute to enhancing both linguistic awareness and competence – for example, the dictionary game (*Call my Bluff* on television), charades (*Give us a Clue* on television), the spelling game usually known as Ghosts, the adverb game often played in drama and the adjective game traditionally known as The Minister's Cat.

For more substantial work even 10 and 11 year olds, as I shall attempt to show in the next section, can learn a good deal from investigating such matters as the speech of young children and the main features of the local dialect. For example, many of the telegraphic two-word utterances of young children, such as 'Dada gone,' follow the pattern S + V and many of the three-word ones, such as 'Dada kick ball,' the pattern S + V + DO. These patterns can also, of course, be observed in non-standard usage. 'Me mum never done nothing' is as much S + V + DO as 'My mother didn't do anything' (although some grammarians would want to classify 'never' and 'n't' as adjuncts).

Whilst favouring specific courses in language awareness for communicating the principal concepts and terminology, I also recognise that pupils' own writing and literature can fulfil valuable supplementary roles. For instance, the ideal time for teaching pupils about complex sentences is the final years of primary and early years of secondary school, precisely because it is during this period that their writing is starting to develop beyond the simple sentence into experiments with subordination and newly discovered conjunctions and ways of linking clauses. Sometimes they get into a mess, producing truncated sentences, never-ending sentences and examples of what my English teacher used to call 'anacoluthon' – sentences whose elements do not cohere properly. In my experience discussion of pupils' writing at this stage is greatly assisted if they know about clauses and subordination and can analyse sentences into their component parts.

I have already given several examples of how literature can contribute to developing linguistic awareness – non-standard English in *Huckleberry Finn* and *Of Mice and Men*; scansion and figures of speech in poetry; proverbs in Graham Greene's 'I Spy'. To support this point the Kingman report pulls some very old chestnuts out of the fire, almost as though some member of the committee had been the first to notice them, whereas at least three – 'making the green one red' (from *Macbeth* – is 'one' a noun or an adjective?), the non-finite sentences with which *Bleak House* opens and the syntactic complexity of the octave in Milton's sonnet on his blindness – were brought to my attention by my English teacher in the 1950s. One other old chestnut in the English teacher's repertoire – Lewis Carroll's 'Jabberwocky' – is worth dwelling on for a moment, because it really can help pupils struggling with grammar and because students in training (in my experience, at least), while aware of its potential for developing linguistic awareness, are often unsure how it might best be taught.

The first point to make is that 'Jabberwocky' should be taught in its context – *Through the Looking-Glass*. Otherwise pupils will be deprived of Carroll's advice on the pronunciation of the nonsense words in the first and last verse, Humpty Dumpty's explanation of them and Alice's initial reaction to the poem ('It seems very pretty . . . but it's rather *hard* to understand. . . . However, *somebody* killed *something*: that's clear, at any rate!'). When I last taught the poem, in the summer of 1991, to the top juniors at the Liverpool primary school as part of the Key Stage 2 Historical Study Unit on Victorian Britain, I began by revising certain parts of speech with them (noun, verb, adjective, adverb and exclamation) and ensuring that they understood the meaning of syllable and syllable stress. They then had in pairs to circle the nonsense words and allocate each a part of speech, in order to underline the point that one of the reasons why Alice was able to make some sense of the poem is that the syntax and morphology observe the rules of standard English. This activity threw up several predictable problems. The pupils were sometimes unsure about which were nonsense words and which were not, partly because they were unfamiliar with words like 'shun' and 'sought' and partly because three of those which were nonsense when Carroll wrote the poem – 'burbled', 'galumphing' and 'chortled' – no longer are. Some of them also had difficulty allocating parts of speech. Are 'whiffling' and 'galumphing', for example, best thought of as verbs, adverbs or adjectives?

The pupils' final task was to rewrite the poem, replacing the words Carroll had invented with ones that actually exist. Their replacements had to fit in grammatically (i.e. be the same part of speech) and metrically (i.e. have the same number of syllables and the same pattern of syllable stress). They were allowed to retain 'burbled', 'galumphing' and 'chortled', and the proper nouns if they wished, and free to preserve or ignore rhyme and to strike their own balance between sense and nonsense. This was undoubtedly a major undertaking for many of the class. Half a dozen rose well to the challenge. This is Laura's poem:

The Dragon Lord
Twas raining and the angry clouds
Did rumble and grumble in the sky.
All frightened were the animals,
And the wind howled away.

Beware the Dragon Lord my son!
The jaws that bite, the claws that catch!
Beware the swooping bird and shun
The snatching dinosaur!

He took his trusty sword in hand:
Long time the dreadful foe he sought.
So rested he by the lilac tree
And stood awhile in thought.

And as in troubled thought he stood,
The Dragon Lord, with eyes of flame,
Came trudging through the greenish wood,
And burbled as it came.

One, two! One, two! And through and through
The trusty blade went clipper-clap!
He left it dead, and with its head
He went galumphing back.

'And hast thou slain the Dragon Lord?
Come to my arms, my lovely boy!
O joyful day! Hoorah! Hooray!'
He chortled in his joy.

'Twas raining and the angry clouds
Did rumble and grumble in the sky.
All frightened were the animals,
And the wind howled away.

The authors whose work is most fruitful for language awareness purposes are: earlier writers whose use of English antedated standardisation; those who write or wrote in non-standard dialect; and those who take or took a particular interest in language and whose use of it is especially creative. In the first category I would single out Chaucer, Shakespeare and the Authorised Version of the Bible; in the second Burns and Clare; and in the third Gerard Manley Hopkins and Dylan Thomas, who stretched grammatical and semantic rules almost to breaking-point.

Above all, I would recommend Shakespeare for the sheer exuberance and versatility of his language use. There is in his plays what Moth in *Love's Labours Lost* calls 'a great feast of languages'. Besides countless variations of Elizabethan prose and verse, and every conceivable kind of image, figure of speech and word-play, there is French in *Henry V*, Welsh in *Henry IV Part 1*, a mixture of English, Latin, French and Italian in the interchanges between Holofernes and Don Armado in *Love's Labours Lost* and an invented nonsense language in *All's Well that Ends Well*, to say nothing of the myriad words and expressions which Shakespeare coined and have passed into the national culture.

A LINGUISTIC AWARENESS COURSE FOR 10 AND 11 YEAR OLDS

In the spring term of 1990 one of the teachers at the Liverpool primary school and I taught a course in linguistic awareness to her mixed ability class of thirty-six top juniors, which I have already drawn on in Chapters 4 and 6. As originally conceived, it consisted of sixteen twice-weekly, half-morning sessions over a period of eight weeks. However, because of a combination of practical difficulties, only twelve were actually taught. The course was based on the Cox report's statements of attainment for levels 5 and 6 and programme of study for Key Stage 2. Its main theme, language variation, was also derived from the report, as were the principles of starting from pupils' implicit awareness and making full use of creative and investigative approaches. The course was essentially macrolinguistic in orientation and was presented to the pupils as preparation for work in English and other languages in secondary school.

Week 1 Individual variation

Session 1 My name   The pupils were asked to identify all the variations on their name, from what appeared on their birth certificates to nicknames, as well as the circumstances in which each was used. After comparing findings, they had to devise a way of presenting them, visually, verbally or through a mixture of media, to the rest of the class. Rosemary Gorry had easily the most variations – ranging from Rosemarie through Rose and Rosey to Mosemary, Robeymary, Rozzy Gozzy and Gozzy Spots. She also noted that what she was called depended not just on the speaker but on the speaker's mood and intentions towards her (wanting to borrow something, for example). She presented her findings in a colourful picture. Others used cartoons, diagrams and word searches. As a research task pupils had to find out the meaning and origin of their first and surnames. All managed to do this in the case of their Christian names (it is a Catholic school, remember) but not their surnames.

Session 2 Idiolect   The children's attention was drawn to the fact that we all have a way of talking which is unique to ourselves – our own speech mannerisms, pet sayings and catch phrases.

They were then asked to jot down the favourite expressions of friends, relatives, teachers and whoever else they wished and again to think of an interesting way of presenting one or all of them. Many took up the suggestion of devising a play scene around the pet saying of someone in the school which the rest of the class had to try and identify. Adele listed the following sayings of classmates, relatives and teachers:

Nana: Have a nice day.
Adele: It was all right.
Grandad: What did you come?
Kirsty: Hiya! Hiya!
Mark: You're not playing.
Christine: So! So! So! So! So!
Peter: No I won't go out with her.
Mrs D.: Stop wandering away.
Rosey: I'm better than you.
Philip: Do you want a ruler game?
Kerri: Hi, kidder.
Mr T.: Hi, love.
Mr H.: Only my best will do.
Mrs H.: Motor mouth.

Week 2 Variation by sex and age

Session 3 Girls' talk and boys' talk   The class were asked if they had noticed any differences in the way girls and boys talked and what they talked about. The girls were quick to say that the boys talked 'rougher' and 'more Scouse', and the boys that the girls talked 'posher, like the Queen'. In small groups, limited to their own sex, they then had to list the topics typical of the conversations of the opposite sex and their own, and concoct a play scene between members of the former on one of their favoured topics. Joanne was given the job of collating, and drawing conclusions from, all the lists. These revealed considerable agreement between the sexes on the main differences. All groups agreed that boys tended to talk about football, films and cars and that girls tended to talk about pop music, television programmes, boys, netball and fashion, although girls surprisingly failed to note that boys liked discussing fighting and girlfriends, while boys greatly exaggerated the extent of girls' interest in babies and marriage.

Below are two girls' version of a typical conversation between boys and two boys' version of a typical conversation between girls:

Andrew: Wow, look at that Porsche
Peter: My uncle's got one of them.
Andrew: So? My uncle's got a Lamborghini.
Peter: My dad's getting a Roller.
Andrew: So what?
Peter: Wow, look at that.
Dawn and
Natasha: Will you two shut up?

Adele: Clare, what do you think I would look like with a perm?
Clare: Um, you'd suit it.
Adele: Come on, be honest.
Clare: I'm being honest.
Adele: I'm getting one anyway.
Clare: So!
Adele: I don't sew, I knit.
Clare: Oh shut up!
Adele: Make me.
Clare: I don't make muck.

Session 4 Differences between the generations The pupils were asked if they had noticed any differences between the way their generation, their parents' generation and their grandparents' generation expressed likes and dislikes, approval and disapproval. They had, but found it far easier, not surprisingly, to give examples from their own use than from that of adults. Dawn represented her observations in a simple framework as follows.

Likes	*Dislikes*
My generation	
boss, brill, cool, sound, well in, custy, better, exo	crap, meff, divvy, you're doing me 'ead in, cracks me up, spaz, mong
Parents' generation	
lovely, gorgeous, nice, chuck, excellent	nuisance, pathetic, pest stupid, silly cow, rubbish

> *Grandparents' generation*
> sweetheart, chicken, lovey,   Don't be cheeky!
> chuck

As a research task the class had to talk to, and if possible tape-record, children of pre-school age and make observations about their language use and development. Those without access to young children at home went to interview those in the school nursery. They noticed the preponderance of one-word, two-word and three-word utterances, the absence of inflections and structural words (as in the 'Dada kick ball' example above), problems with pronunciation (especially 'th' sounds) and the tendency of young children to assume that you know what they are talking about. Unfortunately, for our purposes, no examples of 'good' mistakes ('goed', 'mans', etc.) were recorded.

Week 3 Different Englishes

Session 5 Standard and non-standard English I started this session by giving the class a brief talk about language and the concepts of standard and non-standard English. I explained that language had three aspects: words, the arrangement and form of words in sentences, and the pronunciation of words and sentences. I then drew their attention to the fact that English was a world language and that there were differences in these three respects between English, American and Australian English. They readily provided me with examples of American and Australian usage from their experience of television. From this I turned to differences within England, and within the British Isles, of which they were also well aware, again from their knowledge of television.

When I broached the standard/non-standard distinction, however, and the concepts of dialect and accent, I soon ran into comprehension problems, mainly because of the inherent difficulties in the use of these terms already referred to in Chapter 4. I took examples of 'non-standard' usage from recent ghost stories they had written as illustrations, and it emerged that some of the class simply did not know that 'he never done nothing', for instance, was usually labelled 'non-standard' usage and hence judged by many as inappropriate for written work (apart from dialogue in plays and stories). Most of the class did seem aware, however, that the Queen and television newsreaders would be unlikely to use multiple negation or 'done' for 'did' in speech.

Further evidence of problems in this area was furnished by the research task. The class were asked to watch one regional soap opera on television and note down which characters spoke with a regional accent and which did not and any examples of non-standard English grammar or vocabulary. I watched *Coronation Street* and *Brookside* myself to see what they might come up with. In both programmes there were clear differences as regards accent, with some very obvious 'posh' characters, such as Wendy Crozier and Derek Wilton in *Coronation Street*, and some equally obvious 'rough' ones, such as the Duckworths in the same programme. Though aware of these blatant differences, the class were less sensitive to the subtler variations in the quality or strength of the local accent, except in *Brookside* (as one might expect), and sometimes misread them. They also failed to pick up regional accents from elsewhere (Geordie and Ulster ones in *Coronation Street*, for example) and any cases of non-standard grammar or vocabulary. There were, admittedly, very few of the latter but I was surprised none of the children noticed any of them. In *Coronation Street* I recorded 'happen' for 'perhaps', 'owt' for 'anything', 'any road' for 'anyway' and a very striking 'I knew I were better than her' from Tracey Barlow. In *Brookside* I recorded 'give' for 'gave', 'them' for 'those, 'robbed' for 'stole' and 'ozzy' for 'hospital'.

Session 6 Scouse   Once we started exploring with the class the difficult issue of what exactly is meant by talking Scouse, or Liverpudlian, it became clear that, if an up-to-date description of Scouse is really required, schools are well placed to do the necessary research. We began with the well known booklet on Liverpudlian English, *Lern Yerself Scouse* published in 1965 when Beatlemania was rampant, even though it is more of an exercise in Scouse humour than a serious contribution to dialectology, failing completely, for instance, to distinguish between accent, vocabulary and grammar. I gave the class a list of supposedly Scouse expressions from the booklet to translate into standard English. Some meant nothing at all to them, nor to me for that matter, a member of the Beatles' generation. In fact only one teacher in a largely Liverpudlian staff could translate 'the shawlies were jangling' into 'the old women were talking'. Many expressions most children could translate – 'You what?' for 'Pardon,' 'yocked' for 'spat', 'bevvied' for 'drunk', 'keep dixey' for 'keep a look out' – though there was considerable variation in knowledge between individuals. Some expressions they understood but said were not used by their generation. For these they were occasionally able to supply replacements, though not all necessarily peculiar to Liverpool. For example, several knew that 'scuffers' meant 'police' and 'jigger' meant 'back lane' but said their own words were 'busies' and 'eenog'.

Finally we asked the class whether they thought they could write a Scouse dialogue in pairs and act it out. They responded enthusiastically. This is the one written by Cathy and Jill:

Cathy:	Jill, 'ere.
Jill:	What ye want?
Cathy:	Ye wanna come the park in the car with me mam?
Jill:	Na, don't feel like it.
Cathy:	O come 'ead, it'll be a buzz.
Jill:	Na.
Cathy:	Look 'ere's Dawn.
Dawn:	Hiya la.
Jill and Cathy:	Hiya.
Cathy:	Dawn, will you come the park in the car with me mam?
Dawn:	Yeah, la, it'll be a buzz.
Cathy:	O come 'ead, Jill.
Jill:	All right, la. But I wanna get some dosh.

The interesting question is: how much of this is exclusively or distinctively Scouse? I would say, probably only 'come the park', 'come 'ead' and 'la'.

Week 4   Variations in mode: speaking and writing (a)

Sessions 7 and 8   The work on telling and writing stories has already been fully described in Chapter 4 (pp. 83–7). You might like to refer back to the account at this point.

Week 5   Variations in mode: speaking and writing (b)

Sessions 9 and 10   The oral and written discussion of truancy has already been described in Chapter 6 (pp. 132–5). You might like to refer back to that account too.

Week 6 Variations between languages

Session 11 Different writing systems – The class were shown examples of different alphabets and writing systems. We concentrated on two, the runic alphabet and Chinese characters. In pairs the children practised encoding and decoding messages in each.

Session 12 Greetings in different languages – I taught the children how to greet one another in French, German, Italian and Swahili. They quickly mastered the greetings in the European languages but the sheer unfamiliarity of Swahili (even though its pronunciation is quite straightforward) proved too much for most of the class.

The course finished at this point, though we subsequently added on a single drama lesson in the hall on wordless communication – facial expression, signs and gestures, postures and movement. The untaught sessions 13–16 covered historical variation (the development of English – etymology, place names, versions of the Bible, the language of Chaucer and Shakespeare) and variations from the norm (deliberate mistakes in advertisements, shop signs and trade names, 'Jabberwocky').

The course was essentially an experiment to explore what was possible and likely to be fruitful in teaching about language to 10 and 11 year olds. Looking back, it seems to me that some of the topics we chose (e.g. names, girls' and boys' talk, greetings in other languages) were really no more than good fun, offering little real insight into linguistic structure or use. Three of them, however, revealed considerable potential in this respect – investigating the language of young children, carrying out research into local dialect and comparing the language of speech and writing through examples of pupils' own work in these modes.

FURTHER READING

The best way of learning more about linguistics, grammar and the structure of English, if you feel uncertain about your own knowledge, is to teach, and preferably follow a course in, English as a foreign language. Apart from this, you could have a look at a good up-to-date EFL course book such as the Cambridge English

Course. I would also urge you to continue developing your knowledge of other languages. 'What do they know of English who only English know?' Kingsley Amis once asked, adapting Kipling. I studied Latin, French and German to reasonable levels of competence at school, and have in adulthood added Italian, Swahili and classical Greek (to rather lower levels of competence) to my repertoire. This repertoire has stood me in good stead as an English teacher.

An excellent general introduction to linguistics, written with undergraduates primarily in mind, is *Language and Linguistics* by John Lyons, though you may find parts of it quite tough if you are a beginner in this field. More accessible, perhaps, are the books of David Crystal – *Linguistics*; *Child Language, Learning and Linguistics*; *Rediscover Grammar*. *The Cambridge Encyclopedia of Language*, edited by him, is indispensable both as a reference book and as a source of curriculum ideas. For information on English, as opposed to language in general, I would recommend, in addition to EFL materials, *The English Language* by Robert Burchfield and *The Story of English* by Robert McCrum *et al.*

From the growing pile of books on teaching language awareness you might like to try *Language Awareness for Teachers* by W.H. Mittins. Like everything its author writes, it is informative, readable and entertaining. For work with older pupils, two books which I relied heavily on in the 1960s – *A Grammar of Modern English* by W.H. Mittins (for microlinguistics) and *The Use of English* by Randolph Quirk (for macrolinguistics) – have not been improved on by anything (that I have seen) written since. *Language in Use* (Doughty *et al.*, 1971) did, however, open up some new areas in macrolinguistics and continues to serve as the model for most teachers' understanding of teaching language awareness. Finally, you will almost certainly need a book on word and language games. My own favourite is *The Oxford Guide to Word Games* by Tony Augarde, because it includes much interesting historical information on the games' origins. You will also find some useful ideas in *Grammar Games* by Mario Rinvolucri, though it was written with EFL students primarily in mind.

Afterword: classroom management

Then began the hum of conning over lessons and getting them by heart, the whispered jest and stealthy game, and all the noise and drawl of school; and in the midst of the din sat the poor schoolmaster, the very image of meekness and simplicity . . . the idlest boys . . . growing bolder with impunity, waxed louder and more daring; playing odd-or-even under the master's eye, eating apples openly and without rebuke, pinching each other in sport or malice without the least reserve, and cutting their autographs in the very legs of his desk.

(Charles Dickens, The Old Curiosity Shop, 1841)

'If I were you, Miss Brangwen,' [Mr Brunt] said, menacingly, 'I should get a bit tighter hand over my class.'

Ursula shrank.

'Would you?' she asked, sweetly, yet in terror. 'Aren't I strict enough?'

'Because,' he repeated, taking no notice of her, 'they'll get you down if you don't tackle 'em pretty quick. . . . You won't be here another six weeks . . . if you don't tackle 'em and tackle 'em quick.'

(D.H. Lawrence, The Rainbow, 1915)

A book specifically addressed to those new to teaching needs to say something about classroom management. At the same time it has to be admitted that, in the words of the Newbolt report, 'the ideal teacher is born, not made' and that what there is to learn about this issue is more easily acquired through practical experience or discussion with experienced practitioners than from anything written down. That being able to teach well is a natural gift was easily my firmest conclusion on matters relating to teacher education after observing almost forty students on teaching practice in 1987–8. I usually knew after one visit, and always after three, who would and who would not be a good teacher, although this judgment sometimes contradicted the expectation I had formed of how individual students would perform from seminars and tutorials. Some students seemed to know instinctively how to address a class, how to talk to individual pupils and small groups and how to respond to minor disturbances and major crises; others, almost invariably, chose the wrong option.

The main attributes of the gift are, I would say: a good voice; a classroom presence which pupils 'would fain call master'; a sense of humour; and an unflappable disposition. Anyone seriously deficient in even one of these respects would, in my opinion, be ill advised to go into teaching, though it may take teaching practice to show the deficiency up. They are, of course, necessary, not sufficient, conditions of being a good teacher. On the additional, more directly pedagogic, qualities required there is a striking degree of agreement among pupils, researchers, teacher trainers and teachers themselves. It is widely accepted that a good teacher is one who excels at explaining his or her subject to the whole class and at increasing understanding and stimulating thought among pupils through skilful use of dialogue – in particular, through just the right mixture of 'open' and 'closed' questions.

In today's classrooms, which are often dominated by the philosophy of 'mixed ability' teaching and workshop approaches based on group work, being a good teacher involves excelling both at whole-class exposition and dialogue and at itinerant consultancy to individuals, pairs and small groups – and at moving fluently between these two rather different roles. Crucial to this extension of the concept of teaching is the capacity not only to explain ideas to a range of abilities but to set assignments which successfully challenge the ablest and the least able. Equally important is the establishment of a 'working ethos' and a 'firm, fair and friendly' regime in which rules and routines are clearly laid down.

There is also considerable agreement among pupils, teachers and all others who regularly observe classrooms about what constitutes a good lesson, although the ideal model is not uniformly applicable across the curriculum nor to all types of lesson. Obviously, in the first place, a good lesson is one which has been carefully thought out and planned and whose aims and structure are explained to the pupils. It is also one in which the teacher arrives first, to ensure an orderly entry, and finishes five minutes early, to ensure an equally orderly conclusion and exit. Within the lesson there should be a balance between teacher activity and pupil activity and, in the case of English, between the different modes of language. It should fall into distinct phases (most typically, into teacher presentation, pupil activity and concluding discussion), each of which is clearly signalled so that transitions between them are smooth and trouble-free. In the case of pupil activity children are entitled to expect some negotiating rights, but not complete freedom, in deciding what they are to do and how they are to do it. Lessons, of course, rarely go to plan. Work can prove too difficult or too easy or fail to arouse interest or enthusiasm. Or a pupil may say something which opens up more intriguing paths to follow than those marked out beforehand. Flexibility – the ability to change direction in mid-flight, to think on one's feet and respond to serendipitous eventualities – is as necessary a pedagogic asset as being a good planner and organiser.

Students and probationers can easily be overawed by these models of the good teacher and the good lesson, and by the examples of both which they observe on teaching practice. It is important, therefore, to stress that, although 'the ideal teacher is born, not made' and one cannot change one's personality, the more directly pedagogic aspects of being a good teacher can certainly be cultivated – and surprisingly quickly. A third of my students in 1987–8 were good teachers, in my estimation and in that of the schools they were attached to, by the end of teaching practice. A handful were better then than I was after ten years of teaching. It is also worth adding that I have known a number of teachers – the Miss Brodies of the profession – who fell short of the ideal in certain conspicuous respects or regularly infringed the unwritten code of professional conduct but were still greatly appreciated by their pupils.

My principal advice to my students in 1987–8 was that they should concentrate on doing well what could reasonably be expected of them regardless of their native talents and lack of experience – that is to say, that they should: always be punctual for school and lessons, and absent only when really ill (in which case, no misguided heroics); never fail to plan their lessons (and religiously keep plans and evaluations full and up-to-date in their teaching practice file); set homework regularly and mark it promptly; and abide strictly by school and departmental rules on responding to pupils' writing, record-keeping and assessment, and crime and punishment.

Something else students and probationers can reasonably be expected to achieve is a neat and attractive classroom. On teaching practice, of course, you are working in other teachers' rooms, but you can at least ensure that at the end of lessons all is tidy and orderly, even if chaos has ruled for their duration, and that written work done for you is well displayed. Once into the probationary year you should, unless you are very unlucky, have a room of your own. Making this a pleasure to enter, and conducive to a 'working ethos', is the first, and almost the most important, achievement an inexperienced teacher can aspire to in trying to establish him or herself in a new school. Too many secondary school English classrooms are joyless places – undecorated walls; display boards adorned with the odd piece of illegible written work or torn theatre poster; books, folders and paper strewn higgledy-piggledy; and desks defaced with graffiti. It is not too much to expect that walls should be covered with pictures, posters and photographs, and display boards with regularly changed pupils' work. If you are looking for advice on how best to do this, visit your feeder primary schools. They are the experts on how to display children's work and how to make classrooms attractive workplaces.

Your classroom should also be an effective workplace, which can operate successfully even if you are away and another teacher has to cover for your absence. I emphasised in Chapter 5 the importance of building up a class library. Pupils should be able to use it for reference purposes or taking books out without your help. They should also know where folders, paper and all the utensils they are likely to need for work are kept, and be in the habit of following the routines you have laid down for distributing and collecting in books, written work and other materials.

One essential condition for establishing an effective workplace is an arrangement of chairs and desks which encourages rather than discourages work. An increasing number of secondary school English rooms are following the primary school practice of seating pupils in groups round tables. I would not recommend it, unless they happen to be working on a group assignment. It makes addressing the whole class unnecessarily difficult and encourages idle chit-chat. For most everyday purposes the traditional arrangenent of rows of desks facing the front seems to me best. For drama, if you are using a classroom, you will obviously need to clear a central space, and for full-class discussion and reading literature aloud there is much to be said for a horseshoe arrangement of chairs, with or without desks. For writing I have occasionally experimented with reorganising the room so that it resembles a computer workshop, with desks lining all four walls and pupils seated at them individually and facing outwards.

An important factor in deciding how to arrange chairs and desks will be your attitude towards noise and group work, on both of which I have made some comment in earlier chapters. My own view, you may recall, is that there should ideally be silent sessions for both reading and writing. Michael Marland, an experienced English teacher and headteacher, has outlined the view well in his excellent little book *The Craft of the Classroom*:

> Much individual work, especially reading and writing, requires an atmosphere of concentration. For these activities the silence of a public library is normally far more successful than 'reasonable noise' and is much appreciated by most pupils. Indeed it is more enjoyable to have clearly signed contrasts between 'co-operative talking' and 'library silence' sessions than it is to have all lessons at roughly similar levels of interruptive noise, with the teacher struggling to regulate the volume every fifteen minutes or so.
>
> (Marland, 1975: 64)

As for group work, I suggested in Chapter 4 that you should be niggardly in your use of it, resorting to it only when the educational arguments in its favour are overwhelming and after you have established a working relationship with the class as a whole. I also suggested that you should approach it via pair work and apply strict controls on its implementation.

Whenever I have been present at a discussion on classroom management between students or probationers and experienced practising teachers, the latter have invariably laid particular stress on the importance of the relationship between the teacher and the class as a whole. All classes have a corporate identity, sometimes a very strong one. Making a success of teaching them is heavily dependent on engaging with that corporate identity. Almost the surest sign of a weak student on teaching practice is reluctance to do so, usually manifested in a marked preference for a pedagogy based on the role of the itinerant consultant rather than traditional 'chalk and talk'. 'Chalk and talk' may be despised in some teacher training circles but it is absolutely fundamental to being a good teacher. You need to work at the use of the blackboard and its modern equivalents (whiteboard, overhead projector, etc.) and at using your voice (and eye contact – I once had a student who addressed the class while looking out of the window) to best advantage, both for reading aloud and for explication and discussion, so that it is always authoritative but never a shout or screech.

This brings us on to discipline, on which I can write with some confidence, having never been the profession's most successful disciplinarian. Once again, experienced practitioners are remarkably consistent in their advice. For example, they nearly always stress the positive rather than the negative aspects of discipline – be generous with praise, reward good behaviour and work, get to know names, chat to pupils in corridors and break-times, remain a model of politeness even though sorely tested, and make every effort to re-establish friendly relations with a pupil after he or she has been reprimanded or punished. The keystone to a positive regime is the actual teaching. Observing that 'there exist the two distinct roles of teaching and control', the Bullock report commented: 'the constant aim should be to develop the first to a point where it encompasses the second'. Although it would be naive to pretend that disciplinary difficulties will disappear with the achievement of pedagogic competence, it is certainly the case that they are far less likely to occur in lessons which have been carefully planned and to teachers who try to interest and stretch pupils with imaginative schemes of work.

In considering indiscipline it is necessary to be clear what we mean. All teachers know, and the Elton report of 1989 confirmed, that serious indiscipline of the kind likely to capture media attention – violence and verbal abuse, whether directed against teachers or fellow pupils – is very rare. But it does occur. In the last two decades I have had to break up fights (not only between boys but between girls and between girls and boys), been told to 'fuck off' (once) and been physically assaulted (twice, once as a consequence of trying to break up a fight, as described in Chapter 1). So you do need to be prepared. Your school will amost certainly have a prescribed procedure for such eventualities, involving the immediate removal and subsequent suspension of offenders. If you are female or the offenders likely to resist your own efforts to remove them, do not hesitate to call for help. Serious indiscipline of this kind is very probably not your main concern, however. Your main problem is almost certainly the debilitating and demoralising effect of what the Elton report calls 'a continuous stream of relatively minor disruptions' – unpunctuality, talking out of turn, noisiness, rudeness, jostling, interfering with other pupils' work, etc.

The advice of experienced teachers on dealing with 'minor disruptions' emphasises abiding strictly by school procedures and avoiding making the situation worse through overreaction. Nowadays school procedures are likely to rely on referral to senior members of staff and, if necessary, parents, rather than on punishments such as detention. When referral fails to achieve the desired effect, schools can, of course, turn to the ultimate sanctions of suspension and expulsion, which are much more often resorted to now than they were, perhaps as a result of the proscription of corporal punishment. So far as possible, I would recommend you try to deal with 'minor' indiscipline yourself; involving senior members of staff may simply serve to undermine your authority further. To be avoided at all costs are: shouting at pupils; having classroom confrontations with individuals; being rude or sarcastic to pupils; sending individuals out of the room; punishing the whole class for the misdemeanours of some; and threatening what you cannot deliver. On the positive side, you should try to stay calm, react fast and firmly to the first sign of misdemeanour, insist on agreed routines such as 'hands up, no shouting out' and use command forms rather than questions or statements (e.g. 'Quiet' rather than 'Could you be quiet?' or 'There's too much noise in here').

All this, of course, is easily said but much less easily done, particularly in the kind of schools – 'schools of despair', as I sometimes think of them – in which some of my own teaching career has been spent. There can be little doubt that, although all schools have troublesome pupils and classes, maintaining discipline is a much tougher proposition in some than in others, nor that these 'tougher' schools are invariably situated in inner city areas or on housing estates scoring high on indices of social deprivation. This is not to say, as the Elton report points out, that all schools serving such areas are undisciplined or that all schools serving socially advantaged or heterogeneous ones are disciplined. It is also well known, and confirmed by the Elton report, that the majority of troublemakers are older boys of below average intelligence from disadvantaged backgrounds, which, again, is not to deny that clever boys from middle class backgrounds and girls (especially for male teachers) can be a handful too.

The Elton report comments on the difference in 'feel' between schools (others have preferred the concept of 'ethos'); some schools 'feel' orderly and purposeful, whereas others 'feel' as though they are teetering on the brink of anarchy. Most institutions of higher education do not, as a matter of policy, place students in undisciplined schools, but you may well find yourself teaching in one as a probationer or later in your career and settling for lower standards of discipline than you would in a more orderly school. I know only too well from my own experience how teaching in an undisciplined school affects one's view of teaching. Suddenly it becomes a matter of containment, survival and staying sane – of developing emergency strategies just to cope.

Survival strategies are, of course, necessary for all teachers, particularly given the recent spate of innovation. In my first years of teaching I made the elementary mistake of allowing it to take over too much of my life. I marked books and prepared work most evenings and most Sundays and took school teams on Saturday mornings. I did, however, manage to keep Friday evenings clear for going to the pub, cinema or theatre and Saturday afternoons for playing hockey or cricket; and in the summer holidays I always escaped as far away as possible after a week of lower school camp. Then I realised that I could preserve more of my evenings by getting up early and to school an hour before it began in order to deal with marking and preparation. Later still, when I was a head of department, I tried a different approach to avoid taking work home. I stayed at school to do it, often till the caretaker threw me out at six o'clock. By that time my hockey-playing career was over, so I took to going for long walks or cycle rides on either Saturday or Sunday. It is absolutely vital that you preserve a life of your own outside school which it is never allowed to invade. If you do not, you will soon find that your sense of frustration and harassment increases and that your teaching suffers as a consequence.

FURTHER READING

I have already referred you to the Elton report on school discipline and to Michael Marland's book *The Craft of the Classroom*, though I should warn you that the latter is regarded as fuddy-duddyish in some quarters.

Bibliography

Abbs, P. (1982) *English within the Arts*, London: Hodder & Stoughton.
Adams, A. (ed.) (1983) *New Directions in English Teaching*, Brighton: Falmer Press.
Allen, D. (1980) *English Teaching since 1965: How much Growth?*, London: Heinemann.
Augarde, T. (1984) *The Oxford Guide to Word Games*, Oxford: Oxford University Press.
Barker, C. (1977) *Theatre Games*, London: Methuen.
Barnes, D. (1977) *From Communication to Curriculum*, Harmondsworth: Penguin.
Barnes, D. (1982) *Practical Curriculum Study*, London: Routledge.
Barnes, D., Britton, J., and Rosen, H. (1969) *Language, the Learner and the School*, Harmondsworth: Penguin.
Benton, M. and Fox, G. (1985) *Teaching Literature 9–14*, Oxford: Oxford University Press.
Berry, C. (1987) *The Actor and his Text*, London: Harrap.
Board of Education (1910) *The Teaching of English in Secondary Schools*, London: HMSO.
Board of Education (1921) *The Teaching of English in England*, (the Newbolt report) London: HMSO.
Britton, J. (1970) *Language and Learning*, Harmondsworth: Penguin.
Brook, P. (1968) *The Empty Space*, London: MacGibbon & Kee.
Bruner, J. (1963) *The Process of Education*, New York: Vintage Books.
Burchfield, R. (1985) *The English Language*, Oxford: Oxford University Press.
Crystal, D. (1971) *Linguistics*, Harmondsworth: Penguin.
Crystal, D. (1976) *Child Language, Learning and Linguistics*, London: Edward Arnold.
Crystal, D. (ed.) (1987) *The Cambridge Encyclopedia of Language*, Cambridge: Cambridge University Press.
Crystal, D. (1988) *Rediscover Grammar*, London: Longman.
Daly, M., Mathews, S., Middleton, D., Parker, H., Prior, J., and Waters, S. (1989) 'Different views of the subject: a PGCE perspective' *The English Magazine*, 22.

Davies, C. (1989) 'The conflicting subject philosophies of English' *British Journal of Educational Studies*, XXXVII: 398–416.

DES (1975) *A Language for Life*, (the Bullock report), London: HMSO.

DES (1984) *English from 5 to 16*, London: HMSO.

DES (1988) *Report of the Committee of Inquiry into the Teaching of English Language*, (the Kingman report), London: HMSO.

DES (1989) *English for Ages 5 to 16*, (the Cox report), London: HMSO.

DES (1989) *Discipline in Schools*, (the Elton report), London: HMSO.

DES (1990) *English in the National Curriculum*, London: HMSO.

Dixon, J. (1967) *Growth through English*, London: Oxford University Press.

Doughty, P., Pearce, J., and Thornton, G. (1971) *Language in Use*, London: Edward Arnold.

Evans, T. (1982) *Teaching English*, London: Croom Helm.

Gibson, R. (1986) *Critical Theory and Education*, London: Hodder & Stoughton.

Gibson, R. (1990) *Secondary School Shakespeare*, Cambridge: Cambridge Institute of Education.

Goodacre, E., Harris, J., Harrison, C., Foster, J., and Walker, C. (1977) *Reading after Ten*, London: BBC Publications.

Graves, D.H. (1983) *Writing: Teachers and Children at Work*, Portsmouth, New Hampshire: Heinemann.

Griffiths, P. (1987) *Literary Theory and English Teaching*, Milton Keynes: Open University Press.

Harpin, W. (1976) *The Second 'R'*, London: Allen & Unwin.

Holbrook, D. (1961) *English for Maturity*, Cambridge: Cambridge University Press.

Hourd, M.L. (1949) *The Education of the Poetic Spirit*, London: Heinemann.

Jackson, D. (1982) *Continuity in Secondary English*, London: Methuen.

Jeffcoate, R. (1973) 'Ideologies in English teaching', University of Lancaster unpublished M.A. dissertation.

Jeffcoate, R. (1979) *Positive Image*, London: Writers and Readers.

Johnstone, K. (1981) *Impro*, London: Methuen.

Lunzer, E. and Gardner, K. (1979) *The Effective Use of Reading*, London: Heinemann.

Lyons, J. (1981) *Language and Linguistics*, Cambridge: Cambridge University Press.

McCrum, R. *et al.* (1986) *The Story of English*, London: Faber.

McGregor, L., Tate, M., and Robinson, K. (1977) *Learning through Drama*, London: Heinemann.

Marland, M. (1975) *The Craft of the Classroom*, London: Heinemann.

Marshall, S. (1989) 'Behind the scenes', *2D* 8 (2): 50–8.

Mathieson, M. (1975) *The Preachers of Culture*, London: Allen & Unwin.

Meek, M. (1982) *Learning to Read*, London: Bodley Head.

Michael, I. (1987) *The Teaching of English from the Sixteenth Century to 1870*, Cambridge: Cambridge University Press.

Mill, J.S. (1985 edition) *On Liberty*, Harmondsworth: Penguin.

Mills, R.W. (1977) *Teaching English across the Ability Range*, London: Ward Lock.

Mittins, W.H. (1962) *A Grammar of Modern English*, London: Methuen.
Mittins, W.H. (1991) *Language Awareness for Teachers*, Milton Keynes: Open University Press.
O'Neill, C., Lambert, A., Linnell, R., and Warr-Wood, J. (1976) *Drama Guidelines*, London: Heinemann.
Quirk, R. (1962) *The Use of English*, London: Longman.
Rinvolucri, M. (1985) *Grammar Games*, Cambridge: Cambridge University Press.
Sampson, G. (1921) *English for the English*, Cambridge: Cambridge University Press.
Shayer, D. (1972) *The Teaching of English in Schools 1900–1970*, London: Routledge.
Smedley, D. (1983) *Teaching the Basic Skills*, London: Methuen.
Smith, F. (1986) *Reading*, Cambridge: Cambridge University Press.
Stanislavski, K. (1967 edition) *An Actor Prepares*, Harmondsworth: Penguin.
Stenhouse, L. (1975) *An Introduction to Curriculum Research and Development*, London: Heinemann.
Tallis, R. (1987) *Not Saussure: A Critique of Post-Saussurean Literary Theory*, London: Macmillan.
Trudgill, P. (1975) *Accent, Dialect and the School*, London: Edward Arnold.
Waterland, L. (1985) *Read with Me*, Stroud: Thimble Press.

Index